THE
NORTH STAFFORDSHIRE RAILWAY
IN LMS DAYS

Below: A view looking south at Kidsgrove circa 1935, with the station on the left and the main line on the right approaching Harecastle station. The sidings to the left served (from August 1933) the Premier Artificial Stone Co. Ltd but had been occupied previously by Wagon Repairs Ltd. Note that the station buildings on the far left are not on the platform but at a lower level. The sidings in the centre served the 'Third Line', the Independent line, to Birchenwood. *Author's collection*

Previous Page: In 1926-27, the Loop Line bridge over Scotia Road was rebuilt by the LM&SR and Stoke Corporation took advantage of this opportunity to widen the road at the same time. The new bridge thus had two spans and the majority of the work was paid for by the corporation, as detailed on page 36. Here, a 36-ton crane Ransomes & Rapier breakdown crane, built in 1909 for the L&NWR and normally based at Crewe, positions a support column into the brick abutments, the existing brickwork having been cut out to accommodate this. Note how the wire ties have been wrapped around the column, and around the telegraph and other poles. *Courtesy the Potteries Museum & Art Gallery, Stoke-on-Trent*

THE NORTH STAFFORDSHIRE RAILWAY IN LMS DAYS

Volume 3

Road Deliveries – Buses – The Loop Line
The Biddulph Valley Line – Stoke Works
Rolling Stock – Stoke Round House and Shed
Locomotive Allocations and Use – Traffic Control
The Smaller Canals and Rudyard Lake – The Leek Line
The Leek, Caldon & Waterhouses Railway and Caldon Quarries
The Leek & Manifold Valley Light Railway

Basil Jeuda

VOLUME 3: CONTENTS

Acknowledgements

I have been researching, writing and lecturing on transport and industry, mainly in North Staffordshire and South Cheshire, for more than thirty years, focussing very largely on the origins and history of the North Staffordshire Railway and its canal system. Underpinning this interest for most of this time has been two friends, Allan Baker and David Kitching, and I would like to single them out, in this final volume of my trilogy on the NSR in the LM&SR era, for my appreciation of their support – but without losing sight of NSR historians of an earlier generation, particularly the late Dr Jack Hollick, the late Claude Moreton and the late Robert Keys, each of whom gave me every encouragement and advice over many years.

I would also like to thank the following for their information and support: Paul Blurton, David Bourne, Peter Brown, Robert Cartwright, the late Christine Chester, Mike Christensen, Sheila Cooke, Paul Deakin, Richard Dean, Alan Faulkner, Mike Fell, the late Neville Fields, Albert Finney, Chris Fletcher, David Geldart, David Gibson, Bob Gratton, the late Clive Guthrie, John Hyde, the late Bill Jack, Dr David Jolley, Chris Knight, Gerald Leach, Peter Lead, Roland Machin, Brian Morris, David Moore, Christine Pemberton, Ian Pope, John Ryan, David Salt, the late Ron Simpson, the late Les Smith, Mark Smith, Sue Taylor, Nelson Twells, the late Gordon Walwyn, Martin Welch, and Derek Wheelhouse.

In addition, I am grateful to the dozens of people who have made time available for me to interview them about their reminiscences and experiences; they are too numerous to name but I hope that they will be able to recognize their individual contributions to the book.

I am grateful for the support given to me by the following organisations: The British Library, Cheshire Record Office, Keele University Local Studies Library, Manchester Central Reference Library, Manchester Locomotive Society Library, National Archives, National Railway Museum, Newcastle Museum Archives, North Staffordshire Railway (1978) Limited, North Staffordshire Railway Study Group, Railtrack, the Staffordshire & City of Stoke-on-Trent Archive Services, and The Potteries Museum.

My thanks go, too, to the many people who have supplied photographs and digital images and whom I have acknowledged individually in the captions; I apologise for any omissions in this respect. Over the last thirty years, I have relied on the traditional camera skills of Camera Five-Four, Doug Rendell and Tim Shuttleworth but in the digital age I would also wish to highlight and thank Allan Baker, Paul Blurton, David Kitching, David Moore and Christine Pemberton. I am grateful to Lightmoor Press for agreeing to publish this trilogy and to one of its co-Directors, Neil Parkhouse, for his extremely helpful comments over the best part of twenty years. Finally, to my dear wife, Laura, for her patience and understanding, as ever, as yet another book has made such demands on our lives.

Basil Jeuda, Macclesfield, January 2014

1

Introduction to Volume 3

This is the third and final volume detailing 'What happened next' to the North Staffordshire Railway after its absorption into the London Midland & Scottish Railway on 1st July 1923. This history covers the period from 'Grouping', as it was called, down to 1st January 1948 when, following Nationalisation, the LM&SR too was absorbed into the newly formed British Railways. The contents of the two previous volumes have largely consisted of detailed studies of most of the main and branch lines that constituted the former NSR network, and have attempted to portray the factors that influenced or determined the changes on each line. These factors were considered in detail in the Introduction to Volume 2.

Firstly, there were the operating issues arising from Grouping, including the rationalisation of the different companies, changes in organisation structure and boundaries, and the standardisation of locomotives and rolling stock. Secondly, there were economic factors, including the slump and trade depressions of 1921-22 and 1929-33, the closure of several ironworks and numerous older pits but with the expansion of newer pits, and the development of greenfield sites for newer industry. Thirdly, there was the impact on the railways of the growing competition from buses and road haulage and, with the deterioration in the economy, the threats to the viability of branch lines and services – which in turn led to the cessation of

The popularity of railway excursions can be measured in the 'Public Excursion from Macclesfield & District to Messrs Cadbury's Chocolate Works', which was run on Thursday 12th September 1929, promoted by the L&MSR. The fare was 4s 6d (21¼p) to Birmingham and to Bournville, and included a tour of the works. No fewer than 1,700 people made *the highly instructive and informative visit* and three special trains were run. The following three photographs, depicting each of the trains, were taken at King's Norton carriage sidings:

Above Right: The first portion was headed by former L&NWR 'Prince of Wales' Class 4-6-0 No. 5699. Note the ex-ROD tender.
Above Left: The second portion was hauled by former 'New F' Class 0-6-4T No.173, now LM&SR No. 2049. Built in February 1917, it was one of a class of eight that was built between 1916 and 1919, and was withdrawn from service in July 1934. Passing is former Midland Railway 0-6-4T No. 2025 working a local Up fast.
Right: The third portion, which was headed by former L&NWR 'George V' Class 4-4-0 No. 5356 *Gibraltar*.
All photos Nigel Payton, courtesy Ruth Moston

© Lightmoor Press & Basil Jeuda 2014. Designed by Neil Parkhouse
British Library Cataloguing-in-Publication Data. A catalogue record for this book is available from the British Library
ISBN 13: 9781899889 83 9
LIGHTMOOR PRESS
Unit 144B, Lydney Trading Estate, Harbour Road, Lydney, Gloucestershire GL15 5EJ
www.lightmoor.co.uk
LIGHTMOOR PRESS is an imprint of BLACK DWARF LIGHTMOOR PUBLICATIONS LTD
Printed by BERFORTS INFORMATION PRESS, Oxford

passenger services, to line singling, and to the closure of one third of the passenger stations inherited from the NSR. Fourthly, there was the impact of the First World War on the structure of the railway industry in the United Kingdom, and of the Second World War on the movement of freight, of munitions and of ordnance factory workers to several munitions factories and depots in South Cheshire and North Staffordshire. Finally, the NSR's canal system continued in long term decline, leading to the closure of numerous operating wharves, to the cessation of carrying activities and to the legal abandonment of parts of the canal system, including the Leek Canal.

The factors that brought about the changes to 'T'Owd Knotty', as it was affectionally referred to, can be picked up in this volume, such as competition from buses, locomotive use, the building of locomotives and rolling stock and the closure of Stoke Works, the growth of cartage (road deliveries) and the challenge of competition from road operators, the operating practices and Stoke Control, the cessation of passenger services on the Biddulph Valley and on the Leek to Waterhouses line, the complete closure of the Leek & Manifold Valley Light Railway, and the rundown of traffic on the Caldon and Leek canals.

Left: Former NSR 'K' Class 4-4-2T No. 8, now as L&MSR No. 2180, at Wolverhampton High Level station on 25th May 1932. This was the first of this class of seven passenger locomotives to be built, in November 1911, and was withdrawn from service in December 1933. The class worked some of the longer distance urban passenger workings in the LM&SR era, such as Crewe to Derby and Stoke to Birmingham. *Nigel Payton, courtesy Ruth Moston/SLS*

Top: Stoke Junction with LM&SR 'Compound' 4-4-0 No. 1120 on a Derby to Crewe working on 22nd May 1932. Stoke Junction underwent major track realignment under the LM&SR, which included the replacement of the original McKenzie & Holland signal box with this L&NWR-design box, and related L&NWR signalling. The cost of the engineering work was £9,140; the works were authorised in 1926 and were completed in 1929. Note the newness of some of the brickwork. *Nigel Payton, courtesy Ruth Moston/SLS*

Right: Etruria Gas Works in the spring of 1926. This is a still from a film entitled *City of Stoke-on-Trent 1926, Activities of the Corporation*. It shows the loading of coking coal into L&MSR 6- and 8-plank wagons from the overhead hoppers of the municipally-owned gas works. The Corporation took over this undertaking in 1922, which led to the closure of smaller and formerly independent works, with the consequent supplying of gas to all towns in the Corporation area. Towards the end of the LM&SR era, the gas plant was extensively modernised and three cooling towers built. In the right background is Kerr Stuart 0-4-0ST Works No. 4388, which came new to Etruria in 1926 and was sold to the Brookfield Foundry & Engineering Co. in July 1950. *Staffordshire Film Archive*

William Preston was a member of a long-standing canal family from Runcorn. He worked at different times for the Mersey Weaver & Ship Canal Carrying Co. and Potter & Son (canal carriers between Runcorn and Hanley), as well as working on his own account as a Number One. These two photographs were taken by him circa 1935.

Right: The Mersey Weaver narrowboat *Bethune* at Broken Cross, Northwich, a view looking south, with the Trent & Mersey warehouse in the background. Broken Cross was where the T&M established a transshipment warehouse in 1784, for pottery which was then carried by road to the nearby Weaver Navigation, for onward transport to Runcorn and Liverpool. *Bethune* joined the Mersey Weaver fleet in June 1934 and was registered as Stoke No. 922 on 25th July 1934.

Below: Hardingswood Junction, Harecastle, with William Preston's boat *Rushmere* moored up at the start of the Hall Green Branch of the T&M. In the background, the LMS and GW lettered vans are alongside the Harecastle to Macclesfield line. Preston had contracts for carrying coal from Hardingswood to Marple.
Both Preston family collection

Left: Lucy Gorton (née Bland), seen here on the Burslem Arm circa 1930, wearing the traditional dress of the wife of a boatman. She worked with her husband Ernest (Wood) for the Anderton Carrying Company for more than forty years. The Gortons owned this fine looking horse, which won several first prizes at Northwich and at Rudheath in the early 1930s. In the background can be seen the rucks of china clay which are marshalled into separate pens. Both the Anderton Company and Mersey Weaver had wharves on the Burslem Arm. *Gorton family collection*

Left: Bomb damage on the T&M at Etruria in 1940. In the foreground is Etruria Lock, whilst behind can be seen the roof over the Gauging Lock on the left and the Toll House on the right. Although the T&M Canal at Etruria may have been a deliberate target for the German bombers, it is more likely that they were in fact aiming for the nearby Shelton industrial complex. *Frank Underwood*

This Announcement cancels Bill M 777.
No. M 2584.

LMS
LONDON MIDLAND AND SCOTTISH RAILWAY

Spring Season Excursions, 1925

ON SATURDAYS

MAY 2nd up to and including JULY 4th
(SATURDAY, MAY 30th EXCEPTED).

For 8 or 15 Days,

EXCURSION TICKETS
WILL BE ISSUED TO

PRESTATYN	Corwen	Old Colwyn
RHYL	Abergele	COLWYN BAY
Denbigh	Llandulas	Llandudno Junct.
Ruthin	Llysfaen	Deganwy

LLANDUDNO

Llanrwst & Trefriw	Bangor
Bettws-y-Coed	Carnarvon
Blaenau Festiniog	Menai Bridge
Conway	Bethesda
Penmaenmawr	Afonwen
Llanfairfechan	Chwilog
	and Pwllheli (G.W.)

Passengers are requested to obtain their T...

During the Summer Season, Observation Cars to give facilities for sight... between Llandudno and Bettws-y-Coed, and between Rhyl and Lla... and Sundays excepted. The Cars are fitted with large plate-glas... expansive outlook and taking in the whole panorama of the countr... A Conductor travels in the Cars to point out the various points of i...

40,000. **PLEASE RETAIN THIS BILL FOR REF...**

Right: The NSR published hundreds of handbills each year to promote its excursions. The last Stoke Wakes Holiday, before the NSR was taken over in 1923, was in August 1922 and this handbill promotes Cheap Return Tickets between Loop Line stations and Mow Cop and Congleton. *Ian Walker collection*

NORTH STAFFORDSHIRE RAILWAY. No. 537.

Stoke Wakes Holidays.

Monday, Tuesday, Wednesday and Thursday,
August 7th, 8th, 9th & 10th,
Cheap Return Tickets will be issued to

MOW COP
AND
CONGLETON

TAKE YOUR TICKETS IN ADVANCE.

From	At					Return Fares—3rd Class Available for return the same day only.	
						Mow Cop	Congleton
	a.m.	a.m.	p.m.	p.m.	p.m.		
Hanley	9 8	11 28	12 47	1 43	3 9	1/2	1/8
Waterloo Rd	9 10	11 30	12 49	1 45	3 11	1/1	1/6
Cobridge	9 13	11 33	12 52	1 48	3 14	1/1	1/6
Burslem	9 16	11 36	12 55	1 51	3 17	1/1	1/6
Tunstall	9 20	12 0	1 0	2 0	3 20	1/-	1/4
Pitts Hill	9 23	12 3	1 3	2 3	3 23	1/-	1/4
Newchapel	9 27	12 7	1 7	2 7	3 27	1/-	1/2
Kidsgrove	9 37	12 17	1 17	2 17	3 35	1/-	1/-

Passengers return from Congleton at 8 0 or 9 17, and from Mow Cop at 8 6 or 9 24 p.m.; and also on Monday and Thursday from Congleton at 9 50 and from Mow Cop at 9 57 p.m.

FOOTBALL AT STOKE

STOKE CITY v. CHELSEA—August 26th
STOKE CITY v. PORTSMOUTH—September 9th
STOKE CITY v. DERBY COUNTY—September 23rd
STOKE CITY v. WOLVERHAMPTON W.—Sept. 30th
STOKE CITY v. ASTON VILLA—October 14th
Kick-off 3.15 p.m.

HALF-DAY EXCURSIONS
By LMS to
STOKE-ON-TRENT
SATURDAYS
Aug. 26th, Sept. 9th, 23rd, 30th & Oct. 14th, 1933.

FROM	Times of Departure	RETURN FARES (Third Class)	FROM	Times of Departure	RETURN FARES (Third Class)
	p.m.	s. d.	Milton	p.m.	s. d.
Alsager	2.15	1 0	Mow Cop	2 18	0 9
Aston-by-Stone	1.54	1 3	Newcastle	2.27	0 4
Barlaston	2.27	0 9	(L'pool Rd. Halt)	2.25	0 4½
Blythe Bridge	2.10, 2.30, 2.36	0 6	Nawhapel & G.	1.53, 2.5	0 9
Bucknall	2.22	0 4	Normacot	2.15, 2.37	0 4
Burslem	1.55, 2.1, 2.14	0 6	North Rode	1.44	1 1
Cheadle	2.15	1 0	Norton Bridge	1.33	1 3
Chaddleton	1.33	1 1	Norton Bridge	2.25	1 3
Cobridge	1.58, 2.3, 2.17	0 3	Norton-in-Hales	1.56	1 1
Congleton	1.35, 1.53	1 3	Oakamoor	1.19	1 2
Cresswell	2.33, 2.58	0 6	Pipe Gate	1.49	1 0
Crewe	...	1 3	Pitts Hill	2.9	0 6
Endon	2.11	0 8	Rocester	1.66, 2.7	2 0
Etruria	2.6, 2.20, 2.43	0 3	Rudyard Lake	2.5	1 0
Fenton	2.21	0 1½	Rushton	1.15	1 1
Great Bridgeford	2.20	1 3	Sandon	1.19	1 1
Hanley	2.2, 2.8, 2.22	0 3	Silverdale	1.23	1 2
Harecastle	2.23	0 8	(Crown St. Halt)	2.15	0 2
Keele	2.3	0 9	Stafford	1.45	1 1
Kidsgrove	1.62, 2.6	0 9	Stockton Brook	2.13	0 7
Kingsley & F.	1.28	0 9	Stone	2.32	1 0
Leek	2.0	1 0	Tean	1.29	1 0
Leigh	2.8	1 0	Trentham	2.61	0 5
Longport	2.21	0 3	Tunstall	1.52, 1.56, 2.10	0 6
Longton	2.16, 3.40	0 1½	Uttoxeter	2.14	1 4
Macclesfield (H.R.)	1.34	1 0	Wall Grange	2.9	0 10
Market Drayton	1.50	1 3	Weston & J.	...	1 0
Meir	2.13, 2.34	0 5			

CHILDREN under three years of age, free; three years and under fourteen, half-fares.

Passengers holding day or half-day excursion tickets by special trains are not allowed to take any luggage except small handbags, luncheon baskets, or other small articles intended for the passenger's use during the day. On the return journey only, passengers may take with them, free of charge, goods for their own use not exceeding 60 lbs.

CONDITIONS OF ISSUE OF EXCURSION AND OTHER REDUCED FARE TICKETS.
Excursion tickets and tickets issued at fares less than the ordinary f es are issued subject to notices and Conditions shown in the Company's Current Time Tables.

For suitable return services see overleaf.

Bemrose & Sons Ltd., Derby and London.

PLEASE RETAIN THIS BILL FOR REFERENCE

EVENING EXCURSION

SUNDAY, JUNE 12th
TO

Ashbourne | **Thorpe Cloud**
Tissington | **Alsop-en-le-Dale**
AND
BUXTON

FROM	Departure Times	RETURN FARES (Third Class) TO				
		Ash-bourne	Thorpe Cloud	Tissing-ton	Alsop-en-le-Dale	Bux-ton
	p.m.	s. d.	s. d.	s. d.	s. d.	s. d.
BIRMINGHAM (New Street)	4.5	3 1	2 1	2 1	2 1	2 6
SALTLEY	4 11	3 1				2 6
WATER ORTON	4 15	1 10	1 10	1 10	1 10	2 5
WILNECOTE	4 30	1 7				2 1
TAMWORTH (H.L.)	4 35	1 7	1 7	1 7	1 10	2 1
Arrival Times		p.m.	p.m.	p.m.	p.m.	p.m.
		6 0	6 10	6 15	6 25	6 30
Passengers return same day		p.m.	p.m.	p.m.	p.m.	p.m.
		10 20	10 10	10 10	10 1	9 30

NOTE—PAVILION GARDENS, BUXTON. On presentation of Return Halves of Excursion Tickets, passengers will be admitted at reduced charge of 6d.

CHILDREN under three years of age, free; three years and under fourteen, half-fare.

Day, Half-day and Evening tickets are issued subject to the conditions applicable to tickets of these descriptions as shown in the Company's Time Tables.
For LUGGAGE ALLOWANCES see Time Tables.

CONDITIONS OF ISSUE

TICKETS ISSUED IN ADVANCE AT THE STATIONS AND AGENCIES

Information regarding Cheap Travel and other facilities will be supplied on application to the Stations, Agencies, or Mr. G. R. BRADBURY, District Passenger Manager, New Street Station, Birmingham. Telephone 2740 Midland.

ASHTON DAVIES, Chief Commercial Manager.

May, 1938
(E.A.O. 12302)

LMS

Examples of excursion handbills from the LM&SR era:

Above: Spring Season 8- and 15-day excursions to Llandudno and numerous other destinations in North Wales in 1925.

Right: From Birmingham (New Street) and stations to Tamworth, to Ashbourne and Derbyshire Dales stations to Buxton in 1938.

Far Right: For half day excursions to watch Stoke City play at home in 1933.

Left: The NSR Audit Staff 'checking out' at Leamington in May 1923, at their last reunion. *Author's collection*

Below Left: The 1924 poster of Staffordshire Potteries by Royal Academician Norman Wilkinson, one of eighteen paintings commissioned by the LM&SR from members of the RA. Well know academicians contributed works both for a booklet and a series of paintings which were the basis for colourful posters advertising the LM&SR. The appeal of these posters was considerable, with 26,500 sold in the UK and 3,220 in North America. *Chris Knight collection*

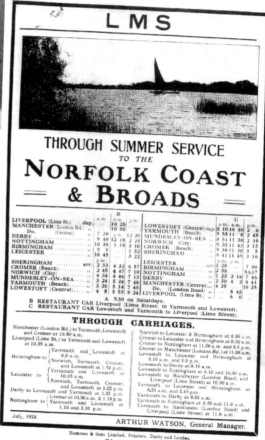

A short history of the Eastern Counties Express appeared in Vol. 2. Further research on this working between Liverpool/Manchester and the Norfolk Coast and Broads has been carried out by David Wrottesley.

Above Right: An LM&SR handbill for July 1923 promoting a through daily summer holiday train service to the Norfolk Coast and Broads. The service ran from Liverpool (Lime Street) and Manchester (London Road) stations, and came to be known as the Eastern Counties Express. It travelled via Derby and Nottingham, running to no fewer than six holiday resorts in Norfolk. A daily morning and afternoon train also ran from Manchester (Central) via the former Midland line, to Derby and Nottingham, thence to Norfolk, whilst separate trains ran daily from Birmingham and Leicester as well. *Chris Bunting collection, courtesy of the Midland & Great Northern Railway Circle*

Right: A northbound express, running from Yarmouth Beach and Lowestoft through to Liverpool and Manchester on summer weekdays, approaching Tutbury station circa 1924, with the twin chimneys of the Nestle & Anglo Swiss Milk Co's factory in the background. The locomotive is former L&NWR 'Jubilee' Class 4-4-0 No. 1923 *Agamemnon*. The first two coaches are a former Midland Railway non-corridor Third and an ex-L&NWR Dining Car. *Author's collection.*

Shelton Wharf looking north circa 1932, with the T&M Canal behind the stack of timber on the left. At the time of Grouping, the NSR operated thirty-two road motors and this number increased on the North Staffordshire Section in line with the rapid increase in their use by all railway companies. One of these early road vehicles can be seen here, centre background, loaded with bales or rolls of some description; the chassis is a Halley, probably ex-War Department. Also, in the centre of the picture is a Ransome & Rapier crane, mounted rigidly to a highly manoeuvrable chassis, which is lifting an LM&SR container. A wide variety of LM&SR wagons are in view, including a 5-plank in the foreground, loaded with barrels of ale. By this time, the major resignalling had taken place and the replacement L&NWR-style signal gantry installed, evidence of the influence of the L&NWR on the resignalling of the North Staffordshire Section. In the background is the former L&NWR warehouse, soon to be let to the Diamond Pottery Company, manufacturers of kiln pottery. In the far right background, some older NSR signalls still survive, beyond which and only just visible is the Winton Pottery. *National Railway Museum*

2

Road Deliveries

Probably the most significant changes in the activities of the railway companies came in the field of road delivery of merchandise. At the time of Grouping, the NSR had a fleet of thirty-two road motors, 291 horse-drawn wagons and carts, and 188 horses for hauling their road vehicles. The Company had, for a decade or so, been increasing the number of 'lurries', with a subsequent gradual reduction in the number of horse-drawn vehicles. For example, as early as 1926, there were plans to withdraw horse cartage from Congleton, even though the LM&SR as a whole continued to place great reliance on horse transport operations. However, through the LM&SR era, motor vehicles became more important; speedy collection and delivery of freight was the strength of the private transport sector and it was in direct competition with the railways for available traffic. The *Wood Mitchell New Penny Railway Time Table* of April 1921 contained an advertisement from the Potteries Electric Traction Company for its 'Tramways Parcels Express' service, with deliveries to all parts, promptly and economically, and '*A Speciality, goods warehoused in bulk and delivered in bulk and delivered as required*'.

In the summer of 1927, the LM&SR introduced containers, where possible, to facilitate the expeditious unloading of goods traffic being moved by rail; these first containers were simple wooden boxes. It was a pilot scheme initially and, after a few months of operation, the other railways simultaneously launched identical schemes. On the North Staffordshire Section, Stoke North Yard was partly converted to a container exchange bay and equipped with an overhead travelling crane, with other locations on the LM&SR system receiving similar facilities. The more common solution, also introduced at Stoke, was the provision of a Walker travelling crane, specifically designed to transship containers and mounted on a 6-wheeled chassis. A wide variety of container types were built to combat road and rail competition, all designed to handle assorted types of goods efficiently, such as services for Household Removals, Farm Removals and Works Removals; between November 1926 and November 1929, no fewer than 2,471 containers were ordered, the most popular being Types A and B, small and large covered steel containers respectively.

The LM&SR offered two distinct services, firstly Farm Collection &

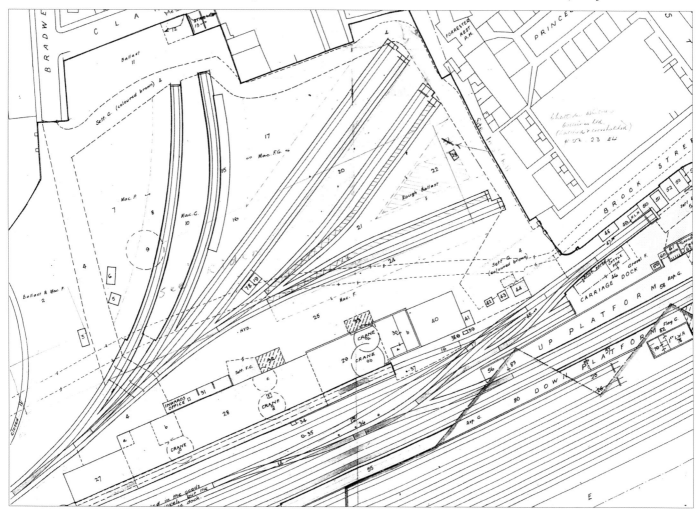

Longport was an important goods station, as shown on this portion from the LM&SR Rating Plan of the late 1920s. In the centre can be seen no fewer than eight sidings; in 1929, there was siding accommodation for 485 wagons. At the bottom of the plan is the long goods shed, which was equipped with four cranes lettered 'a' to 'd' and a fifth, lettered 'e', in the process of being installed or recently removed. Bottom right are the two platforms of the passenger station, with the cattle pen and carriage dock – by this time scarcely used – located behind the Up platform. *Cheddleton Railway Archive*

The former L&NWR warehouse at Nantwich, which the LM&SR leased to Yorke Bros. in October 1926. An ex-NSR Ford T is seen delivering a small load of Bibby merchandise to Yorke Bros, who were local agents for J. Bibby & Sons Ltd., oil, cake and soap manufacturers. The LM&SR lettering and number plate have been added to the photograph, probably on top of the old NSR lettering. The number plate enhancement was probably because the actual plate was old and indistinct, so the draughtsman embellished it for image purposes as well as adding the LMS lettering. *Nelson Twells collection*

Delivery Services for grain, livestock, feeding stuff, packed manure, potatoes and general merchandise; this started in late 1927. The second was a Town Cartage Service and this was first advertised in the Stoke area in 1932. These are now considered separately.

The Country Service operated over a radius of 10 to 12 miles from the nearest station and offered extensive facilities in North Staffordshire and the Moorlands. Typical of the villages served by this initiative were Butterton, Checkley, Ellastone, Ettiley Heath, Fauld, Knypersley, Lawton, Longsdon, Swythamley, Talke and Upper Leigh. Nationally, the LM&SR invested in sixteen livestock motors, of which five were based at Stoke for the short distance livestock market but this initative proved to be unsuccessful. In addition, for a short while, a lorry service had been introduced for all cattle markets within a 17 mile radius from Stoke. Although the movement of cattle by rail in and out of the NSR network had never been significant, in 1939 there were still twenty stations that had facilities for the road conveyance of livestock, including Ashbourne, Cresswell, Endon, Harecastle, Longport,

Sandon, Silverdale, Trentham, Uttoxeter and Weston & Ingestre.

The LM&SR started advertising its Town Cartage New Service in the Stoke area in 1932, for collecting and delivering goods and parcels locally, within the agreed cartage boundaries, of Tunstall, Burslem, Longport, Hanley, Stoke, Longton and Newcastle. The service expanded considerably between 1932 and 1939; initially there were seven depots serving twenty-three towns and villages, increasing to eight with the addition of Kidsgrove in 1934, serving

Promotional postcard, distributed by the District Goods & Passenger Manager, Stoke-on-Trent, to promote the LMS Furniture Removal Service; the reverse invites the recipient to return the card and request further information. The LM&SR trialled this service at Stoke in 1927 and was followed a few months later by the other 'Big Four' railways. In November 1928, the LM&SR announced that, along with the GWR, L&NER and SR, it had agreed to supply containers for furniture removals in order to regain a substantial amount of this valuable business. The vehicle, a Karrier GH5, has a cab-over-engine chassis and could carry up to 6 tons. These were an important heavy lorry class and lasted in regular service through the Second World War. Note the LMS logo on the side, one that lasted until Nationalisation. *Author's collection*

forty-six towns and villages in 1935, with the eight depots serving fifty-two similar destinations in 1939. In 1935, Stoke started to market aggressively the ability of the LM&SR to deliver large blocks of parcels, an early success coming with the delivery of a block of 400,000 parcels.

In April 1931, the list of LM&SR road motor depots included Stoke (at Whieldon Road) and Derby; motor vehicles were employed at Burton, Crewe, Derby, Harecastle, Leek, Longport, Macclesfield, Stoke and Uttoxeter. By the end of the LM&SR era, there were eighteen lorries attached to each depot except Stoke (which had twenty-five), with each depot responsible for its own collections. Each goods yard in the area had its own stables and these had been converted into garages. There was also a bonded warehouse at Hanley that was accessible on Mondays, Wednesdays and Fridays.

The 1928 Road Transport Act had also provided for LM&SR road motor and parcels services over routes that would not now include a section by rail. The commercial rationale behind the significant investment by the LM&SR in containers was justified by the results of two years of operations – £200,000 per annum turnover, with 60 per cent of the traffic attracted

Right: This promotional pamphlet, issued jointly by the 'Big Four' – the Great Western Railway, the Southern Railway, the London & North Eastern Railway and the LM&SR – and, in a foretaste of the future, describing themselves as 'British Railways', was a logical attempt to break into a new market. Jointly, the four companies could offer a country-wide service, since removals traffic would be likely to cross company boundaries, with the most direct route likely to be demanded by those using this facility. The pamphlet was issued probably in the late 1920s and the drawings and photographs contained within illustrated the various steps in furniture removal. For those using the service, fare concessions of one third were offered on fares to the nearest station to their new abode. *Cheddleton Railway Archive*

The LM&SR's Door to Door Container Service in operation, a posed photograph in one of the yards at Stoke in 1936. A Ransomes & Rapier container crane is lifting conatiner No. B1348 on to a trailer hauled by a Karrier 3-wheeled mechanical horse. *Author's collection*

from road and water, 20 per cent held against such competition and with 20 per cent of this traffic hitherto rail borne. The increase in the volume of merchandize carried was reflected in the number of road motors and of articulated units used, such as Karriers and Scammells, which were being continuously introduced. However, the use of horses carried on, albeit on a diminished scale, throughout the LM&SR era and indeed into the 1960s. The LM&SR Traffic Committee approved the purchase of Karrier petrol road motors at fifteen depots, including Longport and Uttoxeter in 1927, to displace horse strength, and this early initiative continued throughout the LM&SR era. The substitution of 'ordinary type motors and horse strength' by mechanical horses was reflected in trials and investment proposals for mechanical horses. In 1934, two national investment proposals for 728 tractors and for 1,400 trailers totalling £260,873 were approved for the LM&SR as a whole; the L&NER had been the pioneers in the use of the mechanical horse.

The LM&SR also introduced to British railways the insulated container for the conveyance of chilled and frozen meat. A further development of this was the introduction of the glass-lined milk container, in collaboration with the GWR and United Dairies, and these were introduced in the late 1920s at Ecton Creamery on the Manifold Valley line and at United Dairies at Uttoxeter.

The biggest capital investment in cartage in North Staffordshire in the LM&SR era occurred in 1937 and was for improved goods terminal facilities at Longport, in order to improve handling facilities in the Potteries and to achieve economies. The proposal was for the bulk shed miscellaneous traffic, then dealt with at Hanley and Tunstall, to be transferred to Longport, whilst the residue of the Hanley miscellaneous traffic would be transferred to Stoke. The cost of these proposals was estimated to be £77,118, including £13,205 for cartage equipment. Amongst the principal features for forwarded traffic was additional siding accommodation for 97 wagons (84 of which were under cover), with four electric gantry trains for received traffic. The reconstruction of the timber goods shed took place in order to provide berthing accommodation for 52 vehicles, whilst yard siding accommodation was to be increased by 140 wagons. Clerical, handling and traffic operating economies were estimated to yield £11,000 per annum.

The former L&NWR warehouse located a few hundred yards north of Stoke station, which was built in 1902 to a standard L&NWR design. The wooden armed loading gauge can be seen on the left, with two wall-mounted cranes on the right, under which can be seen a single-horse dray. The cranes could access both the ground floor loading platforms and the first floor verandahs. The warehouse later passed out of LM&SR use, when it was taken over by the Diamond Company, a local pottery firm. *National Railway Museum*

TOWN CARTAGE.
THE LMS RAILWAY
has established a NEW SERVICE of
Collecting and Delivering Goods and Parcels
LOCALLY
within the agreed Cartage Boundaries of

Tunstall, Burslem, Longport, Hanley Stoke, Longton, and Newcastle

which include the following Towns and Villages:—

TUNSTALL—Pitt's Hill, Chell, Brownhills, Black Bull
BURSLEM—Smallthorne, Cobridge, Bradeley, Ford Green
LONGPORT—Wolstanton, Porthill
HANLEY—Birches Head, Sneyd Green
STOKE—Fenton, Shelton, Trent Vale, Penkhull, Hartshill
LONGTON—Normacot, Sandford Hill, Adderley Green, Florence, Dresden, Meir
NEWCASTLE—Chesterton, Basford

at the following scale of charges:—

Consignments (consisting of one or more packages from one Sender to one Consignee):—

	In usual Cartage Boundary.	Out-boundary.
Not exceeding 7 lbs.	3d.	4d.
Over 7 lbs. and not exceeding 14 lbs.	4d.	6d.
" 14 " " " 28 "	6d.	9d.
" 28 " " " 56 "	8d.	1/-
" 56 " " " 84 "	10d.	1/3
" 84 " " " 112 "	1/-	1/6
" 1 cwt " " 2 cwts.	1/4	1/9
" 2 cwts. " " 3 "	1/8	2/-
" 3 " " " 4 "	2/-	2/3
" 4 " " " 5 "	2/3	2/6

Exceeding 5 cwts. and not exceeding } An additional charge of 3d.
1 ton ... ... } for each additional cwt.

Consignments exceeding 1 ton, and regular traffic, will be subject to special quotations.

The above charges will be increased for articles or packages of exceptional bulk in proportion to weight.

TOWN CARTAGE.
THE LMS RAILWAY
has established a NEW SERVICE of
Collecting and Delivering Goods and Parcels
LOCALLY within the agreed Cartage Boundaries of

Kidsgrove, Tunstall, Burslem, Longport, Hanley, Stoke, Longton, and Newcastle

which include the following Towns and Villages:—

TUNSTALL—Pitt's Hill, Chell, Brownlees, Black Bull, Brindley Ford, Packmoor, Goldenhill, Newchapel
BURSLEM—Smallthorne, Cobridge, Bradeley, Ford Green, Norton
LONGPORT—Wolstanton, Porthill, Chesterton, Audley, Halmerend
HANLEY—Birches Head, Sneyd Green, Etruria, Northwood
STOKE—Fenton, Shelton, Trent Vale, Penkhull, Hartshill, Trentham, Abbey Hulton, Bucknall, Milton, Cliff Vale, Barlaston, Blurton, Ash Bank, Werrington
LONGTON—Normacot, Sandford Hill, Adderley Green, Florence, Dresden, Meir, Blythe Bridge, Weston Coyney
NEWCASTLE—Basford, Silverdale, Westlands, Maybank, Knutton, Cross Heath, Clayton, Seabridge
KIDSGROVE—Butt Lane, Talke, Scholar Green, Dales Green
(HARECASTLE)

at the following scale of charges:—

Consignments (consisting of one or more packages from one Sender to one Consignee):—

Weight per consignment not exceeding	Charge — Destinations within collecting station's usual cartage boundary.	Charge — Destinations outside collecting station's usual cartage boundary.	Weight per consignment not exceeding	Charge — Destinations within collecting station's usual cartage boundary.	Charge — Destinations outside collecting station's usual cartage boundary.
	s. d.	s. d.		s. d.	s. d.
7 lbs.	3	4	9 cwts.	3 5	3 8
14 "	3	4	10 "	3 8	3 11
28 "	4	6½	11 "	3 11	4 2
56 "	6½	9½	12 "	4 2	4 6
84 "	8½	1 1	13 "	4 6	4 9
112 "	11	1 4	14 "	4 9	5 0
2 cwts.	1 1	1 7	15 "	5 0	5 3
3 "	1 5	1 10	16 "	5 3	5 6
4 "	1 9	2 1	17 "	5 6	5 9
5 "	2 1	2 4	18 "	5 9	6 0
6 "	2 4	2 8	19 "	6 0	6 4
7 "	2 8	2 11	20 "	6 4	6 7
8 "	3 2	3 2			

Exceeding 1 ton—subject to special quotation.

For further information apply to the LMS Station Master or Goods Agent.

Above Left & Previous Page Top: Advertisements from the 1932 LM&SR Summer Tourist Guide for the North Staffordshire Section.

Above Right: By 1939, the service had been was expanded to serve fifty-two towns and villages from the original twenty-seven covered. Author's collection

Left: Front cover of a booklet produced in 1939 listing all of the places reached by the LM&SR Country Lorry Service. Covering the whole of the system, contained within was a list of several thousand villages that lay within a ten miles radius of a station, along with the name of the station that each was served from. *All author's collection*

Right: In the first of three delightful views of the Country Delivery Service taken in the Macclesfield area in the mid-1930s, Morris Commercial 10-wheeler flat No. 1712B is seen in Prestbury, with the driver delivering a box of seeds. There are sacks of cattle feed and a box of oranges on the dray as well as a barrel, probably of nails, and a mysterious huge lump covered in sacking. The dray is equipped with a sheeting rail that is not in use, whilst the early canvas roof cab has already been modified by the addition of a windscreen. This photograph was used for several years in a national LM&SR advertising campaign. *Nelson Twells collection*

LMS COUNTRY LORRY SERVICES
FOR FARM
AND VILLAGE

Above: The same lorry is seen leaving Macclesfield (Hibel Road) goods yard, fully loaded with sacks probably containing animal feed. Note the speed restriction of 20 mph. The three cast iron signs visible on the left all detailed the emergency arrangements in the event of a fire breaking out. The lorries were all distinguished by LM&SR fleet numbers, in true railway fashion, as well as by their registration plates.

Left: The order being delivered at a farm in the hills outside Macclesfield on what was clearly a snowy day in the middle of winter. The tyres were solid rubber.
Both Nelson Twells collection

Right: This Great Central & North Staffordshire Railway lettered flat dray was photographed at Bollington circa 1929, some six years after Grouping had seen both companies absorbed, the GCR in to the L&NER. The dray is carrying a newly fabricated dust extractor from the sheet metal fabrication works of Wheeldon & Wrigley. *Author's collection*

Above: LM&SR delivery driver Leonard Moss is seen here at the entrance to Leek goods yard circa 1946, with a horse-drawn delivery to make in the town of a large crate aboard dray No. 18425. Note the beautifully dressed red stone of the goods office and, in the background, one of the gas holders of Leek Gas Works. Leonard Moss delivered by horse throughout Leek and to the edge of the rural areas for a period of thirty-five years. *Paul Blurton collection*

Left: A remarkable photograph taken at Stoke station on 27th April 1964, where not only delivery by horse still survived but the horse proudly carries LMS-lettered horse brasses, although the Company had been Nationalised some sixteen years earlier. The LM&SR continued to invest in the horse-drawn delivery service throughout its existence, despite the expansion of motor services. *Martin Connop Price*

Insets Above & Right: LM&SR period documents from the Chief Goods Manager's Office at Stoke. The top one is an overprint of an NSR letterhead. *Both author's collection*

THE SCAMMELL SCARAB MECHANICAL HORSE (6-TONNER)
WITH FLAT PLATFORM TYPE BODY

Above: This picture of a 6-ton Scarab Mechanical Horse with flat platform appeared in the first edition of the *Scammell Drivers' Handbook for Scarab Mechanical Horse*, **Right**. In 1932, trials of Scammell petrol road motors had proved unsuccessful but the use of mechanical horse units took off in 1934, with a heavy capital programme nationally of over £360,000, when horses and horse vehicles were replaced. In 1939, Scammell 4-wheeled motors, a light mechanical horse tractor with two trailers, were purchased to see if they were cheaper than horse teams but, in the same year, the LM&SR also proceeded with the purchase of horse-drawn vehicles. This handbook was issued to driver Jim Croxall, who drove a Scarab in the Potteries for many years and who was based at Longton. The two pages, **Below**, illustrate the controls and cab layout. *Jim Croxall collection*

THE SCAMMELL SCARAB MECHANICAL HORSE

INSTRUMENTS AND CONTROLS
(See Figure I)

ACCELERATOR PEDAL (Ref. 14).—The right hand pedal which regulates the speed of the engine. Fitted with hand adjusted stop (Ref. 15) to control tick over.

CLUTCH PEDAL (Ref. 12).—The left hand pedal. NOTE.—When driving, do not rest the foot on this pedal or hold out to coast.

FOOT BRAKE PEDAL (Ref. 13).—The centre pedal. Operates the driving axle brakes. NOTE.—On 6-tonners this pedal also operates the trailer brakes which are applied by vacuum servo.

MOTIVE UNIT HAND BRAKE (Ref. 11).—The right hand lever. Operates the driving axle brakes.

TRAILER HAND BRAKE (Ref. 9).—The left hand lever. Operates the brakes on the trailer axle.

TRAILER RELEASE LEVER (Ref. 10).—The centre lever. Pull right back to release trailer. NOTE.—First release the safety catch by pressing down lever situated at base of release lever.

GEAR CHANGE LEVER (Ref. 16).—On right hand side of driver.

CARBURETTOR STARTING CONTROL (See Figure 3).—The Bowden control situated on back of cab. Pull out when starting cold engine.

HORN BUTTON (Ref. 8).—Mounted on right hand side of dashboard.

BRAKE VACUUM GAUGE (Ref. 7).—Registers the amount of vacuum available for braking purposes. Should register approx. 20".

STARTER SWITCH (Ref. 4).—Mounted on instrument panel. Depress firmly and release as soon as engine starts. Do not depress unless engine is stationary.

OIL PRESSURE WARNING LIGHT (Ref. 6).—Mounted on instrument panel. Red light appears when oil pressure falls below 9 lb.

AMMETER (Ref. 5).—Indicates the flow of current into and out of the battery. NOTE.—Owing to the constant voltage control, the ammeter will register a low reading when the battery is fully charged and a high reading when the battery is low.

SPEEDOMETER (Ref. 3).—Registers the speed of the vehicle and mileage covered.

SWITCH BOARD (Ref. 2).—Fitted on instrument panel and has three positions : (1) OFF ; (2) S-Side and tail lamps ; (3) H-Side, tail and head lamps.

IGNITION SWITCH (Ref. 1).—Turn anti-clockwise to switch on.

COMPENSATED VOLTAGE CONTROL AND FUSE BOX.—Fitted on right hand side of scuttle.

WINDSCREEN WIPER.—Turn centre lever clockwise to operate. NOTE.—Ignition must be switched "on."

THE SCAMMELL SCARAB MECHANICAL HORSE

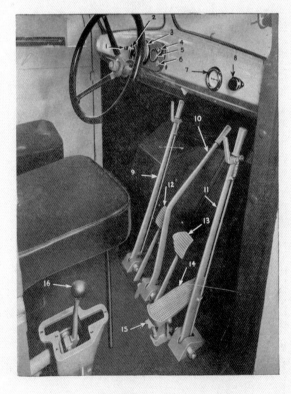

Figure I.—INSTRUMENTS AND CONTROLS

Above: This official LM&SR Works photograph was taken at Wolverton in 1931 and shows a new Karrier GH5 before it had received its registration number. The vehicle, a 4-ton lorry equipped with electric lighting and hand operated tipping gear, was built for the Engineering Department at Stoke at a cost of £860. It was used for carrying material to outlying parts of the District and for taking men to work on Sundays, and was a replacement for an obsolete lorry that was fourteen years old, which was no longer usable nor repairable. *National Railway Museum*

Right: LM&SR van No. 1223-D, seen here in Congleton station yard on 20th June 1953, still in LM&SR livery with shaded numerals. A Karrier Bantam van, its registration number was GRO185. The faded advertisement on the side is for Taverners Fruit Drops. Behind it on the left is horse drawn cart No. M242444 (built at Wolverton in 1936), in black livery and lettered 'British Railways'; note the rubber tyres. In the background is the 1849 Congleton goods warehouse, which still stands and today houses a bathroom design showroom. *F.W. Shuttleworth*

This photograph of a single-decker bus belonging to the North Western Road Car Company, of Stockport, where the vehicle was also registered, also featured in the Introduction to the first volume in this series but is just as relevant here. The destination board indicates a service to Bollington, so the bus would have been in competition with the rail service to the same place. The driver, ticket collector and local inspector all pose for the photographer, along with a number of smiling passengers. Carrying registration number DB5155, the bus was built in 1928 and withdrawn from service in 1936, and had seating for 32 passengers. The chassis was a Tilling Stevens B10A, with a Tilling body mounted on it. Macclesfield (Central station) and the new LM&SR-style Macclesfield Central signal box forms the background to this circa 1935 view. *Author's collection*

3

Buses

The LM&SR, along with the other major railway companies, recognised the threat posed by the expanding bus network. In the expanded region covered by the LM&SR, in one or two locations the L&NWR had run its own bus services and these were carried on by the new company. The LM&SR promoted its own Act of Parliament in 1928 and this received the Royal Assent on 3rd August 1928; similar Acts were promoted by the other three major railways later in 1928. The LM&SR Act empowered it to provide, own, work and use road vehicles to convey road passengers and their luggage, and to enter into agreement with others to provide the same. Of particular relevance to the North Staffordshire District were the acquisitions of shares in two bus companies. All the shares in Crosville Motor Company Ltd were acquired on 1st May 1929 but twelve months later half of these were transferred to Tilling/British Electric Traction

interests. From 1933 onwards, the LM&SR reduced the proportion of its shareholding further, with the GWR acquiring a stake, and this arrangement lasted through the remaining years of the 'Big Four' era. The Crosville area of operations included that part of the former NSR network between Crewe and Market Drayton west of the West Coast main line.

In 1929, the LM&SR acquired, along with the L&NER, a stake of just under 50 per cent in the North Western Road Car Company Ltd, an arrangement which also lasted up until Nationalisation. This bus company operated in Cheshire, Derbyshire and North Staffordshire, serving the former NSR network in many parts. The LM&SR also attempted to acquire the Potteries Electric Motor Transport Company Ltd in 1931 but negotiations were unsuccessful. The passing of the Road Traffic Act in 1932 had the consequence of preventing additional competition with the railways, by prohibiting the expansion of the passenger road transport industry by new road operations. Locally, the LM&SR was able to successfully oppose proposed excursions from Longton and Stoke by Trent Motors.

Above: The LM&SR obtained Parliamentary powers to operate buses in 1928. Whilst it did not exercise these powers in any part of the former NSR network, two of their newly-built small Leyland fleet were photographed in Winton Square, Stoke, around 1929, perhaps on a delivery stop as both omnibuses are carrying trade plates; Stoke station is in the background. They are both Leyland Lions, the bodies for which were constructed at the LM&SR Carriage & Wagon Works at Wolverton; seats were provided for 32 passengers. Livery was crimson lake and white, with black mouldings picked out in gold and vermillion lining on the white. The destination board on the side of the omnibus is for the route between Newark, Southwell and Mansfield, with the top board carrying the LM&SR name. *Manifold collection*

Below: This is typical of the single-deckers that operated in the country areas and small towns in the former NSR triangle of Newcastle-under-Lyme, Market Drayton and Crewe. The bus, LMS Crosville No. 346, is in LM&SR maroon livery and was a petrol-engined Leyland Lion LT1, purchased new in 1929. The livery resembled the LM&SR maroon that was used on its passenger rolling stock. The vehicle, as was typical with many buses of the time, was withdrawn after a short working life with Crosville and sold during 1936. *Crosville Archive Trust*

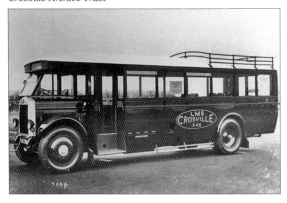

Right: A handbill for 29th June 1929, promoting the LM&SR and Crosville Motor Services 'Grand Combined Rail and Road Excursion through Beautiful Caernarvonshire'. Passengers travelled by Restaurant Car Excursion to Menai Bridge, thence by motor coach to Beaumaris, walking across and back over the suspension bridge, then coach to Bangor and returning by rail from there. *Brian Morris collection*

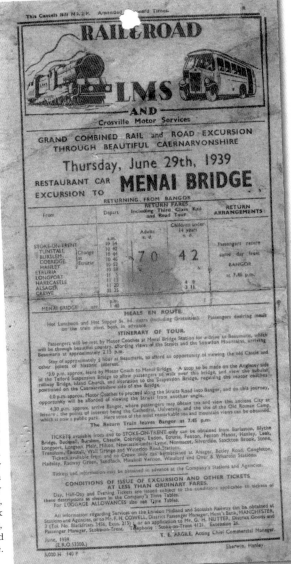

The start of the Loop Line was at Etruria Junction and here, on 31st July 1937, an unidentified Class '4F' 0-6-0 at the head of a mixed freight is seen descending the 1 in 50 gradient to join the main line. From left to right are the massive slag tips of the Shelton Iron & Steel Works, the blast furnace charging hoists and gantries, the steel melting shop with its chimney, and the rolling mills. On the right of the picture are two former NSR houses; the one on the far right, only partially visible here, would have been occupied by the station master at Etruria at this period. *E.R. Morten*

Inset Above: Burslem was one of the stations on the Loop Line. This NSR Stoke to Burslem First Class ticket was issued in 1933. *Author's collection*

N.S.R.—FIRST CLASS
STOKE-ON-TRENT To
BURSLEM
Available for one journey on day of issue only
Turn over   Burslem 72   Fare
1492

4

The Loop Line

The Loop Line was a short line between Etruria Junction and Kidsgrove Junction, seven miles 528 yards long and of considerable economic and industrial importance. Firstly, it connected the principal towns of the Potteries north of Stoke – Hanley, Burslem and Tunstall – with each other. Secondly, it provided the rail connection with several industrial complexes, such as the Shelton Iron Steel & Coal Co. Ltd, Sneyd Colliery and brickworks, and the Birchenwood Colliery Co., and to the large collieries that they owned such as Deep Pit (Hanley) and Sneyd (Burslem). The first section of the Loop Line, between Etruria Junction and Hanley, opened in 1864 and the remainder, north of Hanley, opened in 1873 and 1875. There were two spur lines connecting with the Loop Line: The Pinnox Branch between Pinnox Junction and the private mineral line to Chatterley-Whitfield Colliery and Tunstall Junction, just south of Tunstall station; and the Newfields Branch, which went from Newfields Junction to Newfields

Wharf. These spur lines opened in 1875 and 1874 respectively. On the Loop Line, wagon accommodation was available at Hanley Goods (75 wagons on the Down and 91 wagons on the Up), at Waterloo Road (67 on the Up), at Tunstall (Newfields Junction – 67 on the Down) and at Kidsgrove marshalling sidings (170 on the Up).

It is hard to imagine now just how many passengers it carried on short journeys. In 1922, there were fifty-four trains daily from Stoke; the service was also varied, some originating from Uttoxeter and Cheadle, whilst some went as far as Congleton. The NSR relied heavily on it for passenger traffic and although no separate passenger numbers for the Loop Line are available, it must have contributed a considerable proportion of the 4.1 million Workmen's tickets issued in 1922. There were no passenger trains on Sundays. The motive power used was 'A' or 'B' Class 2-4-0s or rebuilt 2-4-2Ts. From the 1920s, competition from buses was considerable, with the result that, over the years, the Loop Line

An aerial view of the Shelton Iron & Steel Works, looking north west and taken in 1943. The Loop Line runs across the bottom of the picture, heading left to Etruria Junction and right to Hanley. Also visible at the bottom is the Trent & Mersey Canal, which was diverted to the right to allow easing of the Loop Line railway gradient; the original line of the canal passed through what is, in this view, the 32 inch rolling mill building. Above the mill can be seen the blast furnace, with the coke ovens and by-product plant in the centre, and Etruria Hall to the extreme right. To the top right, the Grange railway exchange sidings can just be distinguished, along with the iron ore preparation plant. Note how the canal snakes through the works, bisecting it before heading off to the top right of the photograph. *E.J.D. Warrilow, Keele University Library*

passenger rail service was reduced and, by 1947, the service had more than halved to twenty-five daily, plus the unadvertised Workmen's trains referred to shortly. The passenger service on Sundays during the LM&SR era was to say the least erratic. From no trains at the time of Grouping, in 1924 there were no fewer than thirteen, none in 1931 and 1932, and two in 1933 and 1934; in 1935 and 1937 there were two plus an extra five trains during the summer and in 1939 there were four plus five in the summer. There were none during the war period and still none in 1947.

In October 1922, the availability of Workmen's Daily Return tickets to and from Loop Line stations was considerable. From Burslem, for example, tickets were available to no fewer than ten stations and from the principal Loop Line stops to between seven and nine other stations. In respect of Loop Line stations in the less urbanised areas, Workmen's tickets were available to five destinations from Newchapel & Goldenhill and to four destinations from Pitts Hill. Workmen's tickets were also available to Loop Line stations, from Fenton, Longton and from several others. In addition, in 1922, Workmen's Weekly tickets were available from wider afield, such as Meir, Mow Cop, Alsager, Alsager Road & Talke, Blythe Bridge, Cheadle, Congleton and Normacot. By the summer of 1924, availability had been extended to include

Barlaston, Stone and Trentham, whilst the scheme for Weekly tickets had been rolled out to a much larger number of stations, mainly on the Loop Line; there was a further improvement in availability by 1929.

Wartime saw the introduction of several unadvertised Workmen's trains that served Loop Line stations. For example, in October 1941, there was a Burslem to Norton Bridge train bringing workers to the construction site at Swynnerton (Cold Meece). From April 1942 (with minor variations on Saturdays), to serve two munitions factories, there were two trains from Cobridge and three from Newchapel & Goldenhill to Cold Meece daily and there were two trains daily from Hanley to Radway Green (Mill Lane). On Sundays, there was only a slightly reduced service, four trains to Cold Meece and two to Radway Green; also on

The Shelton Works complex at Etruria and, a few hundred yards to the east, at Shelton, required a large number of industrial locomotives; in 1946, no fewer than thirteen were in use, with nine rostered on a three-shift basis. Depicted over these two pages are several at work during the LM&SR era:

Above: *Lord Faringdon*, an 0-6-0T originally built by Black Hawthorn & Co. Ltd of Gateshead in 1873 (Works No. 242), as a saddle tank locomotive for the North Eastern Railway, their No. 855. Withdrawn in 1911, by which time it was NER No. 868, it was sold into industrial use via locomotive dealer J.F. Wake. It was rebuilt at Shelton in 1930 as a conventional tank engine and is seen here probably only a year or so after that. After a long life, and a reboilering in 1940, it was eventually scrapped on site in 1955. *H.W. Robinson*

Above: *Bowood* was an 0-6-0ST built in 1907 by Andrew Barclay & Sons Ltd of Kilmarnock (Works No. 1113) and delivered new to Shelton Works. It is seen here in the early 1930s at Shelton sidings, with the NSR Loop Line signals prominent in the background; also visible are private owner wagons for Shelton (left) and Tarmac (right). This locomotive was transferred to the Florence Coal & Iron Co. Ltd in 1938. *H.W. Robinson*

Left: *Shellingford*, an 0-6-0ST built at Shelton in 1911, very largely from a Peckett design and with a boiler supplied by Bagnalls of Stafford, was scrapped on site in September 1955. As well as the name, it also carried the number 14, on an oval plate on the side of the cab. *Shellingford* was the third of four locomotives that Shelton built for their own use. The photograph again dates from the early 1930s. *Author's collection*

Sundays there were trains from Newchapel & Goldenhill to Stoke and from Tunstall to Cresswell. After the war, in 1947 there was still a very limited Workmen's service, one train daily to both Cold Meece and to Radway Green.

In order to encourage passenger traffic from Loop Line stations, Cheap tickets on Thursdays and Saturdays were issued to Manchester (London Road) and to Birmingham (New Street), and these continued to be available up until 1939. From 1934, Cheap Daily Return tickets were available along the Loop Line, every day and by all trains, and this facility also continued through to 1939. In 1939, Half Day Excursion tickets were introduced from Loop Line stations to Stafford, Wolverhampton, Dudley Port and Birmingham (New Street). In 1929, there were Cheap tickets available from principal Loop Line stations to Manchester each weekday, and on Thursdays and Saturdays between designated trains.

Above: *Countess*, an 0-6-0ST, built by Peckett & Sons Ltd of Bristol in 1896 (Works No. 630), seen here at Shelton in the 1920s. *Countess* was scrapped in 1935 but some of its parts were used to rebuild sister engine *Shelton*, a Peckett 0-4-0ST of 1889 vintage. *Allan Baker collection*

Right: This 0-4-0 crane tank was built by Dübs & Co. of Polmadie in 1901 (Works No. 4101). It was affectionately known as '*Dubsy*' but never carried any nameplates. It is seen here at work moving a concrete mixer in the 1930s. The locomotive was converted for oil burning in 1962, taken out of use in 1970 and purchased for preservation at Cranmore in 1973 but is now privately preserved on the Foxfield Light Railway. *Author's collection*

These two largely identical Barclay 0-4-0STs, *Buscot* and *Alice*, built in 1899 (Works No. 818) and 1900 (Works No. 884) respectively, were photographed with a train of empty open wagons in the 1930s. They were scrapped in December 1966 (*Buscot*) and October 1963 (*Alice*). *Author's collection*

A significant amount of the freight activity over the Loop Line was reflected in trip working. Shunting engines used were from Longport in the main but also one from Harecastle and three from Etruria. In 1938, there were no fewer than eleven trip workings to destinations on the Loop Line, eight worked by locomotives from Stoke Shed and three from Alsager Shed (all working to Birchenwood). The heavier '4F' Class 0-6-0s and 2-6-4Ts were engaged in colliery work, the lighter loads being performed by Class '3' 0-6-0Ts and 2-6-2Ts.

By 1928, an early morning fish and parcels train over the Loop Line from Macclesfield (Central) to Normacot had been introduced; this did not survive during wartime but, in the autumn of 1946, a Stockport to Normacot (Mondays excepted) parcels train over the route was introduced.

The LM&SR developed its own Town Cartage scheme in the area served by the Loop Line from 1932 onwards. It used three main depots for this, at Hanley, Burslem and Tunstall, and there were several areas along the Biddulph Valley line that were also served from these depots. From Hanley, the area covered initially was Sneyd Green, to which was added Etruria in 1935. From Burslem, Cobridge was served. From Tunstall, the area served initially in 1932 was Pitts Hill, to which was added Newchapel & Goldenhill in 1935

During the 1930s, the LM&SR sought to introduce office modernisation and automation of its clerical procedures. Accordingly, at Hanley, in 1935, office machines for dealing with goods accounting work were acquired for £900, to be financed by the replacement of five male clerks by female clerks at much lower rates of pay.

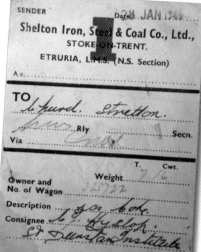

Right: A Shelton Iron, Steel & Coal Co. Ltd wagon label, for a consignment of coke sent to Church Stretton via the GWR in January 1946. *Author's collection*

A builder's photograph of 8-plank wooden mineral wagon No. 1005, one of twenty-five built for the Shelton Company by Charles Roberts in 1935. Note that it is directed to be returned 'Empty to Deep Pits Sidings Cobridge'. These wagons had a red oxide body, with corner plates and door iron work in black, whilst the white letters are edged in black. *Historical Model Railway Society*

A 20-ton steel Hopper, No. 5201, which was built by Charles Roberts as part of an order for fifty iron ore wagons between December 1937 and January 1938. The main lettering is again white edged with black and also painted on the side is the wagon's home address of 'ETRURIA, STOKE-ON-TRENT, LMS'. *Historical Model Railway Society*

Left: Racecourse Pit No. 3, seen here in the early 1930s, was owned by the Shelton Iron, Steel & Coal Co. Ltd. The pit derived its name from the fact that it was located on the old Hanley Racecourse, which saw its last races in the early 1840s, after which the site at Etruria was industrialised; three shafts were subsequently located on it. Over the years, No's 3 and 4 pits were modernised but No. 5 was closed and dismantled in 1921. In 1923, employment at the colliery was 594, increasing to 645 in 1927 but reducing to 560 in 1933 and 405 in 1939. The danger of flooding was an ever-present hazard at the colliery and this, coupled with dwindling reserves, led to its closure in July 1941. In later years, it was mainly ironstone that was mined there. *Bill Jack*

The Flintshire steel making firm of John Summers & Sons Ltd had no blast furnaces of their own, so in March 1920, they took over the Shelton Iron, Steel & Coal Co. which had an overcapacity in steel making. Summers' intention was to increase its iron making capacity, in order to feed Shelton's furnaces and those at Shotton. Modernisation and expansion took place at Etruria at this time, with new mechanically-charged furnaces completed in May 1922. Additional new plant was built at around this time, including new boilers, new foundry extensions to the washers and an additional by-product plant. Shelton Bar at Etruria was a 400-acre site, where 10,000 employees were engaged in steel production but also with five coal mines and a complete internal railway system. As a result of its industrial importance, Shelton Bar was a frequent target for enemy bombers during the Second World War. John Summers & Sons Ltd was Nationalised in 1951, then taken private again a short time later but was Nationalised for a second and final time in 1967.

These two photographs were taken in early 1923 and show the construction of the new by-product plant at Etruria.

Above: A hive of activity with excavation on several different levels. As well as being used to remove spoil, the Shelton wagons are also delivering bricks from the nearby Cobridge Brick Co. On the next level down a chute can be seen in the centre, for pouring concrete behind the timber shuttering a level below; to the right of this is a section of the finished wall or foundation being formed. Note the intense manual nature of the excavations of the foundations for the works, rather surprising at this late date. In the background is the smaller of the two spoil tips of Racecourse Colliery.

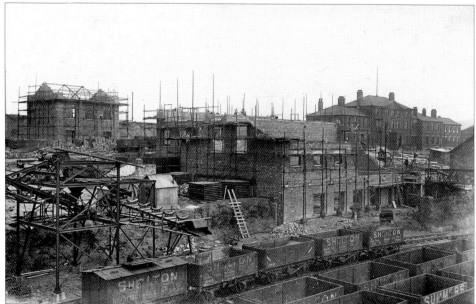

Left: Construction of the new buildings well under way, with Etruria Hall, the offices of the Shelton Company but originally, in the 1760s, the home of Josiah Wedgwood, in the background. The wagons on view are all Shelton-owned, apart from one John Summers wagon just visible in the bottom right corner. The covered wagon bottom left would have been used for the transportation of lime. *Both Steve Birks collection*

Above: An aerial photograph of Shelton Iron & Steel Works taken circa 1937. At the top left of the picture is Racecourse Colliery and its dirt tip, which by this time was the only pit left on the main iron and steel works site, although there had been several others in earlier years. To the right, with the row of tall chimneys, is the steel melting shop, which contained the open hearth steel furnaces, with the 32 inch rolling mill immediately above. In the centre of the picture are the three blast furnaces with their adjacent hot-blast stoves, the area between the two occupied by the elevated railway which served the furnace bunkers. Above the furnaces are the coking ovens and the by-product plant, the construction of which is shown in the two photographs on the previous page; Etruria Hall can be made out just to the right. To the left of the blast furnaces is the power station with its cooling ponds emitting water vapour, whilst the large building in front of the furnaces housed the hot-metal mixer. Notice in the foreground that part of the slag tip is being reclaimed; slag reduction, as it was called, was a common practice with slag deposits at iron works between the wars, the material being variously used as fertiliser, in view of its phosphorus content, along with hard core for construction purposes. The discerning may be able to pick out one of the company's Andrew Barclay 4-coupled saddle tank locomotives, with a train of three slag ladles, just in front of the mixer building – there is another one just in front of the melting shop. The Trent & Mersey Canal passed right through the site and can be picked out on the right, just above the end chimney of the melting shop and then again on the extreme left, by the power station. *Steve Grudgings collection*

Right: NSR Third Class Theatrical ticket Hanley-Euston, 1923. *Author's collection*

Right: A presentation being made by stationmaster Lightfoot to Leonard Rowley in March 1932 in front of the Hanley station nameboard; Rowley, who was a horse-drawn parcel van driver at Hanley, acted extremely courageously when a runaway horse bolted on 16th February 1932. Lightfoot later became stationmaster for the two stations in Macclesfield in 1944. *Author's collection*

Above: Hanley station looking north after being bombed on 26th June 1940. Because of war-time reporting restrictions, this bombing was not reported in the local *Sentinel* newspaper, though there was reference made at the time to damage incurred at an unnamed station in the Midlands. *The Sentinel Newspaper*

Above Right: Hanley station looking south in 1955, showing that the war damaged awning on the right had not been rectified. Contrast the awning on the right with the previous photograph taken immediately after the bombing. *Author's collection*

Inset Above Right: Two Hanley LM&SR luggage labels.
Above: Hanley tickets: Platform; Workman's to Cold Meece; Pram to Lincoln. *Dave Bourne collection*. NSR Third Class Ticket to Hereford GWR issued in 1928; LM&SR ticket to Macclesfield issued in 1930. *Author's collection*

Right: Granville Crossing, where the Shelton internal railway between the main works and Hanley Deep Pit crossed Waterloo Road. Note the unique elevated signal box that controlled the crossing. The gates are also worthy of close study; because the road was wider than the distance between the properties through which the railway passed, the gates had unequal steel sliding extensions, clearly seen here. A mechanical bar, which worked automatically when the gates were opened, pushed the extensions in to position and thus ensured that the road was fully blocked. *Author's collection*

Above: Hanley Deep Pit, looking north from Town Road with the dirt tips dominating the sky line, was the deepest of the pits on or near the Shelton Works site and had one of the deepest shafts in the North Staffordshire coalfield. The colliery dated back to 1854, when it was sunk to meet the needs of the iron works and was served by the internal railway, referred to in the previous picture. Output from Deep Pit fluctuated; in 1930 it was 470,197 tons, in 1935 592,248 tons and 445,986 tons in 1940. Employment was 1,947 in 1930, 1,042 in 1939 and 765 in 1945. On the left, No. 1 Upcast shaft was sunk to a depth of 2,610 feet, whilst the No. 2 Downcast shaft (the coal winder) on the right was 2,661 feet deep. Note the lattice steel headframes. Deep Pit remained in the ownership of Shelton until nationalisation in 1947. The pit was closed in May 1962, when the workings were connected to the nearby Wolstanton Colliery. *E.J.D. Warrilow collection, Keele University Library*

Left: Waterloo Road station, seen here circa 1950, looking north and showing the main buildings situated on the bridge carrying Waterloo Road over the railway, was located only 682 yards north of Hanley station. York Street wharf, on the right, was the site where Shell-Mex carried on an expanding petroleum business throughout the LM&SR era, the siding accommodation here being increased in 1924, 1928 and during the Second World War. William Walker also carried on an oil business nearby and used the sidings at Waterloo Road. The privately owned tank wagons seen here include a 'square' type visible in the rake on the left. The station opened on 1st April 1900 and was closed by the LM&SR on 4th October 1943. *H.B. Oliver, courtesy National Railway Museum*

Right: This view is looking towards Cobridge Tunnel in 1924, with former 'D' Class 0-6-0T No. 57, now with early LM&SR numerals as No. 1570, on a Sunday test train, crossing over towards the Deep Pit sidings on the internal Shelton Works line. *Manifold collection*

Below: Deep Pit signal box circa 1950. The line to the left passes under the Shelton internal railway, with Deep Pit to the left and Shelton to the right. Immediately beyond the bridge on the left, the line curves to the right and then climbed briefly to meet a spur off the internal line. *D Ibbotson*

Inset Right: An LM&SR Cobridge to Blackpool Day Excursion ticket. *Author's collection*

Below: A view of Cobridge station taken on 18th July 1932, looking towards Burslem, with former 'D' Class 0-6-0T No. 129, now LM&SR No. 1569, working an Up coal train. Cobridge signal box can just be seen at the end of platform to the left of the rear wagon on the train. The bottle kilns of Moorcroft Pottery are visible on the right. *Gordon Walwyn*

Below: A snowy scene between Cobridge and Burslem in 1938, with an unidentified 2-6-4T working a Loop Line passenger train. It is seen here approaching the bridge over North Road, with the rear of the train crossing the bridge over Hot Lane and where sidings from Sneyd Collieries connected with the Loop Line. Sneyd Colliery dirt tip can be seen on the right and North Road school is visible between North Road and Hot Lane. The two NSR signals stand starkly against the wintry background. *Harold Bostock*

Sneyd Colliery

The magazine *Colliery Engineer* ran a special feature on Sneyd Colliery in July 1924 and these are some of the fascinating photographs taken for that article. I am grateful to Albert Finney for his enthusiasm to see them reproduced, and to Allan Baker for his technical knowledge and assistance in interpreting the pictures. In 1924, Sneyd Collieries Ltd employed 2,100, both underground and on the surface, including those engaged in brick and tile manufacture. The pit was a major producer in the North Staffordshire coalfield, with an output of 450,000 tons in 1924 and owning 1,000 wagons at that time. In 1927, it employed 1,650 underground and 540 above, and between 1931 and 1945 annual output averaged 448,000 tons. In 1947, output was 400,382 tons and it employed 1,440. Windings ceased in July 1962, when the workings were connected to the new sinkings at Wolstanton Colliery.

Above: Looking east from the public road that ran through the collieries' premises connecting Moorlands Road to the north and Hot Lane to the south; the road just features on the left, as it passes under the bridge taking the standard gauge railway and narrow gauge tramway over it. The railway was little more than a headshunt but the tramway connected with the brickworks. The three sets of headgear are, from right to left, No. 4, a downcast shaft and the main coal winding shaft, 890 yards deep and 15ft in diameter; No. 2, also a downcast, 621 yards deep and 13ft 6ins in diameter also used for coal winding; No. 1, the upcast shaft, used for men and materials only; No. 3, partly hidden and by this time little used, although it had in earlier times been used for coal winding; it was abandoned soon after this photograph was taken. The tall cylindrical structure to the left is part of the dust and slurry extraction arrangements. Note the piles of wooden pit props in the foreground and stacked up by the headgear on the right.

Left: The hydraulic decking gear at No. 4 pit bank. Built by Derby-based George Fletcher & Company and quite new at this date, it enabled the shaft to draw around 1,200 tons in an eight hour shift. The main and secondary cages each had four decks and could between them carry 18 pit tubs, with a combined capacity of 4½ tons per wind.

Above: A view of the coal washing plant, along with part of the aerial ropeway leaving the building to the left of the picture. This plant could handle both the incoming and unwashed coal, as well as the outgoing dirt on its way to the dirt tip. Also new when the photograph was taken in 1924, it was capable of handling 100 tons of coal per hour in six different grade sizes. Notice among the private owner wagons on the extreme left, one belonging to Lovatt Warrington & Company, coal factors of Hanley, possibly the only known photograph to depict one of their wagons.

Below: The brickworks owned by Sneyd Collieries were situated on the opposite or west side of the Loop Line to the pit. At various periods the standard gauge lines and the tramways that serviced part of this site passed both over and under the Loop Line. This particular view is looking north west and is taken from the Loop Line, indicated by the small portion of fencing in the right foreground. A short rake of loaded Sneyd wagons can be seen on the left. Sneyd brickworks manufactured glazed bricks and tiles, fire and silica bricks, common building bricks and sanitary drain pipes. The Sneyd Collieries site was served by a complicated railway system, which totalled 5¾ miles in length.

SPECIAL VALUES
Ladies' Wool Jumpers and Slacks

PITTS
DRAPERS and OUTFITTERS
LONGTON — LEEK — STONE

Evening Sentinel

No. 24,067 Telephone: Stoke-on-Trent 2381 THURSDAY, JANUARY 1, 1942

SERIOUS EXPLOSION AT SNEYD

Forty-Eight Men Trapped and Three Dead

RESCUE TEAMS AT WORK

One Road Blocked by Falls

An explosion of a serious character, but not accompanied by fire, occurred at 7.50 this morning in the Seven Feet Banbury Seam of No. 4 Pit, Sneyd Collieries, Burslem.

There were 53 men in the area involved, and early this afternoon the position in regard to casualties was as follows:—

Two men dead and one died in the Haywood Hospital;

One gravely injured, in hospital;

One suffering from chest injuries and shock, in hospital;

Forty-eight still in the accident area.

Rescue teams have been down the pit and have made an examination. Further teams have gone down to continue investigations up to the coal face.

Mr. I. W. Cumberbatch, Director and General Manager, in giving the information available, stated that the cause of the accident was unknown.

He stated that there are two faces in the district concerned, one 1,000 yards from the pit bottom and the other 600 yards.

Mr. Cumberbatch added that one road is clear, and the other is definitely blocked by falls.

The Lord Mayor of Stoke-on-Trent (Alderman H. W. McBrine) and Mr F. J. Hancock awaiting news at the pithead of the Sneyd Colliery, Burslem, this morning following the disaster there; and (right) one of the rescue teams who had just returned to the surface.

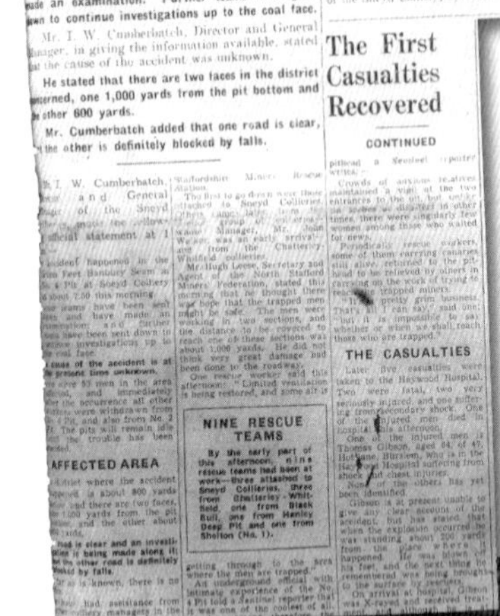

The First Casualties Recovered

CONTINUED

Crowds of anxious relatives maintained a vigil at the two entrances to the pit, but unlike the scenes at disasters in other times, there were singularly few women among those who waited for news.

Periodically rescue workers, some of them carrying canaries still alive, returned to the pit-head to be relieved by others in carrying on the work of trying to reach the trapped miners.

"It's pretty grim business. That's all I can say," said one; "but it is impossible to say whether or when we shall reach those who are trapped."

THE CASUALTIES

Later five casualties were taken to the Haywood Hospital. Two were fatal, two very seriously injured, and one suffering from secondary shock. One of the injured men died in hospital this afternoon.

One of the injured men is Thomas Gibson, aged 64, of 47, Hot Lane, Burslem, who is in the Haywood Hospital suffering from shock and chest injuries.

None of the others has yet been identified.

Gibson is at present unable to give any clear account of the accident, but has stated that when the explosion occurred he was standing about 200 yards from the place where it happened. He was blown off his feet, and the next thing he remembered was being brought to the surface by rescuers.

On arrival at hospital, Gibson was X-rayed and received treatment...

Mr. Hugh Leese, Secretary and Agent of the North Stafford Miners' Federation, stated this morning that he thought there was hope that the trapped men might be safe. The men were working in two sections, and the distance to be covered to reach one of these sections was about 1,000 yards. He did not think very great damage had been done to the roadway.

One rescue worker said this afternoon: "Limited ventilation is being restored, and some air is getting through to the area where the men are trapped."

An underground official with intimate experience of the No. 4 Pit told a Sentinel reporter that it was one of the coolest of all.

NINE RESCUE TEAMS

By the early part of this afternoon, nine rescue teams had been at work—three attached to Sneyd Collieries, three from Chatterley-Whitfield, one from Black Bull, one from Hanley Deep Pit and one from Shelton (No. 1).

AFFECTED AREA

Road is clear and an investigation is being made along it; but the other road is definitely blocked by falls.

Left: A serious explosion occurred at Sneyd Collieries' No. 4 pit on 1st January 1942 and was reported on the same day in the *Evening Sentinel*. The accident occurred at 7.50 am in the Seven Feet Banbury Seam and was caused by the ignition of coal dust, which resulted from a runaway train of underground tubs that derailed and created deadly sparks. The final death toll was 57. *The Sentinel Newspaper*

Sneyd Collieries LD No. 3, an 0-4-4-0T Garratt articulated locomotive built by Beyer, Peacock in 1931, is seen here in almost pristine collection. It was withdrawn from service in 1962 and scrapped on site in 1963. The internal colliery lines had steep gradients and sharp curves, the colliery being situated on rising ground between Burslem and Smallthorne. Sneyd Terrace, Burslem, is in the background. *H.W. Robinson*

Below: An aerial view of Sneyd Collieries taken probably in the late 1930s and looking east, with Burslem cemetery visible top centre. On the extreme left edge of the picture, the washer is just visible, whilst in the yard bottom left are rows of empty private owner wagons, all with the large letters reading 'SNEYD' clearly visible. In the bottom left corner is Sneyd Terrace, to the right of which is the internal line to the brickworks. In the centre of the photograph is the No. 2 shaft, above which, going from far left to centre, is Hot Lane. To the right of the No. 2 shaft is the coal conveyor, from which coal was dropped into railway wagons, with the siding serving it running to the Loop Line off to the right. Top right are the houses at High Lane and below them is the massive dirt tip, at the foot of which is No. 4 pit, the main coal winder and screens. *Author's collection*

This second aerial view of Sneyd Colliery was taken in about 1950 and is looking due north. Running across the top from left to right is Moorland Road, with Burslem town to the left and Smallthorne to the right. At the road intersection at Smallthorne, top right, High Lane (to Chell) runs off to the left to the top of the photograph, whilst the embryo southern end of Bankhall Road is seen as a short stub; the northern end of it had been completed before the war. In the centre, Hot Lane, to the left, becomes Sneyd Hill as it heads across the middle of the picture to the right, with the encroaching dirt tips in the foreground. Notice the various rope and cable railways from the colliery, crossing the road to take the dirt to the ever expanding tips, which were a landmark for miles around. Running through the colliery from top to bottom here is Park Road. To the top right of the pit site is the coal washery, with its distinctive upturned mushroom shaped tower; the numerous railway wagons alongside would contain both unwashed and washed coal. Three of the four shafts at Sneyd can be seen here although one of them is partly obscured by another. Nearest is No. 2, which is also partly hiding No. 3. The complicated railway layout can be party observed although much of it, together with the brickworks and the Potteries Loop Line, which gave the pit its main line connection, is off the photograph to the left. Today, the dirt tip has gone and the colliery site is now Sneyd Hill Park. However, most of the semi-detached and terraced houses alongside and behind Moorland Road survive. The colliery power station is to the right of the chimney and the pit prop storage area to the bottom left. *Steve Grudgings collection*

Left: Burslem station looking north circa 1948, with the early McKenzie & Holland signal box visible at the far end of the Down platform. *Author's collection*

Above: An LM&SR Burslem to Rhyl Third Class Day Excursion ticket. *Author's collection*

Below: Excursion trains off the Loop Line were popular in the LM&SR era. This is a Child's ticket for a Half Day Excursion to Windsor on 24th June 1937. It would have been a long half day, including a trip on a Salter Bros steamer on the River Thames to Marlow with tea on board and then return travel from Marlow station to Burslem. *Dave Bourne collection*

Right: A Loop Line passenger train with an unidentified 'B' Class locomotive at the head and seen here crossing the original Scotia Road bridge in 1925, before the major reconstruction detailed below. Behind the shuttering in the centre of the picture is the start of a tunnel under the line, the preparatory work for the new bridge. One of the many stage-carrying buses is seen here under the bridge and a small flat-bed lorry carrying bottles of mineral drink passes on the right. The road, which is formed of stone setts, has tram rails inset into it and the electric wires for the trams are carried overhead, with two of the cast iron support posts visible on the right hand side of the road. Note that the tram wires rise up and over the railway bridge, with the tramcars having to 'coast' the short distance through the bridge. *G.J.R. Nowell-Gossling*

Left: In the spring of 1926, with the railway bridge over Scotia Road requiring renewal, Stoke Corporation decided to take advantage of this opportunity to widen the road at the same time. The reconstructed bridge had two spans, with a single supporting pier 16ft high. The road was widened with two 20ft lanes passing either side of the pier and there was a separate 9ft 6in wide brick arch for a footpath. The estimated costs of these major works amounted to £17,000, of which the LM&SR were to pay £2,700, this figure representing the cost of renewing the bridge superstructure. Here, former 'New L' Class 0-6-2T No. 156, in early LM&SR livery as No. 2248, is seen on works train duties with the breakdown crane (also seen in the picture on the front title page) positioning the steel face girder on to the new bridge. The girder bears the name 'Horseley B&E Ltd Tipton Staffs', a long-term supplier to the railway industry. *Courtesy the Potteries Museum & Art Gallery, Stoke-on-Trent*

A magnificent view of the engineering work associated with the bridge reconstruction, looking towards Tunstall, with the bottle kilns of the Globe Pottery on the right and, in the background, those of the Alexandra and Unicorn potteries. Prominent in the centre is the LM&SR Civil Engineer's 5-ton crane, marked CD1, beyond which can be seen the ex-NSR Engineer's 5-ton hand crane. Four girders were required for the new bridge, two face girders on each side, with the centre girder being in two parts. One of the new face girders is already in place on the left. In the right foreground, the second face girder can just be seen being delivered on LM&SR Engineering Department wagons. In the background, the original Tunstall Junction signal box at the junction with the short, 427 yards Pinnox Branch can just be seen; in front of the box are the Tunstall Down Home and the Tunstall Yard Distant signals. Note the piles of timber used for scaffolding, at ground level on the left, beyond which are allotments and then out of sight behind them is the Pinnox Branch, a set of signals on which can also be made out. *Courtesy The Potteries Museum & Art Gallery, Stoke-on-Trent*

Left: Tunstall station looking south towards Burslem in 1938, with an unidentified 2-6-4T working bunker first with a three-coach set. The picture is full of interest and detail. There is another three-coach set in the sidings on the left alongside Tunstall signal box. In front of the carriages is the cattle dock, rarely used by this time, with the busy goods yard and warehouse visible on the far right. In the right foreground is part of the stationmaster's house with its well stocked garden. There were several important changes to the station in the LM&SR era. Siding accommodation was increased at the south end in 1933 at a cost of £1,238. In 1946, the LM&SR sold land and property to Johnson Bros (Hanley), earthenware manufacturers, for £10,500, consisting of the former Midland Railway depot (three warehouses), a goods shed and strip of land. In 1947, the LM&SR sold further lands and a warehouse at Scotia Road to the Glazed Floor & Tile Co. for £9,000. Some of these properties can just be made out on the right. *Harold Bostock*

Above: Looking north through the station circa 1948, with the buildings all looking neat and well ordered. Note the LM&SR signals beyond the road overbridge, the bottom one being the 'calling on' arm for the Newfields Branch, some 681 yards beyond the station. The enclosed footbridges at this station and at Burslem were rebuilt in 1938; the 'family likeness' in the design of both stations is very apparent. There is a varied collection of sack trucks and luggage trolleys, along with advertisements for Elasto and Virol. *Author's collection*

Inset Above Left: An NSR Third Class ticket from Tunstall to Longport, issued on 7th March 1926.
Inset Above Right: An LM&SR Tunstall to Burslem Workman's Return ticket. *Both Dave Bourne collection*

Right: There was a serious runaway on the Newfields Branch circa 1923, on the headshunt that ran parallel to the Loop Line immediately north of Tunstall station. The disastrous results are seen here, with an NSR 'D' Class 0-6-0T locomotive in considerable distress, its smokebox embedded in the remains of several wagons, including an L&NWR 6-plank open and a GWR 4-plank wagon. *Manifold collection*

Above: This aerial view dates from the early 1920s and shows part of the Newfields Branch running across the centre, with Newfields Junction just off camera to the right and the bridge over Furlong Road on the left. In the foreground is a fine view of William Adams & Sons Greengate Pottery, with sidings just beyond on the right and mill ponds in the centre. The Loop Line also features top right, heading towards Pitts Hill station, which was located just off the top of the photograph beyond where this line also crossed over Furlong Road. Also visible at the top of the picture is Adams' other pottery, Greenfields, in front of which is the spoil from the former Greenfield Colliery, owned by Adams and closed in 1902. The railway embankment carrying the branch past Greengate Pottery had originally been a viaduct and it is just possible to make out the remains of the timber supports of this. *Author's collection*

Inset Below: An LM&SR Armed Forces on Leave ticket for Third Class travel from Pitts Hill to Stoke. *Author's collection*

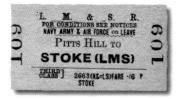

Right: Newfields Wharf, Tunstall in 1947, with the bottle ovens of the Royal Albert and Newfield potteries of Alfred Meakin (Tunstall) Ltd in the background; the potteries were located on the Kidsgrove side of Newfields Sidings. In the foreground is former L&NWR 'Cauliflower' 0-6-0 No. 28460, one of three of the class transferred to Stoke at the end of 1939; their duties were mainly confined to working the steeply graded (between 1 in 37 and 1 in 52) Newfields Branch, 1,342 yards long, which ran from the Loop Line at Tunstall. *Les Smith collection*

Birchenwood

Mining at Birchenwood dated back to the mid 1850s, with ownership of the colliery passing into the hands of Robert Heath & Sons Ltd in 1888. In 1919, a company reconstruction occurred, against the background of the serious situation facing the iron and coal trades after the First World War, and this saw the Heath empire merge with the Yorkshire-based Low Moor Company Ltd. Brunner Mond, the forerunner of ICI, took a financial stake at the same time, as it wanted access to good quality coking coal. Trading difficulties in the succeeding years led to a new company, Kidsgrove Collieries Ltd, being registered and the Heath family becoming owners once again. However, Robert Heath & Low Moor went into receivership in February 1928, the closure of the blast furnaces and ironworks at Biddulph having reduced the demand for Birchenwood coke. Kidsgrove Collieries also struggled and went into liquidation in February 1931, the collieries closing two months later, in April. However, this was followed in May 1931 by the formation of the Birchenwood Coal & Coke Co. Ltd, to operate the remaining coke oven battery, the by-product plant and the brickworks. This new company was jointly owned by Norton & Biddulph Collieries, Sneyd Collieries and Chatterley-Whitfield Colliery. Each of them sought to increase their own markets by the use of their own output for coking.

Above: An aerial view of the Birchenwood complex circa 1928, before the closure of the collieries. The view is looking south, with the Loop Line and the 'Third Line' running down the middle of the picture, in to a deep cutting and then exiting a short tunnel at the bottom; the so-called 'Third Line' was an independent line, nearly 1½ miles long, that went from Kidsgrove Yard to Birchenwood Summit. To the left of the Loop Line is part of the chemical works and the Mond gas producer plant, with No. 4 pit being just off the bottom of the picture. Almost on top of the tunnel is the headgear of No. 18 pit and the screens, with the coal washer to its right. Kidsgrove Collieries at this time employed 1,520 workers (down from 2,350 in 1923), with an annual output of 300,000 tons. Above No. 18 pit are the two coke oven batteries, eighty-four Simon Carves ovens and seventy-two Carl Still ovens, and the remainder of the chemical works, including a tar distillation plant and a benzol rectification plant. At the top of the picture are the brickworks, which had a capacity in 1927 of 180,000 common bricks a week. No. 6 pit can be seen centre right, whilst at the centre bottom is the junction with the 'Third Line'. *Allan Baker collection*

A view of Birchenwood No. 18 coal drawing and downcast shaft, after the official abandonment date of November 1931, the other two pits on site, No's 4 and 6, being closed at the same time. Following the closure of the colliery, the all-steel headgear seen here was sold to Madeley Collieries for re-use. *Bill Jack*

No. 1 at Kidsgrove Collieries circa 1930. This Avonside Engine Co. 0-6-0ST went new to Birchenwood in 1896, was rebuilt there in 1912 and finally scrapped in 1933-34, after the colliery closure. Note the colliery-owned high sided coke wagon on the right and others in the background. *H.W. Robinson*

The final stages in the erection of a new battery of seventeen Simon Carves regenerative by-product coke ovens, replacing earlier ones that had ceased production in 1926. In the centre of this photograph, taken in September 1938 looking south east, are the coke discharge arrangements of the surviving Carl Still ovens; these passed out of use once the new ovens were up and running. A further fourteen ovens were added in 1947, with the final total of thirty-one new ovens able to produce 4,800 tons of coke a week, compared with the 4,500 tons from the 146 older ovens. *Allan Baker collection*

Driver Eli Jones on the footplate of No. 3 *Dido* at Birchenwood in the 1920s, with an unknown shunter also posing alongside. This 0-6-0ST was built by Hudswell Clarke in 1870 (Works No. 88) and spent its early years with the Stanton Ironworks Co. Ltd at Ilkeston in Derbyshire. It was rebuilt by the Avonside Engine Co. in 1887 and arrived at Birchenwood in 1909, initially on hire. The Company later bought it outright and it was scrapped on site in 1945-46. The engine is shunting a Tarmac wagon. *Allan Baker collection*

Tarmac (Kidsgrove) Ltd was formed in October 1922, to operate a slag reduction plant in order to process the tons of old blast furnace slag available locally. The Birchenwood plant was located by the northern entrance of the Harecastle rail tunnel and the slag was brought there by the internal works railway from the Birchenwood, Clough Hall, Black Bull and Norton sites. After the bulk of the slag had been exhausted, the company was wound up in December 1934; the works was closed around that time and the track lifted. Seen here in 1931 in very rural surroundings at the Tarmac plant is 0-4-0ST No. 8, hired from the Biddulph Valley Ironworks for a short period to cover for their own locomotive, *Alexander*, which was away being repaired. No. 8 was built in 1885 by the Falcon Engine & Car Works of Loughborough but was rebuilt by Robert Heath at Black Bull in 1891 and subsequently became the prototype for a further twelve locomotives from this latter

company. It was rebuilt again in 1931, locally by Cowlishaw Walker & Co. Ltd of Biddulph, and probably then came straight to Tarmac at Kidsgrove given the smart condition in which it is seen in this photograph. Note the 12-ton Tarmac steel wagon in the background, a product of the Birmingham Railway Carriage & Wagon Co. Ltd and built at their Smethwick works. *H.W. Robinson*

Kidsgrove Market Street Halt, looking south in the 1930s. The line of rails in the foreground is the 'Third', or 'Independent', line that ran from Kidsgrove to Birchenwood; behind it running past the platform face is the section of the Loop Line from Newchapel which had been singled in 1909. Notice the old 4-wheeled coach body that served as a waiting room. The station opened in 1909 and closed on 2nd September 1950. In the LM&SR era, nearly all of the Loop Line passenger trains and the war-time workmen's trains called at this halt. *National Railway Museum*

Kidsgrove Market Street Halt looking south again, with Stanier 2-6-4T No. 2664, off Stoke shed and still with LMS lettering and livery, on the 4.20pm Stoke to Macclesfield working on 12th June 1948. *W.A. Camwell/SLS collection*

Kidsgrove station circa 1935, looking north towards the junction with the main line. The small hut on the right hand platform housed the tablet instrument for single line working as far as Newchapel. Birchenwood Sidings are to the left of the platform, with two Sneyd wagons in view, whilst at the far end is the water tank. The line from Birchenwood Sidings formed the 'Third Line' to Birchenwood. Kidsgrove Junction signal box can be seen in the background. The LM&SR added Liverpool Road to the station's name in 1944. The title page double spread is a view through the station and along the main line taken from on or near the signal box steps. *Author's collection*
Inset: An LM&SR Cheap Day Return ticket from Kidsgrove (Liverpool Rd) to Etruria. *Dave Bourne collection*

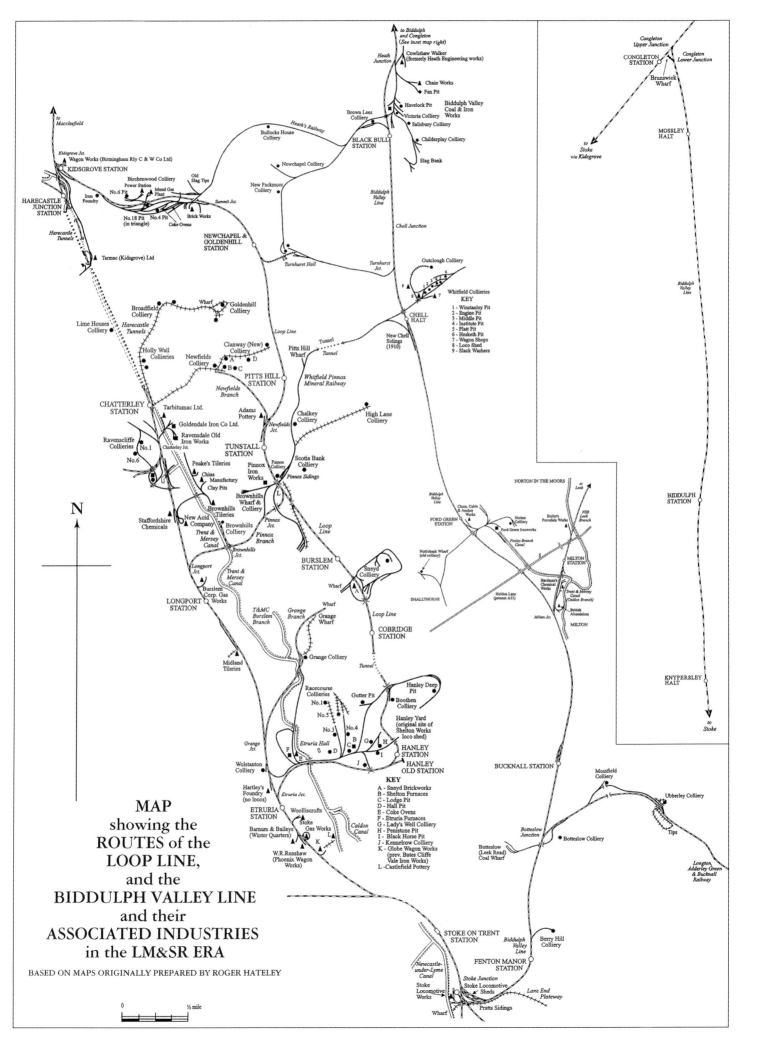

MAP
showing the
ROUTES of the
LOOP LINE,
and the
BIDDULPH VALLEY LINE
and their
ASSOCIATED INDUSTRIES
in the LM&SR ERA

BASED ON MAPS ORIGINALLY PREPARED BY ROGER HATELEY

5

The Biddulph Valley Line and Branches

The Biddulph Valley Line was the first major branch of the NSR to be opened for mineral traffic. It was 13 miles 1,538 yards long and went from Stoke Junction to Congleton Upper Junction, with a spur line (single) from Congleton Lower Junction to Congleton Brunswick Wharf. After it had left Fenton Manor, only a few hundred yards from Stoke Junction, it passed through a countryside punctuated by the numerous collieries and iron works that the line served. The line climbed steadily for eight miles from Stoke Junction to Heath's Junction (just south of Knypersley Halt), with the sharpest gradient the 1 in 68 from Ford Green to Black Bull, followed by a sharp decline for nearly six miles to Brunswick Wharf in Congleton, mainly at 1 in 78 from Biddulph to Mossley Halt (to the south of Congleton). The Biddulph Valley Line opened for freight traffic in 1860 and branching off from it were the NSR's Leek Branch and the private Longton, Adderley Green & Bucknall Railway, whilst a connection with the private Chatterley-Whitfield line was made at Chell. It was typical of the NSR freight lines in that its fortunes were closely tied to and dependent on the fortunes of the industrial customers that it served. In particular, the line was adversely affected by the run down of the iron trade in the 1920s, which in turn lead to the closure of the furnaces at Norton and at Biddulph in 1928. Several large collieries lasted well into the BR era, such as Berry Hill (1960), Norton (1977) and the Victoria at Black Bull (1982), whilst on the LAG&BR, Mossfield closed in 1963 and Chatterley-Whitfield in 1976. One interesting feature of the line in the pre-Grouping era was the freedom with which the two great firms of Robert Heath and Chatterley-Whitfield worked their own trains over certain sections of the line and which collectively extended over most of its length. These arrangements did not last for long into the LM&SR era.

Wagon accommodation on the line was to be found at (i) Pratt's Sidings, storage capacity for 171 wagons on the Down side; (ii) at Botteslow Junction, 61 wagons in the Up yard; (iii) at Ford Green, 175 wagons in the Up marshalling yard; (iv) at Heath's Junction, 102 wagons in the Up marshalling yard; (v) at Congleton Lower Junction, 70 wagons in the Down marshalling yard; and (vi) at Brunswick Wharf, 98 wagons in the yard. All this is evidence of the high volume of freight traffic on the line.

Collieries had the right to mine under the railway lines under the provisions of the Mines (Working Facilities & Support) Act 1923; collieries could be compensated by the railway companies if they waived their rights to do so in order to avoid disturbance and subsidence to the lines affected. In 1924, Mossfield Colliery gave notice of its wish to work seams of coal under Meir Tunnel and the adjoining railway; the cost of opening out the tunnel was estimated at £200,000 and the value of the coal foregone to support the tunnel was a mere £20,000. Common sense prevailed and modest compensation was paid to Mossfield for agreeing not to mine; compensation was also paid to the Duke of Sutherland in respect of the land affected that was owned by him. In 1929, Berry Hill Collieries Ltd sought to exercise similar rights to work under the Biddulph Valley Line, including a section under Fenton Manor Tunnel; agreement was reached whereby the colliery company received compensation for not proceeding to mine under the tunnel.

Passenger traffic was of much lesser importance, since the financial viability of the line was underpinned by freight revenues. Apart from Biddulph, which was a sizeable town, the line served several small villages and, whilst a passenger service terminated at Congleton on the main line, this required locomotive reversals at Congleton Upper Junction. The stations opened for passenger traffic at various times between 1864 and 1919, and included halts at Chell and at Mossley (just south of Congleton), opened to serve colliers' trains for Whitfield Colliery. At Grouping, there were two passenger services each way with an extra two on Saturdays but even this frequency was reduced in the following three years. It was bus competition that killed the Biddulph Valley passenger rail services; by 1922, regular bus services were operating from Biddulph to Tunstall, Hanley and Congleton, and all the outlying parts of the district. The sparse train service and the stations, inconveniently located in respect of the places they were supposed to serve, could not compete with the new form of transport that passed people's doors and ran regularly from early morning until late at night.

On 22nd June 1927, the LM&SR Traffic Committee approved the closure of the line for passenger traffic, which involved shutting specific passenger stations at Ford Green, Black Bull and Biddulph. It was reported that passenger traffic had decreased to such an extent that the running of a passenger service was unremunerative. The number of passengers using the line in 1925 was barely one fifth of those using it in 1913, as the following figures show:

	1913	1925
Passengers	74,516	13,771
Receipts £	2,613	1,344

Prior to the 1926 Coal Strike, there were two trains a day each way between Congleton and Stoke; afterwards, there were two trains a day between Stoke and Congleton only, and there were no public complaints following the taking off of the two trains in the reverse direction. It was reported to the Committee that there were no obligations to prevent the line being closed for passenger traffic and arrangements were put in hand to deal with parcels by motor from other stations in the district. Savings from the closure were estimated to be £2,065 pa. It was agreed not to demolish the stations at that time, as they might be required for the running of excursions but to review the matter later; in 1930, it was agreed to re-use certain structures and platforms that remained at Ford Green & Smallthorne and at Biddulph.

Despite the formal closing of the line for passenger services in 1927, the LM&SR continued to run excursions for Congleton and Biddulph Wakes during the early part of August. For example, in 1935, an excursion train started in Biddulph and called at Ford Green. August 1939 saw three excursion trains run from Biddulph station to Blackpool, North Wales and Liverpool on 12th August, and to Blackpool on 16th August. These excursions were subsequently discontinued, although an attempt was made in August 1952 to resume rail excursions from Biddulph but barely a handful of people travelled.

In 1923, Chatterley-Whitfield Collieries conveyed their own workers between Chell and Biddulph/Mossley Halt; however, these arrangements did not survive long into Grouping. The late Bill Jack recalled:

'The Whitfield locomotive was used on the early morning and late running of the train, while the NSR (LM&SR) brought the noon shift to Chell and took the day shift back again. The colliers' train, after its extension to Mossley Halt, was propelled back empty to Biddulph for stabling as there was no run-round facilities at Mossley Halt. It was similarly propelled empty from Biddulph to Mossley Halt to return loaded to Chell. Biddulph was the weekend stabling point for the coaches as no trains were run on Sundays. In order to prevent congestion at the

lamphouse and at the pithead caused by the simultaneous arrival of both trains at Chell, the Biddulph train was timed to arrive 15 minutes earlier than the train from Pinnox. There was no lighting or heating on either the Biddulph or Pinnox trains and travelling conditions during the winter months were grim indeed. Owing to the inconvenient location of the station at Biddulph, the Biddulph trains very soon began to feel the effects of competition from road transport and the number of men using them steadily declined. By the summer of 1925 the number had dwindled to about 40 and with the closure of Mossley Halt on 13th July 1925, the colliers' train ceased.'

There were no Workmen's tickets issued by Biddulph Valley Line stations in 1922, though Endon, Stockton Brook and Milton did issue tickets to Bucknall & Northwood and to Fenton Manor. In 1924, arrangements were extended whereby Weekly Workmen's Tickets were issued from all Biddulph Valley stations, including Mossley Halt but excluding Ford Green & Smallthorne, and Knypersley and Chell halts; both Fenton Manor and Bucknall & Northwood issued Workmen's tickets to stations on the Leek line. Following the cessation of passenger services in 1927, in 1929 there were Daily and Weekly Workmen's tickets between the remaining Biddulph Valley stations, at Fenton Manor and at Bucknall & Northwood, and the Leek Line stations.

The Biddulph Valley Line was the first major NSR route to close to passenger traffic, on 11th September 1927. The two stations nearest Stoke, Fenton Manor and Bucknall & Northwood, escaped the axe and remained open; they subsequently formed part of the Leek Line and survived until March 1956. Chell Halt closed in 1930, whilst Mossley Halt closed on 13th April 1925 after a short life of a mere 5½ years.

Just prior to Grouping, there were separate ordinary goods workings daily from Pratt's Sidings to Biddulph, Ford Green,

Heath's Junction, Adderley Green and Congleton, and one from Whitfield Sidings to Macclesfield. There were no trip or shunting locomotives allocated to Biddulph Valley duties at the time of Grouping. In terms of freight traffic over the line, in the summer of 1930, there were daily two mineral trains to Stoke, one to Harecastle and one to Crewe. There was one mineral train from Botteslow for Stoke. In September 1938, there were no fewer than seven trips every day, five using Stoke locomotives and two from Macclesfield. Trip workings from Stoke were carried out by Class '4F' 0-6-0s which called at Berry Hill, Norton and Black Bull, and shunted at Botteslow Wharf. From Macclesfield, the trip working to Brunswick Wharf was carried out by a 2-6-2T and that to Chatterley-Whitfield and to Ford Green by a 2-6-4T. There was one stopping freight daily to Stoke, calling at Congleton Lower Junction, Heath's Junction, Ford Green and Botteslow.

The LM&SR developed its own Town Cartage scheme from 1932 onwards. From Tunstall depot, the areas served were Pitts Hill, Chell and Black Bull, to which were added, in 1935, Brindley Ford and Packmoor. The LM&SR Country Service cartage arrangements included Tunstall depot serving Chell Heath, Fegg Hayes and Whitfield.

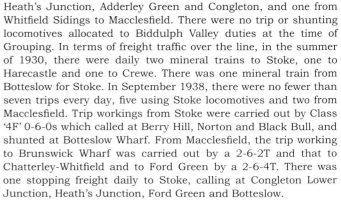

Above: Pratt's Sidings signal box circa 1948, looking towards Stoke Junction, with LM&SR signals visible behind. In the centre of the picture can be seen the cobbles that formed the trackbed of the 4ft 4ins Longton Tramway, which connected the T&M Canal with the town of Longton; this was taken out of use when the Stoke to Derby line opened in 1848 but was only finally lifted in the early 1890s. The brick wall on the left carries a painted advertisement for James M. Brown Ltd, oxides and colours. *Author's collection*

Left: Extract from the 'Local Trip & Engine Shunting Workings' of 26th September 1938, detailing Trip No. 49. It shows, on the left side, the working from Stoke Shed along the Biddulph Valley Line to Congleton and back to Ford Green; thence, on the right, to working along the main line around Cliff Vale and Longport. A Class '4' freight engine – such as a Fowler '4F' 0-6-0 – was allocated for this Trip. *Author's collection*

No. 49.

Class 4 Freight Engine (Standard 0-6-0).

8.15 a.m. (SX) to 11.25 p.m. (SX);

8.15 a.m. (SO) to 6.10 a.m. (Sun.).

	arr.(SX) dep.		arr.(SO) dep.			arr. dep.	
	a.m.	a.m.	a.m.	a.m.		p.m.	p.m.
Stoke Shed	...	8 15 L.E.	...	8 15 L.E.	Ford Green	8 0	8 25
Pratt's Sidings	8 17	8 30	8 17	8 30	Grange Jn.	10 59	11 20 (SX) L.E.
Congleton Jn.	10 35	10 50	10 35	10 50	Newcastle Jn.	11†25	... SX)
Congleton -	10 53	11 7	10 53	11 31	Cliff Vale -	9 49	10 54 (SO)
Congleton Jn.	11 10	11 15	11 34	11 39	Grange Jn.	10 59	11 15 (SO)
Congleton					Longport	11 22	12 30a.m. Assist.
Lower Jn.	11 18	11 33	11 42	11 57			(SuO)
Milton Jn. -	2 5	3 30	2 5	3 30	Tunstall Jn.	12 38	12 42 L.E. (SuO)
Pratt's Sidings	3 45	4 10	3 45	4 10	Longport -	12 50	2 15 (SuO)
Heath's Jn.	4 45	5 5 E&B	4 45	5 5 E&B	Pinnox Jn.	2 20	2 50 (SuO).
Ford Green	5 15	6 15 E&B	...	...	Longport -	2 55	3 55 (SuO)
Milton Jn. -	6 20	7 20	...	...	Pinnox Jn.	4 0	4 31 (SuO)
Ford Green	7 25	...	...	...	Longport -	4 36	6 0 (SuO) L.E.
Ford Green	...	...	5 15	6 25	Stoke Shed	6 10	...
Pratt's Siding	...	...	6 45	7 40			

†—Then works 11.55 p.m. (SX) to Burton.

Left: A panoramic view of Stoke engine shed near the start of the Biddulph Valley Line, looking back towards Stoke Junction in September 1939. The sidings on the left had been laid in around two years earlier, on the site of the wagon repairs shop. The brake van is at the rear of a goods train coming off the Up Biddulph Valley Line, with the Down line immediately to the right of it. Next is the line into the motor shed and then the six lines into the 'long shed', the section on the right being roofless as the result of a fire. The Second World War delayed the repairs to this until the early 1950s. Stoke Round House can just be made out behind the motor shed. *A.G. Ellis collection*

Fenton Manor station in 1950, looking towards Bucknall, with the dirt tip of Berry Hill Colliery dominating the sky line and the chimneys of its brickworks just visible beyond the tunnel. An LM&SR signal stands in the right foreground and part of the station master's house can be seen at the top right of the picture. The station opened in 1889; although originally part of the Biddulph Valley Line, when this line was closed in 1927, the station then became operationally part of the Leek Line, until that too closed for passenger traffic on 6th March 1956. *F.W. Shuttleworth*

Inset Above: An NSR Third Class Return Workman's ticket from Fenton Manor to Leek, issued in January 1923. *Author's collection*

Above: Aerial view of Berry Hill Colliery, Fenton, in 1933. This colliery was extensively developed in the early 1930s, a new shaft, No. 1, being sunk in 1930 and drawing coal from January 1933, with modern screening and washing facilities being introduced. In 1924, the colliery employed 941 underground and 206 above ground. In 1934, the colliery drew 207,669 tons with 909 men, whilst in 1947, 295,055 tons were drawn with 1,089 men. The Biddulph Valley Line just features running across the top left corner of the photograph, with Stoke off to the bottom and Biddulph to the top. Immediately alongside the line is Railway Pit, followed by the twin No. 4 pits known as Ash and Knowles, and then the new No. 1 pit with its bright new winding engine house. Above this can be seen the power house, the screening and washing plant, and the original winding engine house; the dirt tips are in the foreground. The colliery closed in April 1960. The Berry Hill brickworks was situated just off the bottom right of the picture. *Manifold collection*

Above: This advertisement for Berry Hill Brickworks appeared in *The Sentinel Yearbook* for 1926 and shows *Berry Hill No. 1* marshalling a heavy load. These works were located to the south east of the colliery and manufactured firebricks, kiln quarries, fire tiles and cupola blocks, as well as preparing saggar clay. *Hanley Archives*

Left: An early 1930s portrait of *Berry Hill No. 1*, an Avonside Engine Co. 0-4-0ST built in 1892 (Works No. 1343). This locomotive spent its entire career at Berry Hill and was rebuilt there twice over its life, in 1898 and 1931; this photograph may well have been taken shortly after the second rebuilding. The arrival of newer motive power in 1947 and 1954 saw it fall out of use and it was scrapped on site in the latter half of 1955. A Berry Hill 7-plank wagon is on the left and an LMS-lettered 5-plank wagon is on the right. *H.W. Robinson*

The Ash and Knowles pits of Berry Hill Colliery in June 1933; the pits were named after the seams of coal worked. There is a good selection of the colliery company's own wagons in the foreground, which were painted bright red with white letters. Coal drawing here ceased in 1931. *Bill Jack*

The Longton, Adderley Green & Bucknall Railway

The Longton, Adderley Green & Bucknall Railway was promoted as a private line in 1866. It comprised a loop railway to the east of Stoke, linking the Biddulph Valley Line at Botteslow Junction with Millfield Junction at Normacot on the Stoke to Derby line; serving numerous collieries, it opened in 1875. In 1894, an Act of Parliament was passed abandoning 398 yards immediately beyond Stirrup & Pye Colliery which, as a consequence, severed the link between the two major NSR lines; the northern section, two miles 928 yards long, served in the LM&SR era two collieries, Mossfield and Stirrup & Pye, whilst the southern section, only 1,606 yards

long, served Park Hall Colliery. The NSR acquired the line in its two sections in 1895. It was single throughout and on a climbing gradient of 1 in 48 to 1 in 57. Traffic was lost with the closure of Stirrup & Pye in 1935 but Mossfield Colliery was one of the few to increase its output during the Second World War. The official closure date for the line was 6th July 1964.

At Grouping, there were two daily workings to Adderley Green but, in 1930, there was only one daily train that came off the branch. There were trip workings to Mossfield Colliery and from Stirrup & Pye to Harecastle, the latter ceasing after 1935.

Mossfield Colliery, seen here around 1930, was sunk circa 1850 and originally was served by a tramway to Sutherland Wharf on the Stoke to Derby line. The old wooden headgears are shown in this view but they were later replaced with steel frames. These were tandem headgears, with a pair of shafts being worked by one winding engine; both shafts were on the same side of the winding engine. A new screening plant was installed in 1925 and pit head baths in 1930. In 1923, there were 613 workers underground and 133 above ground, and output was 343,675 tons; output in 1939 was 449,556 tons with 960 workers in total and there were 1,050 men working there in 1946. The colliery closed in October 1963. *Bill Jack*

Left: This Mossfield Colliery private owner wagon, No. 874, was built by the Gloucester Railway Carriage & Wagon Co. Ltd and was purchased second hand from them in May 1933. The cost of 100 second hand wagons was only £4,850, roughly the same as forty brand new ones. The livery was black with plain white lettering; the italics in the bottom right hand corner read 'Empty to Mossfield Colliery, Adderley Green Sidings, L.M.S. (N.S.Section)'. *Gloucestershire Archives*

Below: The front page headline from the *Evening Sentinel* of 21st March 1940, following the Mossfield Colliery disaster; eight men were killed. *Hanley Archives*

Below: The Hilton Gravel Co. operated from 1943, using Valley Sidings at Mossfield Colliery but on LM&SR property. The company entered into an agreement with the LM&SR, in respect of a right of way to give access to a tipping dock, for the movement of gravel by rail. Percy Trentham Ltd (contractors of London and Birmingham) was another quarry operator to operate on the LAG&BR, using the Stirrup & Pye Colliery siding until 1954. *Author's collection*

Works at Longton, Stoke-on-Trent

Right: A view of Adderley Green Colliery, known locally as Stirrup & Pye, in the 1930s. This was a long established coal mining site, mining operations having commenced here in 1799. The colliery was acquired by local factors Settle Speakman in 1935; they purchased the rights to several other local collieries at the same time. The pit was merged with Mossfield Colliery on 18th April 1940, so as to concentrate the available workforce at other nearby pits with higher outputs per man shift. Notice the tandem headgear. The shafts were retained for pumping and ventilation until the closure of the nearby Mossfield Colliery. Annual output averaged 150,000 tons and in 1933 there were 528 employed here. *Bill Jack*

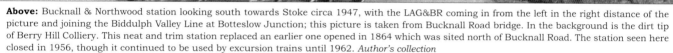

Above: Bucknall & Northwood station looking south towards Stoke circa 1947, with the LAG&BR coming in from the left in the right distance of the picture and joining the Biddulph Valley Line at Botteslow Junction; this picture is taken from Bucknall Road bridge. In the background is the dirt tip of Berry Hill Colliery. This neat and trim station replaced an earlier one opened in 1864 which was sited north of Bucknall Road. The station seen here closed in 1956, though it continued to be used by excursion trains until 1962. *Author's collection*

Inset Above: LM&SR Special Day Return ticket from Bucknall to Leek. *Author's collection*; **Inset Below:** LM&SR Child's ticket from Bucknall to Stoke. *Dave Bourne collection*

Below: Bucknall & Northwood 1864 station and station master's house, looking towards Biddulph and taken at the same time as the previous photograph. The original platforms of the station can be seen on either side of the tracks. In the background, the line enters the former goods yard to serve Northwood Colliery and John Cadman's Bucknall Saw Mills. The overhead gantry on the left supports the travelling crane used by the saw mills, whilst Bucknall signal box can be seen in the right middle distance, facing the goods yard. *Author's collection*

Right: A view just to the north of Milton Junction, where the Biddulph Valley Line separates from the Leek Line, showing the former crossing keeper's house. This dated from when the railway opened in 1859, with Milton Road at that time crossing the line here on the level but this was replaced by the bridge, seen here in the foreground, some years later. Careful study of the house shows that the original building was single storey, with the later brick second storey extension clearly visible. *Author's collection*

Above: One of the 0-4-0ST locomotives built by Robert Heath pictured here engaged in providing craneage for culvert repairs in 1946. There were fourteen locomotives built at the Black Bull fitting shop between 1904 and 1926, twelve 0-4-0STs and two 0-6-0STs, originally for their own use but later, in the LM&SR era, by Robert Heath & Low Moor Ltd and then by Norton & Biddulph Collieries. *Metcalfe collection*

Above: Just south of Ford Green station in the mid-1930s, a view looking towards Biddulph. In the foreground, the bridge carrying the private line from Norton Colliery, on the right, to the landsale wharf at Nettlebank, Smallthorne, is under repair. Behind on the left is the ex-NSR goods shed, beyond which can be seen the station master's house. *Manifold collection*

Below: A former NSR 'New L' Class 0-6-2T passes through Ford Green and Smallthorne station with a train of coal empties in the late 1920s. The view is looking towards Bucknall, with the station master's house in the background. On the left is the loading dock that served the Taylor Chain & Cable Works. By this time, the line had closed for passenger traffic and the station nameboard had been removed. During the LM&SR era, Thomas Kirkham traded as a coal merchant from the station yard. *Author's collection*

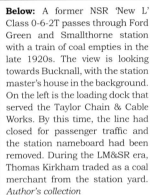

Above: This calling card for Herbert Peacock, goods and passenger agent, Ford Green station, is evidence of the growing commercialisation of the LM&SR as increasing numbers of its traffic staff canvassed for business. *Author's collection*

Right: The station staff at Ford Green and Smallthorne station photographed in the mid-1920s alongside a fine example of an NSR station nameboard. James Peacock, the station master, stands at the back, and behind him is his place of abode whilst employed here. *Author's collection*

Ford Green and Smallthorne station looking north towards Biddulph on 12th June 1948. On the left is the single storey crossing keeper's house and on the right Ford Green signal box, behind which are the level crossing gates and Ford Green road. The LM&SR signals frame the footbridge, behind which can be seen the Up platform, staggered so as to accommodate the needs of goods and mineral traffic from the yards south of the station. *W.A. Camwell*

A mid-1920s aerial view of Ford Green looking north, with the Biddulph Valley Line off the picture to the left. Ford Green ironworks, in the centre of the picture, commenced operations in 1854 and was taken over by the Heath empire in 1890. The furnaces closed between 1925 and 1928, and the mills, forge, steelworks (which had only opened in 1924) and the remainder of the plant in September 1928. To the left is the chain and cable works of Samuel Taylor & Sons of Brierley Hill, which also closed with the ironworks. On the right is Norton Colliery which, together with pits at Black Bull, were formed into a new company, Norton & Biddulph Collieries, in 1929. Norton Colliery passed into NCB ownership in 1947 and eventually closed in June 1977. It employed 1,295 underground and 353 above ground workers in 1923; in 1947, it had 1,346 workers and its output was 407,151 tons. Tarmac (Kidsgrove) Ltd was formed in 1922 to recover and process ironworks slag at Norton and at Childerplay (Biddulph); these operations ceased at the end of the 1920s. Norton was subsequently worked by a new company, the Five Towns Macadam Co. Ltd (a Tarmac and Derbyshire Stone consortium), which also had operations at Shelton; it was wound up in 1935, its operations being then carried out by Tarmac. *Manifold collection*

No.10, an 0-4-0ST built at Norton between 1904 and 1912, pictured at the colliery circa 1950. The locomotive was scrapped in 1965. *Industrial Railway Society, K.J. Cooper collection*

The Chatterley-Whitfield Railway

The Whitfield Colliery mineral railway, a private line, had its origins in the need to connect coal output with its principal user, the Chatterley Iron Company. The railway ran between Whitfield, located between Tunstall and Biddulph, and Chatterley, situated on the NSR main line south of Harecastle. The railway, in its final form, was two miles 1,210 yards long and commenced at Pinnox Junction, where it connected with the Pinnox Branch of the NSR that in turn connected with the Loop Line at Tunstall Junction. The Whitfield Railway opened in 1878 and had extensive sidings at Pinnox Junction, Scotia Road and at the colliery itself; the colliery also had sidings on the Biddulph Valley Line at Chell.

In addition, there were landsale wharves at Leek Road (Ubberley), Brownhills (Tunstall), and Greenhead (Burslem).

The colliery had two types of locomotives, the first of which were used mainly for shunting at the colliery or working to and shunting at the coal wharves, and also for working the colliers' trains. The second were the 'main line' engines and these were engaged in the haulage of heavy trains from the colliery and the return workings with empty wagons. A colliers' train was introduced in 1887 and this service ran until 29th December 1930. Its objectives were to induce men from Burslem and Tunstall to work at the colliery. Pick up points were at Greenhead Wharf, Pinnox Crossing and Pitts Hill Wharf and the service ran in connection with the day and noon shifts only; the train service was variously referred to as the 'Paddy Train' or as the 'Monkey Train' (on account of the use of ex-Barnum & Bailey circus vans).

The site of Chell Halt, bottom left, a view looking south circa 1950 from the North Stafford bridge that carried the Chatterley-Whitfield private line into the colliery. The Biddulph Valley lines and NSR signal box are to the left and the Chatterley-Whitfield Railway's Chell Sidings are to the right. The colliers' train used to arrive here from Biddulph (and latterly Mossley Halt); Chell Halt opened in 1890 and closed circa 1930. There were further sidings at Botteslow Junction and, for nearly thirty years, a Chatterley-Whitfield locomotive had running powers between Chell and Botteslow; this arrangement ceased in 1924, very shortly into the LM&SR era. *Manifold collection*

Above: A view at Scotia Road in the early 1930s, looking west towards Trent Vale with Fowler 2-6-4T No. 2344 working a train of empties for Sneyd Collieries across the Loop Line viaduct. On the left, *Minnie*, an 0-4-0ST built by Hudswell Clark in 1912, is hard at work propelling its short heavily loaded coal train up the Chatterley-Whitfield branch to Greenhead landsale wharf at Burslem. In the centre is the Chatterley-Whitfield line to Pinnox Junction, the set of rails to the right went to the Company's Brownhills landsale wharf, whilst branching off to the far right is White & Taylor's siding. *Author's collection*

Left: Scotia Road Crossing at Tunstall, a view looking north towards Tunstall and Chatterley-Whitfield Colliery. Scotia Road, now the A50, is the principal road through the Five Towns, and here links Burslem on the right and Tunstall on the left. Although a private line, the Chatterley-Whitfield Railway adopted McKenzie & Holland signalling (they were also signalling contractors to the NSR), as evidenced by the home starter in the foreground and the signal box in the background. Pinnox Sidings, beyond the gates, was a significant marshalling yard, and saw expansion in the LM&SR era. The building at the side of the signal box housed the traffic office; other sidings on the private line included White & Taylor (timber merchants), the Anglo-American Oil Co. and Walter Sylvester Ltd, motor, mining and general engineers. *Manifold collection*

Left: Chatterley-Whitfield Collieries had a very significant stock of their own wagons. In 1914, they owned a fleet of 2,262 main line wagons, with a further 200 others which were restricted to internal use. The size of the fleet obviously did not vary a lot over the years, however, as in 1935, they owned around 2,200 wagons with a further 400 on hire. The final design of Chatterley-Whitfield wagon and livery is seen here on No. 4055, an 8-plank open with side, end and bottom doors, built by Charles Roberts of Wakefield in 1937; they were coloured dark grey. The wagon is marked 'EMPTY TO PINNOX JUNCTION. LM&S (NS)'. Following the outbreak of the Second World War, wagon pooling came into operation and this enormous fleet had left the collieries within a few weeks. *Historical Model Railway Society*

Right: Pinnox Sidings circa 1930, with the bottle banks of Tunstall on the far right of the photograph. The locomotive is *Dolly*, an 0-4-0ST built by the Yorkshire Engine Co. in 1891, which had arrived here at Chatterley-Whitfield by 1896; it was transferred to Berry Hill Colliery in 1951-52, where it worked until 1954. These smaller locomotives were used for shunting and marshalling at the sidings and at the various landsale wharves. Between 1896 and 1924, *Dolly* worked between Chell and Botteslow under running powers granted by the NSR. *H.W. Robinson*

Left: Seen here in the mid-1930s is another Yorkshire Engine Co. product, *Alice*, an 0-6-0ST built in 1876 (Works No. 283) and which went new to Whitfield Colliery. *Alice* was to be rebuilt by Chatterley-Whitfield Collieries circa 1940, along with sister engine *Katie*, when it lost the ogee-shaped boiler seen here and was fitted with a conventional saddle tank instead. Bagnall's also supplied new enclosed cabs for both locomotives. *Alice* was transferred to the NCB in 1947 and was scrapped in late 1964. Behind the locomotive is Queen's Bridge, Tunstall, the then newly-built concrete bridge linking Queen's Avenue with the new Greenbank Road. *H.W. Robinson*

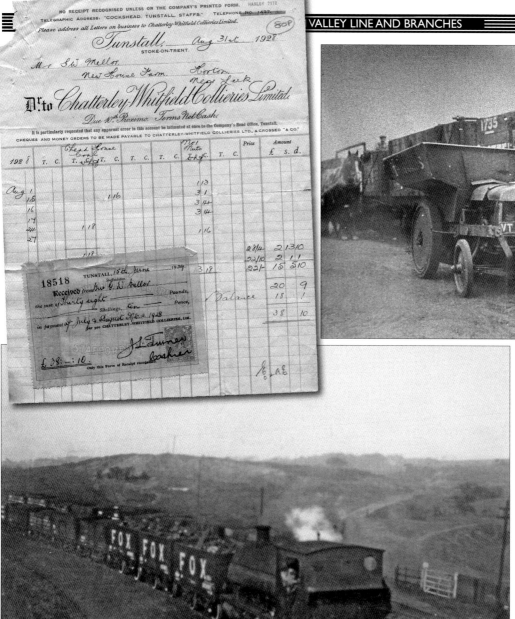

Above: Chatterley-Whitfield Collieries had landsale wharves at Ubberley (on the Leek Road), Greenhead and Brownhills. This is a typical view taken at the first named of these wharves in the mid-1920s, with a Foden tipper tractor belonging to Twyfords being loaded with coal by the driver direct from a wagon in the siding; behind can just be seen the motive power for a more conventional road delivery vehicle – a horse-drawn coal dray. *Author's collection*

Above Left: A 1928 example of a Chatterley-Whitfield invoice letterhead. Note the location of the Head Office as Tunstall at that time; this was later transferred to Whitfield around 1934. *Author's collection*

Centre Left: Seen arriving at Queen's Avenue, Tunstall, in the early 1930s is *Edward VII,* hard at work propelling a train of private owner wagons to Chatterley-Whitfield, with three very new looking Fox wagons to the fore. *Edward VII* was an 0-6-0ST built by Hawthorn Leslie and new to Chatterley-Whitfield in 1902; transferred to the NCB in 1947, it was scrapped in 1964. This was one of the larger locomotives in the fleet and had the responsibility for hauling trains from Chatterley-Whitfield to Scotia Road. On the right hand side, above the wisps of steam, is the former line to High Lane pits, long since lifted, whilst above the Fox wagons is the site of the old Chalkley pit. The train is about to enter the 404 yards tunnel under the High Lane ridge. *Bill Jack collection*

Left: A JE-owned 12-ton wagon in the course of being repainted. The firm of James Edge, with its sales office in Manchester, were the selling agents for much of the coal mined at Chatterley-Whitfield Collieries. They first took a stake in the Chatterley-Whitfield Co. in the 1920s and gradually bought out all the interests of the company that had owned it. *Mark Smith collection*

Left: Whitfield Colliery from the south in 1926. In the background are the ventilation shafts, in front of which are the locomotive sheds, with the old power house in the centre and on the right the Winstanley Shaft, and then the coal washery.

Below: This second aspect of Whitfield Colliery is looking north-west in 1930. From left to right are Winstanley Shaft (which dated from 1914), Engine Pit (circa 1850), the old power house, Ragman Pit (circa 1850), Middle Pit (1863), Bellringer Pit (1874), Institute Pit (circa 1850), Platt Pit (1853) and, just off picture, Hesketh Pit (circa 1915). In 1923, Whitfield Colliery employed 4,369 workers, which had risen to 4,810 in 1927 but then fallen to 2,778 in 1947. Output reached one million tons in 1937, with a slight drop to 950,051 tons in 1947. *Both Bill Jack collection*

Left: 'Kruger' was the last pit pony at Institute Pit and is seen here on 9th June 1931, with ostler A. Lovatt, leaving work for the last time. The steps on the left lead to the cage upper landing deck and the pulleys are for the North Cockshead haulage engines. *Bill Jack collection*

Above: *Roger*, an 0-6-0ST built by Nasmyth Wilson in 1886 and which arrived at Whitfield in 1905, is seen here at the extensive sidings at Chatterley-Whitfield Collieries in the early 1930s. This was another locomotive rebuilt by the colliery company, in late 1930, so is seen here in its rebuilt form. It was taken out of use sometime in 1964 and scrapped on site by local scrap merchant Geo. Singer Ltd in December 1965. Note, in the background, the rural surrounds to the sidings. *H.W. Robinson*

Right: *Phoenix* was an 0-4-0ST built by Chapman & Furneaux Ltd of Gateshead in 1899 (Works No. 1172), arriving here at Chatterley-Whitfield from the Chatterley Iron Works in 1901. Rebuilt at Chatterley in 1931, it is seen here in the late 1930s, possibly not long before it was also fitted with a new boiler, supplied by Bagnalls, in 1938. Note the colliery ventilation shafts on the left. *Phoenix* was taken out of use in 1962 and scrapped on site in the November of the following year. *Author's collection*

Right: *Edward VII*, the 'main line' engine, is seen here outside the Chatterley-Whitfield locomotive shed in 1945. Built by Hawthorn, Leslie & Co. Ltd in 1902 (Works No. 2539), it spent its entire working life at the collieries, passing in to NCB ownership in 1947. Taken out of use in 1963, it was scrapped on site by GFM Co. Ltd in late 1964. *J. Birchenough*

Left: *Katie*, seen here at Whitfield in the early 1930s, was a sister engine to *Alice*, seen a little earlier. Although completed the following year to *Alice*, in 1877, it was allotted the preceding Works number, 282, by the Yorkshire Engine Co., suggesting that the two locomotives were ordered together and allotted Works numbers at that time. Note the distinctive Ogee saddle tank. *H.W. Robinson*

Right: *Katie* again, in the form she exhibited after being extensively rebuilt in the Chatterley-Whitfield workshops in 1940, with a new saddle tank and a fully enclosed cab. Taken out of use in 1963, the engine was scrapped on site by GFM Ltd in late 1964. *H.W. Robinson*

Left: A view at Canada Dock, Liverpool, on 3rd February 1927 with the Lamport & Holt steamers *Browning* and *Balzac* being loaded with 2,600 tons of Chatterley-Whitfield 'Thirds' for bunkering. The private owner wagons in the picture all belong to either Chatterley-Whitfield or James Edge. The wagons were lifted bodily over the ship by the large crane and then tipped to shoot the coal out of the end door. For full participation in the shipping trade, Chatterley-Whitfield used a 12-ton wagon with side, end and bottom doors. Most of the lettering was in white with black shading, whilst in later years, a darker grey shade was used on the main body, as it was found to weather better. *Manifold collection*

Left: An unidentified ex-NSR 'New L' Class 0-6-2T running bunker first at the head of a goods train approaching Chatterley-Whitfield Colliery in the late 1920s. In the background is the former Turnhurst line embankment at Chell, one of Robert Heath's private lines, which ran from Turnhurst Colliery to the Biddulph Valley Line north of Chatterley-Whitfield. *Manifold collection*

Left: No.15, an 0-6-0ST built in 1915 by Robert Heath, was photographed at Biddulph Valley Iron Works in the late 1920s. This engine spent much of its working life at Victoria Colliery and passed in to NCB ownership in 1947. Bagnalls supplied a new boiler for it in 1948 and No. 15 then spent nearly a year under repair at Chatterley-Whitfield in 1954-55. It was scrapped on site at Victoria in 1965. Behind the locomotive are the blast furnaces, whilst the headgear of Victoria Colliery can also be seen in the left background. *H.W. Robinson*

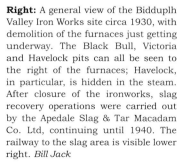

Right: A general view of the Bidduplh Valley Iron Works site circa 1930, with demolition of the furnaces just getting underway. The Black Bull, Victoria and Havelock pits can all be seen to the right of the furnaces; Havelock, in particular, is hidden in the steam. After closure of the ironworks, slag recovery operations were carried out by the Apedale Slag & Tar Macadam Co. Ltd, continuing until 1940. The railway to the slag area is visible lower right. *Bill Jack*

Right: A view of Black Bull Colliery taken in 1929, from the west side of the pit looking east. In the background, from left to right, is the Havelock upcast shaft, then the Victoria shaft winding engine house, and then the Victoria coal winding shaft. The four wagons in the centre of the picture illustrate well the changes in ownership in the Heath empire occurring in the middle and late 1920s. From left to right they comprise an LMS lettered 5-plank wagon and then wagons belonging to the short-lived Kidsgrove Collieries (1925 to April 1931), Robert Heath & Low Moor (from January 1920 to January 1929) and Norton & Biddulph Collieries (from January 1929 through to Nationalisation in January 1947). Employment at Black Bull was 841 in 1923, whilst in 1933 it was 1,150 and 1,422 in 1947. Output in 1928 was 179,641 tons, and in 1947 496,396 tons. The colliery was closed in August 1982. James Cadman purchased Victoria and Norton collieries, along with the nearby engineering and machine shops at Black Bull, in 1929. Cadman transferred his engineering works, Cowlishaw Walker & Co. from Etruria to Black Bull; over the years this firm rebuilt several of the Heath locomotives which had been manufactured there originally. *Bill Jack*

Right: A Norton & Biddulph Collieries 12-ton wagon, No. 3201, built by Chas Roberts & Co. Ltd in 1938 and lettered '*Empty to Norton & Biddulph Collieries, Black Bull, L.M.S. Railway (N.S. Section)*. *Historical Model Railway Society*

Far Right Below: A Norton & Biddulph Collieries Ltd wagon label, dated 9th January 1946, for a load of coal destined for Church Stretton. *Author's collection*

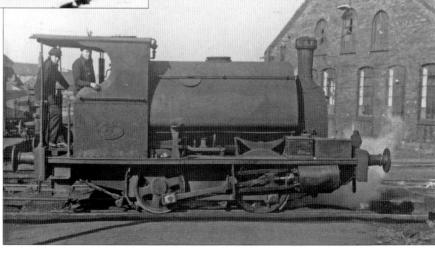

Above: Seen in wintry conditions at Black Bull Colliery on 18th January 1936 is No. 11, an 0-6-0ST, built by Black Hawthorn Ltd in 1888 (Works No. 949). By this date, No. 11 probably looked nothing like it had done when it first emerged from Heath's works, having been rebuilt no less than four times in the interim: at an unknown date by Kerr, Stuart, then by Heaths in 1902 and again in 1914, and finally by Chatterley-Whitfield in 1932. Passing to the NCB in 1947, at which time it was to be found at Norton Colliery, it came back to Black Bull circa 1952, after being fitted with a new boiler supplied by Bagnalls in 1951, and was finally scrapped on site in 1965. *Author's collection*

Right: Another Robert Heath product and the last to be built, 0-4-0ST No. 9 is seen here outside the engine house of Victoria Colliery on 28th February 1953, by which time it was in NCB ownership. Built in 1926, a new Bagnall boiler was fitted in 1951; No. 98 was taken out of use circa 1961 and scrapped in 1964. *Harold Bowtell*

STOKE TO BUCKNALL					
STATIONS	Week days				
	a.m.	a.m.	p.m.	p.m.	p.m.
Stoke .... dep.	8 25	10s30	7s20	4 25	8s52
Fenton Manor ...	8 40	10s34	7s25	4 29	8s56
Bucknall	8 44	10s38	7s29	4 38	9 s 0
Ford Green	8 53	10s46	7s35	4 39	9s 6
Black Bull	9 2	10s53	7s55	4 46	9s13
Knypersley Hlt	9 6	10s57	1 59	4 50	9s17
Biddulph	9 10	11b 7	2 3	4 54	9s27
Mossley Halt ..	9 16	11b 7	2 8	5 0	.....
Congleton arr	9 28	11b76	2 22	5 6	9s34

FORD GREEN BIDDULPH AND CONGLETON.						
STATIONS	Week days					Notes.
	a.m.	p.m	p.m	p.m	p.m	
Congleton dep.	10 50	12s35	1 s 5	3s10	6 55	9s42
Mossley Halt ..	10 39	12s44	1s14	3s19	7 4	.....
Biddulph	10 46	12s51	1s27	3s 6	7 11	9s56
Knypersley Hlt	10 50	12s55	1s25	3s30	7 15	'0s 0
Black Bull	10 54	12s59	1s19	3s34	7 19	10s 4
Ford Green	11 1	.....	1s36	3s41	7 26	10s11
Bucknall	11 7	.....	1s43	3s47	7 82	10s17
Fenton Manor...	11 12	.....	1s47	3s51	7 86	10s21
Stoke .. arr	11 16	.....	1s51	3s54	7 39	10s24

Notes.
S—Saturdays only
B—Saturdays excepted.

This photograph of Biddulph station was taken in 1912, so is strictly well outside the LM&SR period that we are studying in this series but it is included here simply because of its rarity value; with the passenger service ceasing in 1927, views showing the station in use are extremely scarce. Looking towards Stoke, an NSR 'D' Class 0-6-0T is seen at the head of a local passenger working about to depart for Congleton, via Congleton Lower Junction and Upper Junction. Note the standard NSR kissing gates on either side of the level crossing. All the station buildings are single-storey, the architect's feature for the Biddulph Valley Line and there are two signs reading Booking & Waiting Hall, with another for Telegrams. The signal box was to a standard early McKenzie & Holland design and was similar to the box at Congleton station on the main line. *Biddulph Museum, courtesy of the late Miss Oakes*

Inset Above: The March 1923 timetable for the Biddulph Valley line, taken from the Wood Mitchell bus and railway timetables. *Author's collection*

Left: This advertisement appeared in the *Congleton Chronicle* on 11th August 1939 for railway excursions from Biddulph station to Congleton and Biddulph Wakes in August 1939. Those on 12th and 13th were combined excursions from Biddulph and Congleton stations for Blackpool, North Wales and Liverpool, whilst the excursion to Blackpool on 16th August (at the foot of the advertisement) was from Biddulph only. This was the last excursion from Biddulph during the LM&SR era, whilst the final excursion from the station took place in August 1952. *Cheshire Archives & Local Studies*

Above: An overall view of Biddulph station on 28th February 1953, looking north towards Congleton. Although the station closed for passenger services in 1927, goods facilities continued until December 1964 and holiday excursion trains occasionally called. On the left, in the background beyond the level crossing is the crossing keeper's house. The goods shed and loading dock are in the centre, with the loading gauge over a second siding on the right. *Harold Bowtell*

Left: The Biddulph Down Home signal, in the first of two photographs taken in September 1950. This was a Mackenzie & Holland product, with a 16ft post, and dated from when the signalling was provided in NSR days. *John Alsop collection*

Right: The Biddulph Up Home bracket, a most unusual signal with two lower arms on the main post. *John Alsop collection*

CHEAP LMS TRIPS

Congleton Wakes
1939

At Specially Reduced Fares for

Congleton and Biddulph Wakes

(August 11th to 18th inclusive, 1939)

MONTHLY EXCURSION TICKETS will be issued from CONGLETON BY ANY TRAIN AUG. 11th to 18th INCLUSIVE TO ALL STATIONS in ENGLAND, SCOTLAND and WALES, and will be available for return BY ANY TRAIN on ANY DAY within ONE CALENDAR MONTH of the date of issue.

Special Excursion Trains will run on Saturday August 12th, 1939

		From			Return Fares
			am	am	
BLACKPOOL	dep	Biddulph	6.40	9.0	
	"	Congleton	7.0	9.17	
	arr	BLACKPOOL	9.49	12.10 pm	

			Rhyl	Colwyn Bay	Llandudno
NORTH WALES	dep	Biddulph 6.40 am	10/6	12/7	12/1
	"	Congleton 7.0 am	10/0	12/1	11/7
	arr	LLANDUDNO 9.42 am			

			Liverp'l	Doug-las	New Brigt'n	South-port
LIVERPOOL	dep	Biddulph 6.40 am	9.5	23.6	10/6	11/7
(for Isle of Man, New Brighton, Southport)	"	Congleton 7.0 am	8.11	23.0	10/0	11/0
		change at Crewe				
	arr	LIVERPOOL 8.58 am				

LONDON	dep	Congleton	12.19 night	27.10
	arr	LONDON	4.50 am	

FOR RETURN TIMES and FARES TO OTHER POINTS SEE HANDBILLS

CHEAP TRIPS for

BIDDULPH & CONGLETON WAKES, 1939.

EACH DAY, MONDAY, AUGUST 14th TO FRIDAY, AUGUST 18th.

		Congleton dep.	Biddulph dep.	Third Class Return Fare.
BLACKPOOL		7-41 a.m.		8/3
		8- 5 a.m.		
PRESTATYN		8- 5 a.m.		6/9
RHYL		8-35 a.m.		7/3
COLWYN BAY		10-12 a.m.		7/9
LLANDUDNO				8/3
SOUTHPORT		7-41 a.m.		6/3
BLACKPOOL		9-35 a.m.	Sun. Aug. 13th.	4/9
		12-15 p.m.	Wed. Aug. 16th.	
		12-15 p.m.	Thur. Aug. 17th.	
CHESTER		9-55 a.m.	Sun. Aug. 13th.	3/2
RHYL		11-24 a.m.	Thur. Aug. 17th.	4/9
COLWYN BAY				5/3
LLANDUDNO				5/3
CHESTER		4-15 p.m.	Sun. Aug. 20th.	1/10 Evening Excursion.
RHYL				2/5
COLWYN BAY				2/5
LONDON		10-59 p.m.	Sun. Aug. 13th.	9-Crewe 3/2 Lichfield 3/8 Tamworth 3/6 Nuneaton 4/9 Rugby Northampton 6/9
MANCHESTER		10-20 a.m.	Sun. Aug. 13th.	2/8
		12-29 p.m.		
SHREWSBURY		7-16 a.m.	Wed. Aug. 16th.	5/3
		12- 1 p.m.	Thur. Aug. 17th.	3/6 Floral Fete
TRENTHAM PARK		9-20 a.m.	Sun. Aug. 17th.	5/3
		4-15 p.m.	Sun. Aug. 13th.	1/4 Including Garden Admission.

THROUGH HALF-DAY EXCURSION FROM BIDDULPH STATION.
Wed. Aug. 16th. BLACKPOOL. Biddulph dep. 12- 2 p.m. 4/9

Ask for Handbill NSR/R Congleton Wakes Excursion.

Right: The 1928 Rating Plan for Mossley Halt. This was the most basic of facilities, with a platform about 100 yards long, a waiting shed and booking office, and a platelayers' hut. By the time of Grouping, the service on the Biddulph Valley Line was very modest; on weekdays, two trains a day each way between Stoke and Congleton, and a late evening train which did not call at Mossley Halt; of the two Saturdays only trains, only one called at Mossley Halt and there was a Saturdays only mid-day train from Congleton to Black Bull. Also of interest was the provision of a service by the Chatterley-Whitfield Company for their own workers between the Whitfield Sidings at Chell and Mossley Halt, two trains a day each way, Mondays to Fridays. The halt was located about 1½ miles south of the main line station at Congleton, on the Congleton to Biddulph road, and because it was located on a high embankment, was reached by a

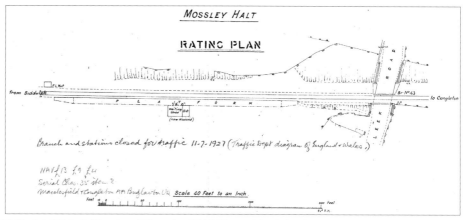

steep path. Opened in 1919, it closed on 13th April 1925. The late Bill Jack, historian of Chatterley-Whitfield, noted that '*After the opening of Mossley Halt, a Whitfield locomotive worked the early morning and late running of the train, while a NSR (LM&SR) locomotive brought the noon shift and took the day shift back again. The colliers' train, after its extension to Mossley Halt, was propelled back empty to Biddulph for stabling … There was no lighting in the colliers' trains and travelling conditions during the winter months were grim. Because of the inconvenient location of Biddulph station and the competition from buses, the numbers using the colliers' trains had dwindled to 40. The trains never resumed after the national coal strike was over.*' Cheddleton Railway Museum

Right: Private Siding Agreement from the mid-1920s for Brunswick Wharf, Congleton, between the LM&SR and Robert Heath & Low Moor. The line came in on the left from Congleton Lower Junction and served three wharves: Robert Heath & Low Moor (top), the Congleton Industrial & Equitable Co-operative Society (centre) and H. Hargreaves & Co. Ltd, coal, coke and lime merchants. Robert Heath and its successor companies had operated a coal siding here since 1886, and this arrangement continued throughout the LM&SR era as Norton & Biddulph Collieries. James Edge, sales agents for Chatterley-Whitfield also used sidings at Brunswick Wharf at this period. *Author's collection*

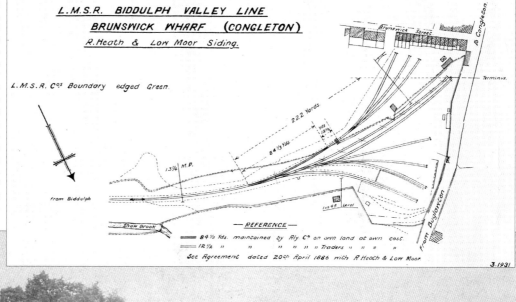

Brunswick Wharf, Congleton circa 1926. The Congleton Industrial & Equitable Society coal lorry is about to commence deliveries and one of their wagons is also on view. From left to right are: Harry Walton, ? Minshull (Yard Foreman), John Butler, Charles Yates, Jack Holland, unknown. On the left is one of Hargreaves' wagons, who operated from here for many years. Brunswick Wharf closed in April 1968. *Author's collection*

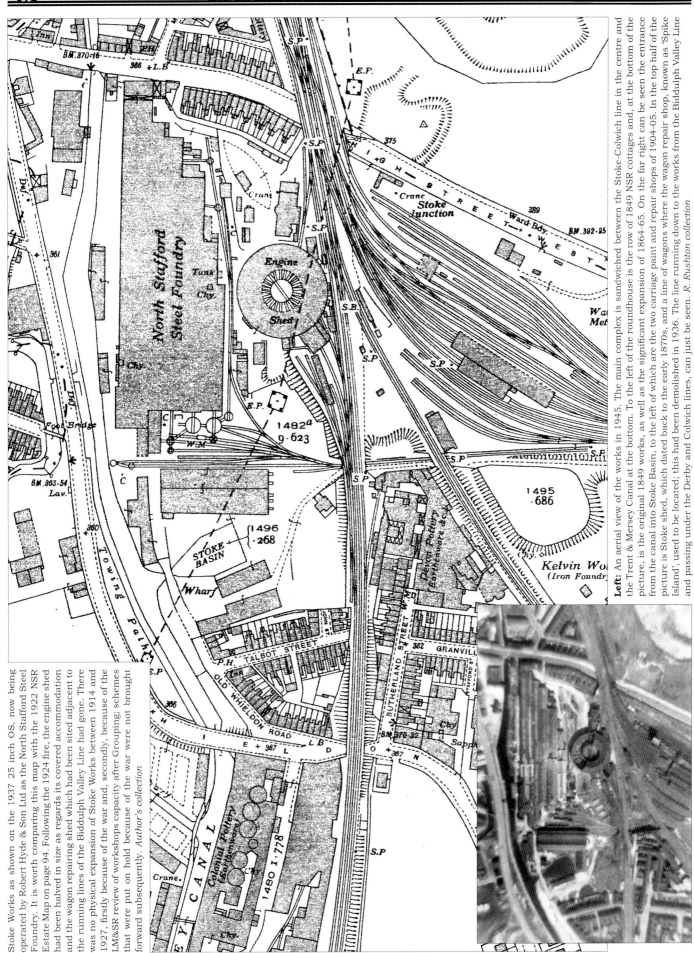

Stoke Works as shown on the 1937 25 inch OS, now being operated by Robert Hyde & Son Ltd as the North Stafford Steel Foundry. It is worth comparing this map with the 1922 NSR Estate Map on page 94. Following the 1924 fire, the engine shed had been halved in size as regards its covered accommodation and the wagon repairing shed which had been sited adjacent to the running lines of the Biddulph Valley Line had gone. There was no physical expansion of Stoke Works between 1914 and 1927, firstly because of the war and, secondly, because of the LM&SR review of workshops capacity after Grouping; schemes that were put on hold because of the war were not brought forward subsequently. *Author's collection*

Left: An aerial view of the works in 1945. The main complex is sandwiched between the Stoke-Colwich line in the centre and the Trent & Mersey Canal at the bottom. To the left of the roundhouse is the row of 1849 NSR cottages and, at the bottom of the picture, is the original 1849 works, as well as the significant expansion of 1864-65. On the far right can be seen the entrance from the canal into Stoke Basin, to the left of which are the two carriage paint and repair shops of 1904-05. In the top half of the picture is Stoke shed, which dated back to the early 1870s, and a line of wagons where the wagon repair shop, known as 'Spike Island', used to be located; this had been demolished in 1936. The line running down to the works from the Biddulph Valley Line and passing under the Derby and Colwich lines, can just be seen. *R. Rushton collection*

6

Stoke Works

The origins of the NSR's Locomotive, Carriage & Wagon Works date back to 1849 when, three years after the NSR gained its Parliamentary Powers, the spine of the NSR network had been opened: Macclesfield to Colwich, Crewe to Derby and North Rode to Burton-on-Trent, some 111 miles and 63 chains. The site chosen for the NSR's locomotive roundhouse and works was Whieldon Grove, an area of wooded parkland located within a triangle formed by the road going from Stoke to Fenton, the T&M Canal and the 1804 Lane End plateway, which ran for 2¾ miles from a canal basin to Longton. This constriction was later to prove the site to have been poorly chosen, as it came to be very cramped but with no room for expansion.

From 1849 to 1859, the NSR appointed a contractor, Joseph Wright & Sons, '*an extensive coachbuilder of Saltley, Birmingham*', to maintain the rolling stock and work the traffic. Stoke Works opened in 1849, whilst Wright's firm later became the Metropolitan Railway Carriage & Wagon Company.

The NSR in those early years purchased its locomotives and rolling stock but the Company's decision to build its own motive power, caraiges and wagons, as far as capacity would allow, and to repair its ever increasing stock of them, led in 1865 to a major expansion of the works. This consisted of new erecting and boiler shops for locomotives, and new facilities for carriage and wagon building and repairs. Accordingly, the first carriage was built in 1861, the first wagons in 1863 and the first locomotives in 1868.

Subsequently, over the years down to Grouping, the NSR built nearly all its own locomotives, the main exceptions being when increased activity led to a shortage of motive power. In its lifetime, the NSR built 192 locomotives, a very modest number compared with the L&NWR and the Midland Railway. A shortage of materials, as a result of restrictions during World War One, resulted in only ten locomotives being built between 1915 and 1919, with the final batch of six 'New L' Class engines being completed in the spring of 1923.

The increase in the number of wagons being built and repaired resulted in the construction of separate carriage and wagon shops alongside the T&M Canal in 1865. To increase the capacity of the works, a section of Whieldon Road, which bisected the original

Below: An LM&SR First Class Pass, issued to Mrs Hookham and family, which expired on 31st December 1924. It was in respect of travel over the former NSR network and to some locations where the NSR had running powers, including Manchester, Birmingham, Derby and Buxton (via Middlewood). *Manifold collection*

John Hookham in his panelled offices at the works with his highly polished table and chair. On the wall can be seen photographs of various NSR locomotives and the main chart is a 'Diagram Showing the Age of Engines'; this diagram was introduced by Hookham in 1916, and then annually until Grouping, and originals can be seen at the National Railway Museum at York. Hookham started his career under William Kirtley at the London, Chatham & Dover Railway, where he became a draughtsman. On the formation of the South Eastern & Chatham Railway, on 1st January 1899, he was transferred to Ashford. He then spent two years in Brazil, before being appointed Works Manager at Stoke in 1902. He was appointed Locomotive Superintendent in 1915, a position he held until the NSR was amalgamated with the LM&SR in July 1923. He then became Mechanical Engineer, Stoke, until his retirement in December 1924. He had a good reputation as an engineer on the works side and as being ahead of his time in such operations as machining piston rods and packing. He was also considered a leader in using cast-iron gland packing rings, supplying Gresley with information leading to their use on the Great Northern Railway, and later on the London & North Eastern Railway. *Author's collection*

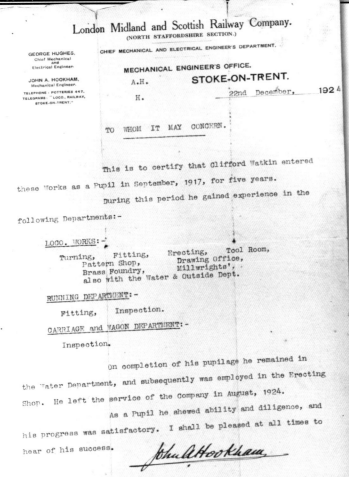

London Midland and Scottish Railway Company.
(NORTH STAFFORDSHIRE SECTION.)

GEORGE HUGHES.
Chief Mechanical
and
Electrical Engineer.

CHIEF MECHANICAL AND ELECTRICAL ENGINEER'S DEPARTMENT.

JOHN A. HOOKHAM.
Mechanical Engineer.

MECHANICAL ENGINEER'S OFFICE.
A.H.   STOKE-ON-TRENT.

TELEPHONE : POTTERIES 447.
TELEGRAMS : "LOCO. RAILWAY,
STOKE-ON-TRENT."

H.   22nd December,   1924

TO WHOM IT MAY CONCERN.

          This is to certify that Clifford Watkin entered
these Works as a Pupil in September, 1917, for five years.

          During this period he gained experience in the
following Departments:-

   LOCO. WORKS:-
       Turning,   Fitting,   Erecting,   Tool Room,
               Pattern Shop,   Drawing Office,
               Brass Foundry,   Millwrights',
               also with the Water & Outside Dept.

   RUNNING DEPARTMENT:-

       Fitting,   Inspection.

   CARRIAGE and WAGON DEPARTMENT:-

       Inspection.

          On completion of his pupilage he remained in
the Water Department, and subsequently was employed in the Erecting
Shop. He left the service of the Company in August, 1924.

          As a Pupil he shewed ability and diligence, and
his progress was satisfactory. I shall be pleased at all times to
hear of his success.

                              John A. Hookham

Left: A letter of reference from John Hookham, in respect of Premium Apprentice Clifford Watkin, who had served a five year pupilage from 1917 to 1922. The letter is dated 22nd December 1924, just a few days before Hookham retired as Mechanical Engineer for the North Staffordshire Section of the LM&SR. Formerly Locomotive Superintendent of the NSR from 1915 to 1922, he was appointed Mechanical Engineer under George Hughes, the Chief Mechanical & Electrical Engineer of the LM&SR, in January 1923. The letter details experience gained in the Loco Works, Running Department, and Carriage & Wagon Department, before subsequently being employed in the Erecting Shop. It is likely that Hookham was providing references for his former pupils prior to his retirement. *Watkin family collection*

market) and the tight space required the construction of a traverser to move the carriages around.

World War One and the restriction of materials resulted in a significant slow down of activity in the works. The details below show builds between 1915 and 1923:

	Locomotives	Coaching Stock (bogie stock, milk vans & carriage trucks)	
1915	2	5	
1916	4	3	
1917	-	1	
1918	4	-	
1919	-	10	
1920		5	7
1921		5	18
1922		3	-
1923		4	-

One of the early NSR casualties of the LM&SR era was the Locomotive, Carriage & Wagon Works at Stoke. Initially, in terms of the future organisation of the LM&SR's carriage and wagon building and repairs, this part of the Stoke operation was hived off from the locomotive section. The works was at that time still under John Hookham, the former NSR Locomotive, Carriage & Wagon Superintendent but the hived off section was placed under W.J. Smith, Superintendent of Works, Carriage & Wagon Department, Derby, whose responsibilities included Stoke and Crewe; William Sinclair became Stoke Carriage & Wagon Works manager. The function of the former works changed; no new locomotives were built at Stoke after March 1923, nor any new carriage stock and wagons. Repair work continued and some painting occurred of locomotives

building and the 1865 carriage and wagon shops, was closed in 1883 and roofed over. A new and separate wagon repair shop, again to cope with the increased need for new build and repairs, was built in 1883, alongside the Biddulph Valley Line, opposite Stoke shed.

Carriage building continued to expand and a separate carriage and erecting shop was built some time between 1878 and 1893. Two replacement carriage shops, on the same site, were opened in 1905, specifically to accommodate the introduction of bogie stock (initially for the longer distance leisure

Henry George Ivatt, the son of H.A. Ivatt, Locomotive Superintendent of the Great Northern Railway, is seen here in his office at Stoke Works. He was a Premium Apprentice at Crewe Works, subsequently becoming Assistant to the Crewe Works Manager. He took up the post of Deputy Locomotive, Carriage & Wagon Superintendent at Stoke in September 1919, before becoming Works Manager of the Locomotive Works in 1923. In July, upon the closure of the works, he was appointed Special Assistant to Sir Henry Fowler, the Chief Mechanical Engineer of the LM&SR, at Derby. A career with the LM&SR saw his appointment as CME on 1st February 1946. In June 1951, he retired to start a new career in the manufacture of diesel locomotives. In the photograph, the 'Work in Progress' board on the right (only partially visible) indicates dates when various tasks were completed; from left to right, engine on pit, axle boxes, big ends, little ends, connecting rods, eccentric straps, eccentric sheaves, pistons and piston valves. Note how sparse this office looks, compared to Hookham's, though a telephone can be seen at the side of Ivatt's left elbow. *Author's collection*

into the new LM&SR livery. With its comparatively small facilities, it was always likely that the prospects for the works would be bleak. There is no evidence of any capital expenditure in excess of £200 being authorised between 1923 and the summer of 1927, when the works formally closed.

Operationally, it had ceased to function a short time before, with some of the carriage and wagon workers transferring to Derby, whilst 308 men from the locomotive works transferred to Crewe early in May 1927. A special train service from the Potteries, initially just for them, was introduced from Stoke and lasted until 1989. The closure of the works followed a major review by the LM&SR in 1925, of the scope for closing down some of its workshops. This review was carried out by Ernest Lemon and John Aspinall, who visited Stoke Works not to question the inevitable closure but to see if any of the machinery was worth rescuing; apparently not was the answer.

Ultimately, a significant report came to the Board in July 1926, entitled *The Concentration of Works and Closure of Workshops'*. The initial intention was for the works to close on 1st November 1926 but, as a result of lobbying from the City of Stoke on Trent Council, this date was put back some months; a favourable consequence of this was that many workers were thus able to find new employment at the Michelin Tyre Company, which was opening up nearby. A modest amount of new investment at Crewe took place to cope with the work transferred. At Stoke, meanwhile, the larger wagon repair shop was given over to storing locomotives but was eventually demolished in 1936; other repairs remained at Cockshott, just north of Stoke, until 1933.

Robert Hyde & Son Ltd, foundry engineers, who manufactured castings for axle boxes and other products for the railway industry, leased the locomotive works from 1928 for fourteen years and the successors of that company own it down to the present day. Hydes were attracted to the site because of its rail access for incoming materials comprising sand, coal and scrap steel, and for the despatch of axle boxes and other products. The Company transferred its casting business from its Abbeydale Foundry in Sheffield to Stoke on 1st October 1928. Trip working that was carried out daily to and from the former Stoke Works continued for Hydes, Trip No. 12,

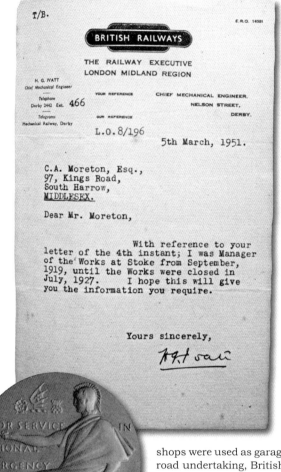

known as *'T'owd mon's shift'*, being worked by an elderly driver and a young fireman; they would work the 336 yard section at 1 in 30 from Pratt's Siding down into the works. Depending on the volume of traffic, shunting could last most of the day and, to the end of the steam era, a Class '3F' 0-6-0T was allocated to this trip. The track work and turntables remained and were used until 1967, when the manufacture of castings was transferred to Chesterfield.

Documents dealing with the renewal of Hydes' lease contain details of a significant amount of internal standard and narrow gauge track that dated back to the NSR era being still in situ in the mid 1940s. The Company contributed to the war effort in the same way that the NSR had done nearly thirty years earlier, Hydes' works at Stoke and Chesterfield between them producing nearly 350,000 castings for tanks, guns, bomb loading trolleys and armoured cars. That part of the former carriage and wagon works which was located alongside the Trent & Mersey Canal was used by the LM&SR for storage and as a garage; Rolls Royce leased it during the Second World War for the manufacture of parts used in the assembly of Merlin and Lancaster aircrafts. The two former carriage shops were used as garages, passing on in 1948 to the nationalised road undertaking, British Road Services.

Above: This letter, to Claude Moreton, one of the five co-authors of the first major history of the North Staffordshire Railway, was written by George Ivatt, known in Stoke Works as 'The Major'. In it, he confirms the official date of the closure of the works as being 31st July 1927. At least half the employees had transferred to Crewe or to Derby some weeks before that. *Manifold collection*

Left: The commemorative medallion issued to George Ivatt by the LM&SR to recognise his service in the National Emergency of May 1926 – the period of the General Strike and its aftermath. These were issued to all employees who worked through the period of the strike and were presented with a citation and a letter of thanks. *Author's collection*

Left: The two NSR employees who progressed furthest in the LM&SR and who really made their mark on its development, both emanated from Stoke Works. George Ivatt was one, whilst the other was Tom Coleman. Coleman served an apprenticeship at Kerr, Stuart & Co. in Stoke and then moved literally down the road to Stoke Works, on 1st May 1905. Starting as a draughtsman, he became works plant draughtsman and, by the time of Grouping, was Chief Draughtsman for the NSR. In September 1926, he was transferred to Horwich and for the remainder of his career he was involved in locomotive design and re-design, and later carriage and wagon design. In 1933, he was moved to Crewe as Chief Draughtsman with continuing control of Horwich; in March 1935, he was transferred to Derby as Technical Assistant and Chief Draughtsman of the LM&SR. He retired at Derby in July 1949 and, in retrospect, has acquired a reputation as one of the best railway company designers of the century. *Paul Blurton collection*

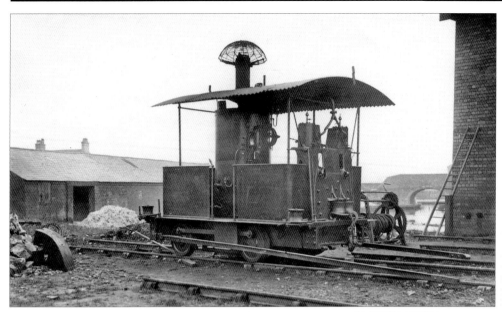

Left: This steam traverser was used for moving carriages into position for entry into the coach painting and repairing shops, the wall of which can be seen on the right. In the right background of this circa 1923 photograph is Stoke Basin, on the Trent & Mersey Canal; the bridge carries Whieldon Road over the waterway. *W.H. Whitworth*

Below: The erecting shop in 1923, with 'B' Class 2-4-0T No. 1446, formerly NSR No. 48A, on the left hand of the three lines. In the centre is an ex-NSR 5-plank wagon, now painted in LM&SR livery whilst, on the right, is the cab interior of an unidentified locomotive. *Author's collection*

Below: Former NSR 0-6-0ST No. 58A, now carrying LM&SR No. 1600 on its tank, poses in front of the wagon repairing shop. No. 1600 is in the pre-1927 style livery, with the cabside insignia panel and 14 inch numerals on the saddle tank sides. *Author's collection*

Above: A view of the six-lane 'Long Shed' in 1936, with the section on the left without its roof. On the far right is another glimpse of the wagon repairing shed, which was nearly the length of the engine shed and, by this date, providing storage for withdrawn locomotives. This was to be its final role and the building was demolished later that year. *W. Potter*

Left: A 1933 advertisement for Hyde axle boxes, as fitted to the carriages used on the electrified London to Brighton line.

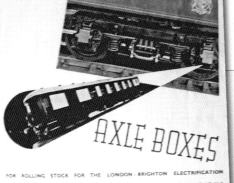

Right: The entrance to the former NSR Locomotive, Carriage & Wagon Works at Stoke in the early 1930s, now bearing the name of the lessees Robert Hyde & Son, Ltd, who had taken it on in 1928. Above the archway, the only entrance to the works, was the former time office, with the mess room to the side. *Hyde archive*

Left: This photograph was taken in 1928, at the time that Robert Hyde took out a lease of the erecting shop. The main erecting shop is to the left, with the main machine and fitting shop barely visible on the extreme left; note the twin wagon turntables in the left foreground. Of particular interest is the presence on the right of an ex-NSR 12-ton implement wagon, one of two built in 1919 at a cost of £400 each and adapted from an earlier (1913) Midland Railway design. The wagon depicted here is No. 3484. Behind is a small hand crane, here numbered 1, which was mounted on a 4-wheeled chassis; although running on standard gauge track, it is unlikely to have ventured much farther than this outside the building. There is no clue as to its origins, although it was certainly not built at Stoke Works. *Hyde archive*

Far Left: A 1948 advertisement by Hydes from *Overseas Railways. Hyde archive*

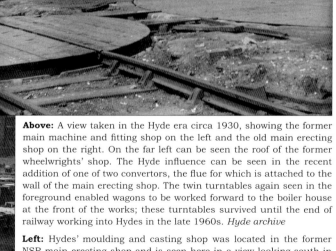

Above: A view taken in the Hyde era circa 1930, showing the former main machine and fitting shop on the left and the old main erecting shop on the right. On the far left can be seen the roof of the former wheelwrights' shop. The Hyde influence can be seen in the recent addition of one of two convertors, the flue for which is attached to the wall of the main erecting shop. The twin turntables again seen in the foreground enabled wagons to be worked forward to the boiler house at the front of the works; these turntables survived until the end of railway working into Hydes in the late 1960s. *Hyde archive*

Left: Hydes' moulding and casting shop was located in the former NSR main erecting shop and is seen here in a view looking south in 1932. All over the shop floor are sand moulds waiting to be filled with steel. At the rear are two convertors, one on either side, which made the steel that was poured into ladles and then into the moulds. On the right hand side, the archways led into the old main machine and fitting shop. *Hyde archive*

Right: Looking north inside the former main erecting shop and taken probably shortly after Hydes moved in during 1928. Some interesting features of the NSR/LM&SR era can be seen, such as the inspection pits in the foreground and background, and the standard gauge internal works railway running down the centre of the shop and going through to the engine room behind. One of the two Craven Bros electric cranes can also be seen. The steel stanchions on the right of the shop are evidence of the mid-1890s extension and in-filling of the works, reflecting its piecemeal development. Note too the wooden floor on the left. *Hyde archive*

Below: Another view taken inside the old main erecting shop in 1932, this time looking north. The standard gauge track is still in situ and the two 1907 Craven Bros electric cranes can be seen; the last one of these was finally removed in 1978. A residual amount of line shafting, no longer in use, can be seen on the back wall, whilst evidence of the former pit road can be seen on the right. By this time, it had become Hydes' moulding shop and in the background is where manual shot blasting or heat treatment took place. Across the centre of the picture a new internal railway track has been installed. On the left, moulding boxes are seen stacked up. *Hyde archive*

Above: Hydes' moulding shop, seen here in 1932, was formerly the small (original) erecting shop; in the background, to the right of the door, is the cupola for smelting iron. The standard gauge rails are still in situ in the centre of the picture but the overhead crane had by this date been dismantled. In the right foreground, the ladles are stacked on a bogey which connected with the former main erecting shop on one of two recently installed sets of connecting rails. Note the set of newly built substantial shutter doors on the right. *Hyde archive*

Left: Another 1932 picture, showing the former boiler shop which Hydes had converted in to a machine shop. Bogie wheels and other castings can be seen around the shop floor, with a lathe and milling machine in the background, and a couple of seated machinists apparently caught enjoying a 'snap' (food) break. *Hyde archive*

Above: A comparison between the NSR and Hyde eras is given in these two photographs of the former NSR wheeling section of the erecting shop. Note the narrow gauge works tramway running down the centre in both (note that it uses one rail of the standard gauge system), the wooden turntable and the two manually operated, swivelling, pneumatic cranes. This first view shows part of the wheel shop. On the left is the marking out table, on which rests several brass-faced gauges; behind it, axle grinding is taking place. In the front centre is a crank axle, whilst behind is a leading or trailing axle being lifted above the works tramway. In the distance several plain axles are just visible. On the right are wheel lathes for turning the wheel sets and also tyres of various sizes ready to be fitted; several wheel lathes can also be seen. The works built no new locomotives after Grouping, activity instead being reliant on maintaining existing rolling stock and painting it in the new LM&SR livery. None of the NSR's substantial investment in plant and equipment was transferred to other workshops. *Author's collection*

Right: A view looking the opposite way about eight years later, after the locomotive section of the works had been leased to Robert Hyde & Son Limited, showing what had now become Hydes' machine shop. The LM&SR had left behind some of the NSR's plant and machinery – noticeably, on the left, the 8ft diameter pairs of plates with gear teeth, at the back of which were the wheel turning lathes. One of the pneumatic cranes can be seen, top left; the internal works railway, tramway and turntable are all prominent and much of the NSR's internal rail systems were still in place in 1945, though not necessarily in use. Note also the NSR installation of line shafts high up on both sides, which were used to drive a multitude of diverse machines. The machine in the right foreground looks like a slotter, for making keyways in bores. *Hyde archive*

Left: Hydes' newly established pattern shop, looking north in 1929. Of particular interest is the narrowness of this workshop; it was created from the original Whieldon Road which ran between the carriage and wagon works and the locomotive shops, and pre-dated the building of the original works in 1849. Whieldon Road was closed by Act of Parliament in 1883 and a series of narrow workshops established along its former route, several of which are still in use today. A roof was built spanning the road between the workshops and drain pipes on their 'exterior' walls can still be seen. In later NSR days (1913), the pattern shop was the wagon shop extension. *Hyde archive*

An LM&SR plan of the former works, the bold lines delineating the boundaries of the property occupied by Hydes. The different workshops are shown with their 'new' uses. Hydes occupied only one of the canalside workshops, probably to allow for the delivery of timber by the canal path. The standard gauge lines and various turntables clearly show the reliance by the works on the rail system; the hatched section of track was worked by LM&SR locomotives and the unhatched section, including turntables, by Hyde's tractors. *Hyde archive*

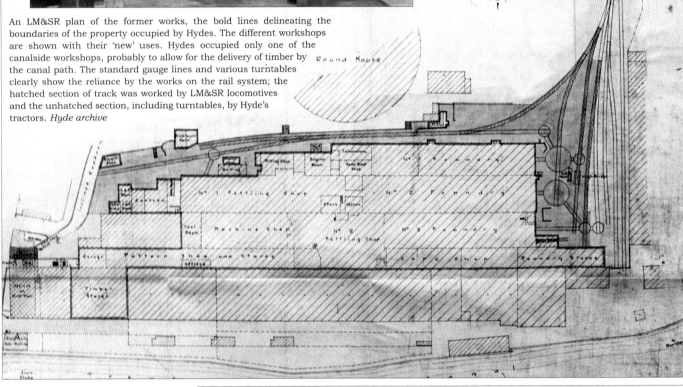

Right: Much of the former Stoke Works complex can be seen in this view of Hydes' factory, taken on 8th January 1965. It shows the works buildings as they existed and were used by Hydes during the LM&SR era. On the left are the two 1905 carriage sheds (coach painting and repairing), which were built over the trackbed of the former Lane End plateway. The running lines in the centre go straight on to the Trent & Mersey Canal but delivery of materials to the works via the waterway had largely ceased under the NSR. Stoke shed's veteran Class '3F' 0-6-0T No. 47596 is on its daily trip working; this took the form of coal, sand and scrap iron being brought into the works for smelting and forging, with finished axle boxes, buffer castings, etc, being moved out. The gantry and track for the magnet crane are prominent on the centre right. The tops of the two convertors that fed into Hyde's moulding shop can just be seen, whilst the coke piled on the right is waiting to be hand-barrowed across. *R.H. Brough*

7

Rolling Stock

The NSR's Locomotive, Carriage & Wagon Works occupied a very cramped site, located as it was between the NSR main line from Stoke to Stone and Colwich (at a higher level) and the Trent & Mersey Canal. For most of its operational life, the works built a very high proportion of the NSR's locomotives, carriages, wagons and other rolling stock. It also carried out rebuilding of the locomotive stock (such as the 'B' Class) and the rebuilding, repairing and conversion of some of its own coaching and wagon stock. The NSR was never self-sufficient, purchasing in rolling stock when it had physical capacity problems – such as the 1911 purchase of six 6-wheeled milk vans from the Metropolitan Railway Carriage & Wagon Co. Ltd and numerous bogie passenger coaches from the same supplier between 1919 and 1921 – and when it needed specialist wagons, such as bolster wagons or large timber trucks. The NSR also regularly assessed the competing demands being placed on the works, of commercial opportunities, space and finance.

The following is a summary of the NSR's rolling stock, as presented in the Company's final Annual Report of 31st December 1922:

Passenger Carriages
Carriages of uniform class	267
Composite Carriages	74
	341

Other Coaching Vehicles
Luggage, Parcel and Brake Vans	16
Carriage Trucks..	24
Horse Boxes...	47
Miscellaneous	106
	193
Total Coaching Stock	**534**

Merchandise & Mineral Vehicles
Open Wagons	
8 and up to 12 tons	5,336
Covered Wagons	
Under 8 tons.	9
8 and up to 12 tons	336
	345
Mineral Wagons	
Over 12 and up to 20 tons	18
Cattle Trucks.	66
Rail & Timber Trucks	350
Brake Vans....	127
Miscellaneous	6
Total Merchandise & Mineral Vehicles	**6,248**

The LM&SR acquired a large number of workshops and the fate of Stoke Works is considered in much greater detail elsewhere in this volume. Suffice it to say that, from July 1923 to July 1927 (when the works officially closed), no new rolling stock was built there, activity instead being concentrated on the repair of existing rolling stock, along with the repainting and renumbering into LM&SR livery of NSR rolling stock transferred over, and possibly other non-NSR LM&SR stock. At the end of the NSR's life and the start of the LM&SR era, the works carried out the conversion of 6-wheeled Full Brake vans to Brake Thirds.

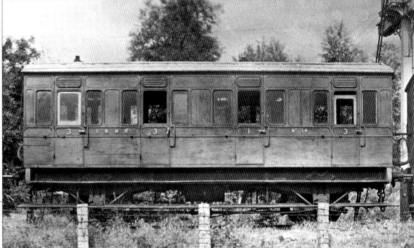

Above: This First/Third 4-wheeled Composite, photographed on the Shropshire & Montgomeryshire Railway in 1935 and bearing the lettering S&MR No. 14, was one of three carriages purchased from the NSR in 1917 and shortly afterwards. Seen here with one First Class and three Third Class compartments, it was originally one of four built between 1880 and 1887 to Diagram 14. *S.H.P. Higgins*

Left: A First/Third 6-wheeled Composite coach, seen at the former 'North Western' Yard at Stoke in 1933. It was built to Diagram 9 in 1907 and was one of seven of its type constucted between 1895 and 1907, all of which were in service in 1933. It was given LM&SR No. 14876 in 1923, 27219 in 1933 and was finally withdrawn from service in January 1937. *S.H.P. Higgins*

This three-compartment 6-wheeled Brake Third, built in 1891 to Diagram 5, was photographed at Cliffe Vale carriage sidings, in immaculate condition in June 1933, before being given its new LM&SR No. 27775. It was withdrawn from service in June 1938. *S.H.P. Higgins*

Passenger Carriages

The following table demonstrates the age profile of the coaching stock that was transferred to the LM&SR in 1923. It excludes the NSR duplicate stock (*i.e.* withdrawn from normal service) and those coaches that were made available for the private workings over the NSR by two colliery companies, and is drawn from the detailed analysis of available records for each carriage:

Date of Build/Purchase	6-wheelers	8-wheelers	Total
1890-1899	70		70
1900-1909	76	41	117
1910-1919		58	58
1920-1922		36	36
	146	**125**	**271**

The quantities of 6-wheeled stock are split fairly evenly between the two decades up to 1909, the last 6-wheelers, five in total, being built in 1907. From 1906 onwards, 8-wheeled bogie stock was introduced and, of the 125 that arrived, ninety-seven were built in Stoke Works, with the balance being acquired from the Metropolitan Railway Carriage & Wagon Co., twelve in 1907, two in 1908 and fourteen in 1920; the high numbers for 1920 reflected the need for the

NSR to modernise and increase its fleet after the freeze on carriage building during the First World War. The Metropolitan RC&W Co. had previously supplied 6-wheelers in 1891, in 1897 and in 1900, some of which survived into Grouping.

The new livery of crimson lake that was adopted by the LM&SR for its carriage stock was virtually the same as the madder lake of the NSR. The NSR passenger vehicles were placed in the LM&SR numbering scheme in date order. Some older vehicles in the NSR duplicate list were given duplicate numbers in the same LM&SR series and prefixed '0'. Vans, carriage trucks and horse boxes numbered in passenger stock were given LM&SR numbers, again with duplicates prefixed with an '0'; milk vans in the duplicate series were put back into LM&SR capital stock.

It has not been straightforward to trace what happened to each carriage due to incomplete records but, from accumulated research carried out over many years by the late Dr Jack Hollick, the late George Chadwick, the late Bernard Holland, Dr David Jolley and Mark Smith, it has been possible to draw some general conclusions. Whilst some of the records are incomplete, coaches

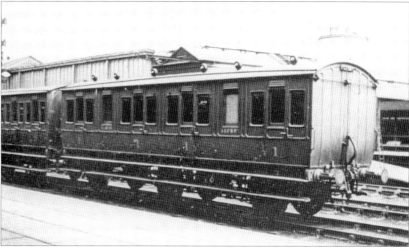

Right: A Radial 6-wheeled First with two lavatory divisions, built by the Metropolitan Railway Carriage & Wagon Co. in 1897; its original design does not appear in the Diagram Book. It was probably built as a First/Second Composite but, following the abolition on the NSR of Second Class travel in 1911, was upgraded after that date. It is seen here at Crewe with its 1923 LM&SR No. 14757, receiving No. 27400 in 1933, before being withdrawn from service in May 1935. *S.H.P. Higgins*

Below: A five-compartment Third, built to Diagram 12 in 1902, at Cliffe Vale carriage sidings and also in immaculate condition, in June 1933; these were the most prolific of the types of coaching stock used by the NSR, fifty-seven of which were in service in 1923. It is here carrying its new LM&SR No. 26619. This coach was built in 1902 and was withdrawn from service in September 1936. *S.H.P. Higgins*

A four-compartment Brake Third, built to Diagram 22, at Cliffe Vale sidings in 1933. It was one of twenty-four 8-wheeled bogie vehicles built to this diagram, of which four had arc roofs, the other twenty being fitted with elliptical roofs. This is one of the elliptical roofed versions, which were built over an extended period between 1910 and 1920. This example was one of the last built, being turned out from Stoke Works in 1920; it received LM&SR No. 14970 in 1923, was renumbered 24129 in 1932 and was the last NSR coach to be taken out of service when withdrawn in May 1959; in its final years it had been part of the Thames Haven set of workmen's train from 1956 to 1959. *Manifold collection*

withdrawn from service were as follows:

Period built:	1890-99	1900-09		1910-19	1920-21
	6-wlrs	6-wlrs	8-wlrs	8-wlrs	8-wlrs
Withdrawn					
1923-1932	32	18			
5/1931-12/1939	34	49	12		
1/1940-12/1949	2	7	26	10	
1/1950- 5/1959	1	1	4	48	27

From the above analysis, the 6-wheeled stock was withdrawn steadily down to 1939, with only a small number surviving after then. Of the bogie stock, all 8-wheelers, only twelve were withdrawn before December 1939, thirty-six in the following decade to December 1949 and seventy-nine in the final period to May 1959. What is clear from this analysis is that, whilst there were sizeable withdrawals down to 1939, wartime saw a slackening in the numbers withdrawn. In the late 1940s and through until the mid-1950s, some of the surviving NSR coaches continued to be grouped in train sets (many

NSR train sets had operated during the LM&SR era because of the compatibility of their electric systems) and were used for carrying workers on industrial railways, such as at Tredegar (between 1946 and 1949), Abergavenny (between 1946 and 1951), Thames Haven (between 1956 and 1959) and Moor Row in Cumbria (in 1954).

A Diagram Book was issued in 1912 for coaching stock. It was divided into two sections, from 1 to 20 being 4-wheeled and 6-wheeled stock, and 21 to 37 being bogie 8-wheeled stock. The coaching stock illustrations are in a sequence that reflects the change in style and appearance over a fifty year period from the 1870s down to Grouping.

Right: Two 8-wheeled bogie Third coaches at Uttoxeter on 25th August 1953. They were built to Diagram 26 and were amongst thirty of the type built between 1906 and 1920, all of which remained in service in 1933. The coaches bear their 1933 numbers with the prefix of M (Midland Division), with 15289 in front built in 1920 and 15275 in the background built in 1913. They were withdrawn from service in July 1954 and July 1953 respectively. *Dr Jack Hollick*

Right: A two-compartment, 8-wheeled, bogie Brake Third coach, photographed outside the Cliffe Vale carriage sheds when newly painted in 1933. It was built in 1908 to Diagram 29 and was one of thirteen of its type built between 1908 and 1921. Its 1923 LM&SR number was 14890 and its new 1933 number was 24095. The coach was withdrawn from service in September 1947. Note the chimneys of the Shelton Coal Coke & Iron Co. in the background on the right. *G.N. Nowell-Gossling*

Left: A First/Third, 8-wheeled, bogie, non-corridor Composite carriage, one of two built in 1914 to Diagram 33. This was an unusual vehicle, having six First Class and one Third Class compartments, and it is seen here at Gloucester on 22nd July 1949. It was given LM&SR No. 14946, 17782 in 1933 and was broken up in Scotland in June 1959. *Author's collection*

Right: This First Class 8-wheeled six-compartment bogie coach, seen here at Cliffe Vale sidings in 1933 with a Shelton chimney in background, was one of three of its type built to Diagram 35 between 1913 and 1921. It was given LM&SR No. 14937 in 1923 and 10601 in 1932. This coach was built in 1913 and withdrawn from service in September 1951, the body later being sold at Inverurie. *S.H.P. Higgins*

A five-compartment 6-wheeled Third Class coach on fire at Froghall Junction, on the Churnet Valley line, in 1929. The fire was caused by an overheated wheel bearing but, fortunately, no-one was hurt and no other stock was damaged. The coach was built to Diagram 12 and was one of approximately sixty built between 1891 and 1907; fifty-seven of this type survived into Grouping and there were still thirty-two in use in 1932. The last coach of this type to be withdrawn was in November 1941. *Jim Plant*

The bleak Cumbrian landscape provides the backdrop for this former NSR/LM&SR set of 8-wheeled bogie stock at Moor Row on 16th May 1954. From left to right they are: No. M24104M, a two-compartment Brake Third, built at Stoke in 1921 to Diagram 29 and withdrawn from service in March 1957; No. M15281M, an eight-compartment Third, built to Diagram 26 in 1920 by the Metropolitan Railway Carriage & Wagon Co. and withdrawn in June 1956; No. M15293M, another eight-compartment Third, again to Diagram 26 in 1920 by Metropolitan RC&W and withdrawn from service in June 1956; No. M17780M, a First/Third seven-compartment Composite, one of nine built between 1907 and 1912 to Diagram 27, itself built in 1912 and withdrawn from service in November 1958; No. M19927M, a First/Third six-compartment Composite, with twin lavatory, one of three built to Diagram 37 in 1919 and 1920, itself built in 1919 and broken up in May 1957; No. M15277M, another eight-compartment Third, to Diagram 26, built in 1914 and broken up by June 1956; and lastly, No. M24097M, a First/Third six-compartment with two twin lavatories, one of eight built between 1906 and 1911 to Diagram 24, itself built in 1910 and broken up in Scotland in 1955. *H.M. Livesey*

At Whaley Bridge station shortly after Grouping on 10th September 1923, as an unidentified former L&NWR 4-4-2T leaves with a train of NSR coaches and is about to pass a goods train arriving from Buxton. The coach on the left is an eight-compartment Third, Diagram 26, with its NSR crest and No. 231 clearly visible; the leading vehicle is a two-compartment Brake Third, built to Diagram 29. *H.G.W. Household*

This First Class six-compartment twin lavatory coach was one of three built between 1914 and 1921 to Diagram 36. This example was built in 1914 and had a long life, being finally withdrawn in September 1955 as No. M18595M. Its body was sold from Inverurie in December 1955 for use in a boat builder's yard at Banff, where it was photographed on 9th July 1957. *R.M. Casserley*

Colliery Trains

During the North Staffordshire Railway era, some of the older 4-wheeled coaching stock had been withdrawn from normal service and used by contractors to carry workmen to site (*e.g.* on the Asylum Railway at Cheddleton in the late 1890s). Later, around the time of the Grouping, some were also used on colliery trains, known locally as 'Paddy trains', to Chatterley-Whitfield Colliery and to the Midland Coal, Coke & Iron Company at Apedale. In 1920, there was still a stock of fourteen of these older carriages, all dating back to 1878, if not earlier, and nearly all Brake Thirds.

This ex-NSR 4-wheeled Second/Third Composite coach formed part of the Chatterley-Whitfield colliers' train and is seen here around the time of Grouping. The train, consisting of four coaches, travelled between Mossley Halt, Congleton and Chell Halt (described in the Working Time Tables as Whitfield Sidings), and was hauled by a Chatterley-Whitfield locomotive. Mossley Halt closed in April 1925 and this private rail service lasted barely a couple of years into the LM&SR era before being replaced by a special colliery bus service. *Manifold collection*

Carriage Bodies

The NSR operated a policy of using old carriage bodies for a variety of purposes but mainly as waiting shelters. This policy was introduced in circa 1907 and, at Grouping, such shelters could be found at Leycett (cricket pavilion), Rudyard Lake (caddies' hut for the golf course), Hulme End (for storing bicycles), Winkhill Halt (as a mess room) and Froghall Basin (for storage), and at Consall, Beeston Tor, Redhurst Crossing and Caldon Low Halt (all as passenger waiting shelters).

In 1907, the body of a pre-1880 4-wheeled Composite coach was transferred to Leycett on the Audley line, to serve as a cricket pavilion and it is seen here still reasonably intact although no longer in use in 1952. It shows the square panelling style used in the 1870s, whilst the painting of it as a pavilion in white above the waist gives the appearance it must have had when repainted into the NSR's 1880s livery. *Author's collection*

Above: The Manifold Valley line was a popular destination for redundant NSR carriage bodies, as shown by the two featured here, both looking in remarkably good condition. Firstly, at Hulme End circa 1930, this former 4-wheeled coach had been substantially modified and had lost its characteristic end framing; it had been mounted on two old crossing timbers and was used mainly as a cycle store.

Below: At Redhurst Crossing, this former three-compartment, 4-wheeled, First Class coach, built to Diagram 16 in the late 1870s/early 1880s, was used as a passenger shelter. This view is looking in the Waterhouses direction and was taken at the time when the line was being lifted in the spring of 1937, after its closure in March 1934, in preparation for its final use as a route for walkers. *Both Bob Gratton collection*

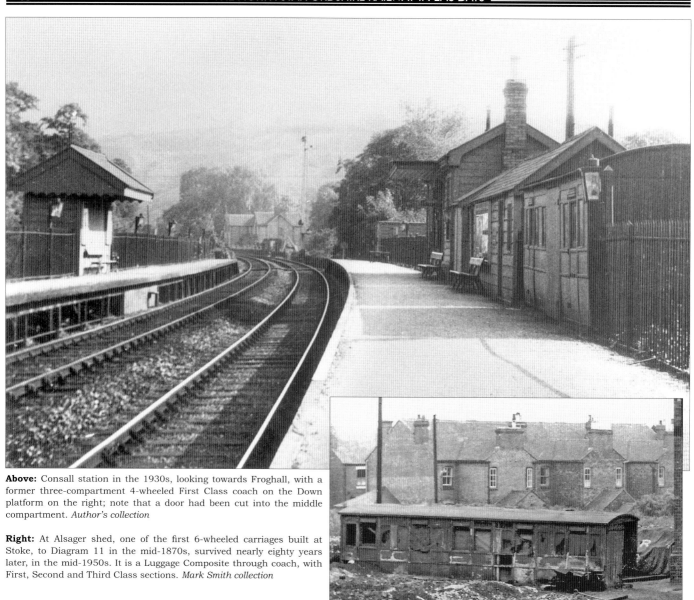

Above: Consall station in the 1930s, looking towards Froghall, with a former three-compartment 4-wheeled First Class coach on the Down platform on the right; note that a door had been cut into the middle compartment. *Author's collection*

Right: At Alsager shed, one of the first 6-wheeled carriages built at Stoke, to Diagram 11 in the mid-1870s, survived nearly eighty years later, in the mid-1950s. It is a Luggage Composite through coach, with First, Second and Third Class sections. *Mark Smith collection*

Saloons

There were twelve Saloons in total in the NSR's stock that passed to the LM&SR at Grouping: four bogies and seven 6-wheelers – the Directors' Saloon and eleven Third Class Saloons – along with one 4-wheeled Engineer's Inspection Saloon. Of these, seven were built between 1896 and 1901, and four as bogies in 1909. Five of the Third Class Saloons were still in use in 1932 but they were mostly to be withdrawn between June 1937 and circa 1940. However, one was retained in Departmental Service at least until 1956.

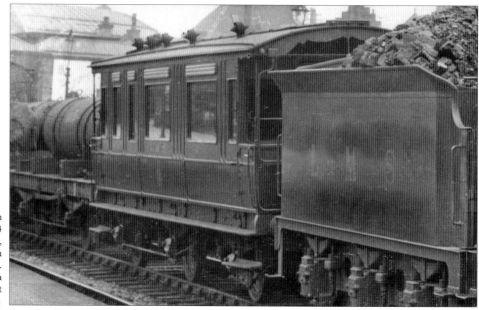

The NSR 6-wheeled Directors' Saloon, built in 1896 to Diagram 3. It is seen here circa 1924 at Stirling, in its new LM&SR livery and crest, on a mixed stock train; it was used as an Inspection Saloon in Scotland for some years. It received both a 1923 number, 14747, and a 1932 number, 45040. It is not known when it was withdrawn from service. *F.W. Shuttleworth*

Left: The Inspection Car for the NSR Engineer's Department posed near the turntable (at the south end of Stoke station), over which wagons were manhandled into the Engineer's workshops on the opposite side of Station Road. It was built in 1921 by the Drewry Company as an open car and substantially rebuilt in 1924 at Stoke Works to the form seen here. Visible are the horn fitted on the roof and an adjustable searchlight fitted to one corner, both additions to the original design. It was withdrawn from service in 1934. *G.J.R. Gossling*

Below: This Third Class 6-wheeled Saloon was one of seven built between 1896 and 1901 to Diagram 8. It is seen here carrying its 1923 number, 14744, in the early 1930s; it received No. 962 in 1933. Built in 1896, it was withdrawn from service in August 1937. *S.H.P. Higgins*

Bottom: A Third Class 8-wheeled bogie Saloon, one of two built in 1909 to Diagram 32. It was given LM&SR No. 14905 in 1923 and 966 in 1933. It is seen here alongside Platform 3 at Stafford station and was withdrawn from service in December 1940. *S.H.P. Higgins*

Goods Stock

Most NSR goods stock, described in the December 1922 Annual Report as 'Merchandise & Mineral Vehicles', was of a conventional pattern, conforming to the latest specifications laid down by the Railway Clearing House. The bulk of the goods stock consisted of open wagons of various sizes, mainly with side doors, there being at Grouping 5,336 such wagons out of a total goods stock of 6,748. The 8-ton wagons had two planks and most 10-ton wagons had three planks. A lot of the goods stock was merged with the same type of wagons of other railway companies in the new LM&SR. Photographs of former NSR goods stock have not survived in great numbers and so the illustrations in this section are not as comprehensive as would have been liked. Open wagons of 8- and up to 12-tons accounted for approximately 93 per cent of all the goods stock.

Above: A 2-plank 8-ton wagon, bearing the 1912 NSR wagon logo, seen here in the late 1920s on the sidings behind the breakdown shed. Just visible behind it are two 'New L' Class locomotives. The chalked '15' on the end is the siding number in the marshalling yards. *Author's collection*

Open Wagons

Two 3-plank 10-ton wagons, both fitted with oil axle boxes and external diagonal strapping:
Left: No. 4051.
Below Left: No. 01113.
Both R.J. Essery collection

Bottom Left: A former NSR 3-plank 10-ton wagon bearing the LM&SR No. 193309. The vehicle had oil axle boxes and internal diagonals, and a tare weight of 5.0.2. It is seen here fitted with plain buffer castings and V-hanger brakes. The LM&SR cast new number plates for all inherited wagons in a characteristic 'D' shape and all of the old rectangular plates were removed. *G.H. Platt*

Bottom Right: This former NSR 3-plank 10-ton open wagon, carrying LM&SR No. 197177, was photographed in the goods yard at Renfrew, loaded with a container on 10th March 1946. It has external diagonals and was built at Stoke in 1920. It has the LM&SR wartime austerity style of one line lettering on the lower plank, while one of the top planks has been replaced and not painted. This and the previous wagon were painted in bauxite livery, which was similar to their NSR colouring. *A.G. Ellis collection*

Below & Right: Side and end views of an ex-NSR 2-plank 8-ton open wagon, with LM&SR No. 193134, taken on 29th April 1939.

Left: Former NSR locomotive coal wagon No. 1607, built in 1913 and seen here at Burton shed in the late 1920s. It was one of a batch of 7-plank, 15-ton wagons and was fitted with spring buffers, oil axle boxes and V-hanger brakes on both sides. *Author's collection*

Vans

Right: A former NSR 10-ton van, with brakes on both sides but fitted with new axleboxes. It is seen running in its new guise as LM&SR No. 196734. *Bob Essery collection*

Brake & Tool Vans and Tool Vans

Above: This former NSR 6-wheeled Brake & Tool van was still very much a survivor when photographed, in remarkably good condition, at Willesden in March 1959. It is bearing No. 195848. In its original guise, it formed part of the NSR breakdown train. *The Transport Treasury*

Left: An ex-NSR 4-wheeled Tool van, built in 1892, which later received LM&SR No. 196929. It is seen here as late as 29th April 1958 at the former Cheshire Lines Committee goods yard at Shore Road, Birkenhead. The van was built on a 4-wheeled coach underframe. *Jim Peden*

Milk Vans

The movement by rail of milk reflected the increased demand from London and from the northern cities and towns, and this in turn can be seen in the growth and decline in the number of milk wagons. At Grouping, the NSR had eighty-nine milk vans, and the following table shows the age profile of the fleet:

Date Built	4-wheelers	6-wheelers
1876	1	0
1890-1899	24	6
1900-1909	9	15
1910-1919	1	25
1920-1921	0	8
	35	54

As demand for milk increased from London and Manchester, and from elsewhere in north west England, so the number of milk trains increased, as did in consequence the number of milk vans to meet that demand. This reflected in the new build in the 1906-1921 period. Whereas most were built at Stoke Works, six were built in 1911 by the Metropolitan Railway Carriage & Wagon Co. (the NSR's favourite suppliers). The peak years for Stoke-built milk vans were six in 1906, seven in 1910 and eight in 1921.

One particular feature is the continued mix of new 4-wheeled and 6-wheeled stock, and in most years there was at least one milk van added to the fleet. The table below shows the age profile of the surviving milk vans in 1932, when

Right: Ex-Caledonian Railway Pickersgill 4-4-0 No. 76, still with all its CR insignia, is seen here at Annan in 1924 at the head of a mixed goods train. The first wagon is a former NSR 4-wheeled milk van, of short style, with three panels either side of the door; the brake lever is just visible. *Manifold collection*

Below: This former NSR 6-wheeled milk van, with inside doors and deep slatted sides, was carrying its LM&SR duplicate stock number 01848 when seen at Leek. It was in use as a Mobile Warehouse and designated for 'Storage at Wayside Stations'. *Author's collection*

they received new LM&SR numbers. It indicates the rapid decline in the number of such vehicles in use by then, as the market for the movement of milk by rail in 'traditional' vans (as distinct from the new glass-lined containers) contracted and also as major dairy companies, such as United Dairies, collected milk from farms direct:

Date Built	4-wheelers	6-wheelers
1876	1	0
1890-1899	0	4
1900-1909	4	11
1910-1919	0	22
1920-1921	0	8
	5	45

There were still one or two milk vans in use as parcel vans as late as 1956.

In addition to the above, there were ten 6-wheeled passenger coaches converted in World War One, to carry parts for Avro 504 aeroplanes from Manchester to the south, and these were known as Aeroplane vans. After the war ended, they were used as milk vans, eight of which were placed in the duplicate stock and given LM&SR numbers; all were withdrawn from service by 1932.

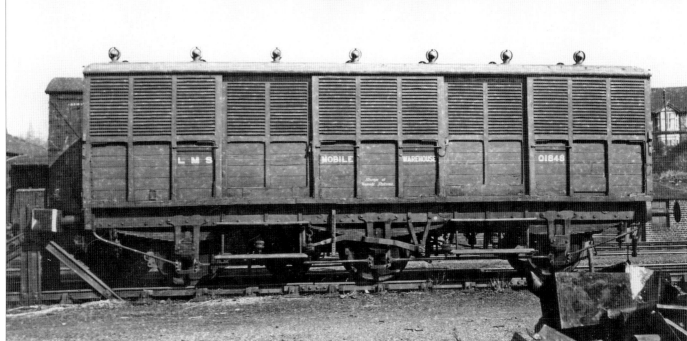

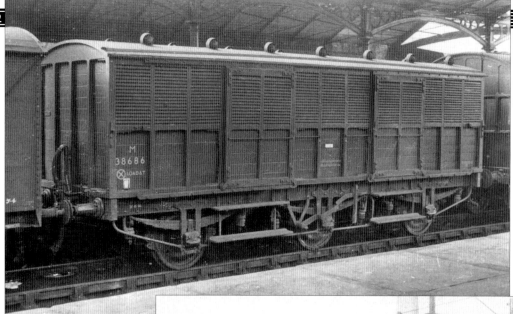

Right: No. 38680, seen at Uttoxeter in 1954, had begun life as NSR milk van No. 92. *P.J. Garland, Roger Carpenter collection*

Horse Boxes

At Grouping, there were forty-five 4-wheeled horse boxes which, by the time of the 1932 LM&SR renumbering, had been reduced by only four. Of the forty-five, twelve were on the duplicate list, nearly all of which had been built prior to 1900. Stoke Works carried out a modest building programme in the occasional years when new horse boxes were being built, although in 1913, there was a major new build programme, when no fewer than twelve were constructed. The last horse box in service was withdrawn in 1952. The age profile of the horse boxes at Grouping was as follows:

Date Built	
1886	1
1890-1899	8
1900-1909	23
1910-1919	13
	45

A former NSR arc-roofed horse box, seen here at Crewe in LM&SR livery as No. 43705. It was built in 1902 and withdrawn from service in July 1939. Note the oil pot, and also the roof steps and rails at the compartment end. *G.N. Nowell-Gossling*

Cranes

The former 15-ton NSR breakdown crane acquired in 1895 from Cowans Sheldon, is seen here at Llandudno Junction on 10th September 1953. It was given LM&SR No. MP40 and then, from May 1941, was numbered RS1027/15. It was based at Stoke until around 1938, when it was transferred to Shrewsbury. It was sent to Birkenhead (Dock Road) from 10th May 1940 until 24th November 1943 and was then at Llandudno Junction from 11th May 1944 until 1957. It was withdrawn on 16th January 1961 but was noted working at Patricroft shed in 1963; it was cut up one year later. *Author's collection*

One of several small 4-wheeled hand cranes that were used by the Engineer's Department, photographed in the late 1920s; it is thought to have been supplied by Cowans, Sheldon. Note the wooden jib, the use of chains and not wire ropes, the counterweight and the axle which was fixed to a wheel truck. The crane itself could be swung round and the truck was permanently coupled to a 5-plank wagon. *N. Nowell-Gossling*

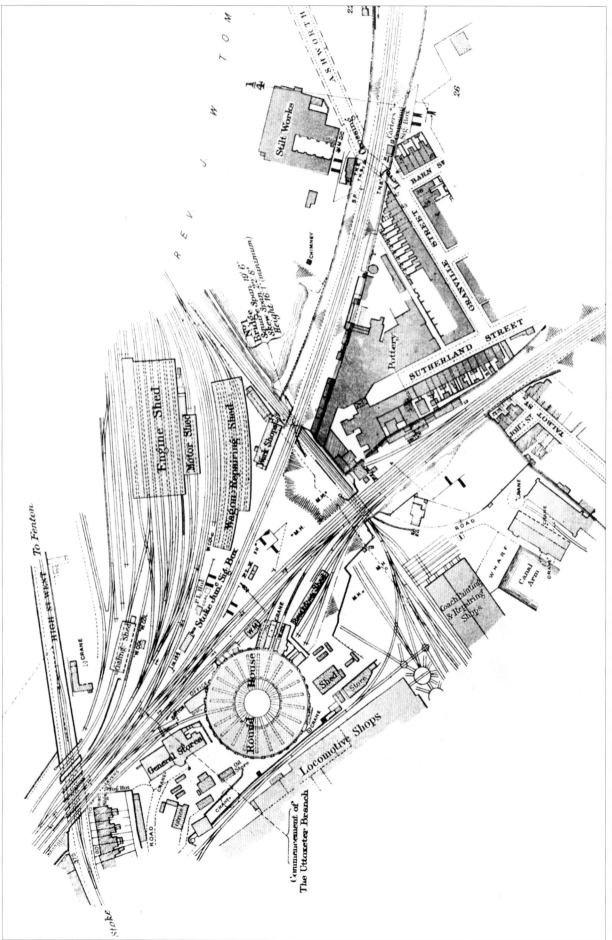

Extract from the NSR Estate Map of 1922, showing the site layout of the Round House, engine and motor sheds. The Round House was sited close to the works and note the single road breakdown shed adjacent to its main entrance entrance. Only part of Stoke Works is shown here, the map not quite detailing the locomotive shops complex, centre left, or the coach repairing and painting shops, centre bottom. The traverser provided access to the five lines into these shops. Also omitted from this map is part of the locomotive works and the carriage and wagon shops which lay alongside the Trent & Mersey Canal. The large wagon repairing shed can be seen in the centre of the map, beyond which are the running lines of the Biddulph Valley Line. To see how the engine shed and Round House complex changed during the LM&SR era, comparison should be made with thbe OS map extract on page 66. *Author's collection*

8

Stoke Round House and Shed

The dual facilities provided for locomotive care at Stoke on a daily basis comprised, firstly, the 1849 Round House on the Down side of the main line at Whieldon Road and, secondly, the Long Shed built alongside the Biddulph Valley line. The Round House was an imposing structure, forming a complete circle, the 50 foot turntable in the centre being wholly or partially open and unroofed for much of its later existence. There were twenty-three roads, two of which provided an exit or entrance. Intended as the NSR's main maintenance or repair centre, a Ransome & Rapier 60-ton travelling crane was provided, moving on rails through 360 degrees to serve any road. By 1913, the practice was to use it on only thirteen roads, occupying the western half of the building. The building overlooked Stoke Works, and its basement housed the works' tinsmiths and the iron store. By the south side of the Round House was a shed for the breakdown train. The Long Shed had six through roads and alongside was a smaller shed with two through roads for the rail motors.

This was the inheritance of the L&MSR from the NSR, with Tom Longsdale, the Locomotive Running Superintendent at Stoke, being effectively responsible for the entire NSR locomotive stock; he retired in 1927, being replaced by Tommy Whitehead as Running Shed Foreman.

A major fire occurred on 12th July 1924 in the rail motor shed that gutted it, badly damaging three locomotives shedded there and destroying more than 700 creosoted sleepers; it required three local fire brigades and two railway fire brigades (from Stoke and from Crewe) to put it out.

The NSR allocation at Stoke at Grouping was 125 engines and, by 1929, this number had dropped to 112, reflecting the decline in the number of NSR locomotives in service. On 1st March 1926, Stoke shed, along with others, was given a Western Division code and, alongside the closure of Stoke Works in the spring of 1927, lost many of its repair and maintenance duties, becoming officially 'a garage of Crewe North'.

The Traffic Committee, in June 1933, embarked on a major works programme within its motive power department, initially amounting to £177,037 for eleven sheds but not including Stoke; all this was intended to yield annual savings of £14,801. It was part of a more ambitious scheme covering forty-seven depots and costing £750,000. The objective of the scheme was to improve the efficiency of the running department, which had an annual locomotive mileage of 230 million that incurred an annual expenditure of £12 million in running alone. The programme was very much geared towards reducing to a minimum the unproductive time of each locomotive, by reducing the time under and awaiting repair, and by improvements in terminal facilities, such as coaling, watering, ash disposal and preparation.

The next stage in this modernisation programme was the approval in 1934 of a further seven motive power depots (MPDs), at a cost of £135,540; this included Stoke shed, where a project costing £17,750 was approved, with anticipated annual revenue savings of £2,269. In November of the same year, a further thirteen sheds were approved, at a cost of £129,257. The implications for Stoke were that new ash disposal and coaling plants were erected, as well as a new water tank with a capacity of 75,000 gallons. The demise of 'The Parlour' and a portion of land that it occupied were to lead to new offices, the second phase of which was postponed with the outbreak of war in 1939.

In November 1938, approval was given for a major programme of capital works at Stoke, consisting of the renewal of the roof of the Long Shed, the demolition of the Round House and the erection of new offices, at a total cost of £22,217. The Chief Operating Manager submitted a critical report that covered the following: (i) that the MPD was split in two, on either side of the main line; (ii) that the offices, stores, machine shop and staff amenities were unsatisfactory and inadequate; (iii) that there was the loss of time and accident risk for staff crossing three sets of lines to get from one shed to another; (iv) that there was inconvenience to engines occupying main lines to pass from one portion of the depot to another.

This report also referred to the need for extensive repairs to the Round House, adding that the roof of one of the bays of the straight shed had already been demolished some years ago for

Footplate staff on parade outside the Round House in 1930, in front of a former Midland Class '2F' 2-4-0. Second from the left is Les Hemstock, whilst to his right is Tom Edge (leading fitter). The first three in the back row are Jack Bandell (fitter), Mo Carter (mate) and Norman Lowe (fitter). Stoke Junction signal box can just be seen on the right. *Leslie Smith collection*

safety reasons. The report stated that the renewal of this roof was urgent because of the adverse working conditions, especially in bad weather. Because the main activities of the MPD were at the Long Shed, the report recommended that, in the interests of efficiency and economy, a substitute office, machine shop and other facilities should be provided in a convenient location to the Long Shed. The principal recommendations were that: (i) the Round House and certain buildings be removed, with the turntable and radiating lines being retained for engine stabling in busy periods; (ii) the roof of one of the bays of the Long Shed be renewed and altered; (iii) additional siding and pit accommodation be provided at the Long Shed; (iv) a two storey building be constructed alongside the Long Shed, for offices, stores, machine shop and amenities; (v) a footbridge be constructed over the traffic sidings to give access to the proposed new offices etc from Fenton Road.

A later report came to the LM&SR Board in January 1941, with revised costs and estimates of £22,248. The steel work for the new roof had been acquired before the war had started but all other work was put on hold during the course of the hostilities. The Round House was used less frequently but was not demolished until 1973, with the Long Shed re-roofing finally being completed in the early 1950s.

In 1946, the LM&SR introduced a major national programme of water softening, the cost for the Stoke area water supplies being £3,228.

Top: The Breakdown Shed was located in front of the Round House and can be seen here in the background, behind former L&NWR 'Experiment' Class 4-6-0 No. 5466 *Glendower*. This engine was one of six members of the class which were transferred to Stoke in late 1928. *Author's collection*

Above: Former NSR 'G' Class 4-4-0 No. 87 is seen here inside the Round House circa 1924, wearing its first LM&SR livery and carrying its new No. 596. The engine is in the fully lined out crimson lake passenger livery of the LM&SR. Built in 1910, No. 596 was to be withdrawn from service as early as June 1929. Note the absence of a roof to the Round House. *W.H. Whitworth*

Left: The interior of the Round House circa 1936, with former L&NWR 'Prince of Wales' Class 4-6-0 No. 25767 about to be lifted to fit the pair of front wheels seen adjacent to the wall on the right. Behind the locomotive and executing the lift is the Cowans & Sheldon breakdown crane acquired by the NSR in 1895; note the wires are strapped around the boiler and apparently causing the handrail to bend. Several of the 'Prince of Wales' Class arrived at Stoke in 1931 and four more came between September 1935 and January 1936; however, these latter locomotives stayed only for a few months. With no roof as protection against the elements, the interior fabric and brickwork of the Round House are showing signs of deterioration. *Leslie Smith collection.*

Above: An interior view of the Round House taken in around 1933, with several ex-NSR types on shed. From left to right, they comprise former 'New C' Class 0-6-4T No. 174 now as LM&SR No. 2045 and shortly to be withdrawn (in May 1934); former 'New F' Class 0-6-4T No. 114, now as LM&SR No. 2048 (withdrawn in July 1934); former 'New F' Class 0-6-4T No. 119 now as LM&SR No. 2053 (withdrawn in April 1935); and former 'K' Class 4-4-2T No. 55 now as LM&SR No. 2183 (withdrawn in December 1933). *Manifold collection*

Right: This elevated view of the Round House was taken on 13th May 1939 from the top of the coaling tower, with Stoke Junction signal box bottom left. The chimney on the left served the boiler house of the former carriage and wagon works and the one on the right served the former locomotive works. An impression of the length of the works can be gained from the roofs of the workshops visible immediately behind the Round House, to the left and to the right. *A.G. Ellis*

Right: A view of the offices and, on the right, the general stores, with the Round House behind, looking southwards across the main line on 13th May 1939. *A.G. Ellis*

Below: A distressed but rare enamelled Stoke (40) LM&SR era shedplate. *Chris Knight collection*

Above: The interior of the Round House on 4th October 1947. By this time, the use of it was declining, as is evident from the photograph, although the smaller engines were frequently deposited in here. In the centre immediately beyond the pillars is the 50 foot turntable. Note the corks attached to the strings hanging down; these were intended to advise footplate men of the clearance of pillars and arches. *Harold D. Bowtell*

Left: A close up view of the ex-NSR Cowans & Sheldon brakedown crane, in immaculate condition in the mid 1920s. It was photographed outside the breakdown shed, a timber building with a brick base. Standing far left is Tom Edge. This crane was given LM&SR No's MP40 and RS102715 and was transferred to Birkenhead in 1939; it was eventually withdrawn from service in 1961 and cut up in December 1964. It was replaced here at Stoke by a former Midland Railway Cowans & Sheldon crane, built in 1893 and transferred from Birkenhead in 1938. This crane stayed at Stoke until 1961 and then transferred to Llandudno Junction, where it was finally cut up in March 1965. *Leslie Smith collection*

On Saturday 12th July 1924, a major fire occurred at the rail motor shed, adjoining what was described as the new shed. It was believed to have been caused by a spark from a locomotive and it led to the rail motor shed being completely gutted, with only one wall of it left standing after the fire had been extinguished. The general structure of the new shed was not badly damaged but the four engine roads inside were temporarily taken out of use. Three engines were burned and blistered and badly damaged but a fourth was rescued. The roof of the adjoining new shed was almost completely wrecked. In addition, between 700 and 800 creosoted sleepers were destroyed in the Engineer's Yard, about 200 yards way. After a recent spell of dry weather, all the wood and woodwork had been very dry. The fire was attended by three local fire brigades, from Hanley, Stoke and Fenton, and two railway brigades, from Stoke and Crewe. Large crowds of spectators saw cascades of smoke carried 150-200 yards by a strong wind.

Top Left: A view inside the severely damaged rail motor shed looking east towards Fenton Manor. The engine on the right is an an outside framed 0-6-0 and beyond it is the 4-cylinder 'D' Class locomotive.

Above: Looking west towards the Round House, with dampening down still taking place; note the water pipes in the centre and the damaged roof.

Right: Smoke emanating from some of the piles of creosoted sleepers which caught fire. *All Tom Longsdale, the Manifold collection*

Left: The article in the *Staffordshire Sentinel* of Monday 14th July 1924, detailing the fire. *The Sentinel Newspaper*

RAILWAY WORKS FIRE AT STOKE.

Damage Amounting to Thousands of Pounds.

Locomotive Shed Destroyed.

Although the amount has not yet been definitely assessed, it is estimated that some thousands of pounds of damage was done by fire on Saturday at the L.M. and S. Railway locomotive works at Stoke (briefly reported in Saturday's "Sentinel.")

The fire broke out in the early afternoon, and it is believed to have been caused by a spark from an engine, which led to the motor shed being completely gutted, three engines badly damaged, and the roof of what is known as the New Shed, adjoining, almost demolished, while between 700 and 800 sleepers were destroyed.

The outbreak originated in the motor shed, which is part of the extensive works just within the Fenton boundary, on the main road from Stoke to Longton. It was first discovered by an employee in the stores at the locomotive sheds, who informed Mr. F. J. Owen, the lodgeman. He quickly prepared the fire-fighting apparatus kept on the works, and fire brigades were immediately summoned. Five fire brigades were soon on the scene—from Hanley, Stoke, Fenton, and two railway brigades. In the meantime workmen were busily engaged in removing twelve locomotives from the New Shed, which, with the motor shed ablaze close by, was in immediate danger. The gang of workmen was able, by great efforts, to get these engines clear of the building, but three others were in the motor shed, which was burning furiously and provided the firemen with a very difficult task. Following the recent spell of hot weather, all woodwork was very dry, and the flames, once they had gained a firm hold, spread rapidly, fanned by a strong south-westerly wind. Hard though the firemen worked, only one wall of the motor shed remained standing when the flames were subdued, and the three locomotives in it were badly burned and blistered. Although a detailed mechanical examination has not yet been made, it is believed five engines are fairly sound, and a fourth engine, which was "rescued" while the building was actually burning, suffered little damage beyond blistering of the paint.

Attention was concentrated, with success, upon saving the New Shed, the wooden roof of which became ignited by sparks from the building where the fire originated. The roof was badly burned, and this will make the use of four engine tracks under it temporarily impossible, but the general structure was not badly damaged.

Large crowds of spectators saw cascades of sparks carried for a distance of from 150 to 200 yards by the strong wind, and these set fire to a huge stock of sleepers in the engineer's yard, which were to have been sold. The sleepers are creosoted timber and blazed fiercely, and when the 700 or 800 were well alight the flames leapt to a great height, and there were dense volumes of smoke and myriads of sparks. Owing to the creosote in the wood the flames could not be extinguished, and the pile was still burning on Sunday.

The smoke and sparks were a danger to those passing along the main road from Stoke to Longton, and the police stopped all traffic a long there. The train service was greatly interfered with, and motor 'bus traffic was diverted by way of Wheildon-road and Regent-road. The working of trains was not affected.

NEWCASTLE LAY PREACHERS' ASSOCIATION.

From left to right, this panoramic circa 1925 view shows 'the Parlour', the Long Shed and the fire-damaged rail motor shed. In the foreground, with its LM&SR No. 2320 executed in 14 inch transfers, is former NSR 'E' Class 0-6-0 No. 74, with outside framed tender, built in 1871 by Stoke Works; it was withdrawn from service in June 1934 as No. 8650, having been renumbered again in 1928. Behind, in its early LM&SR livery and with LM&SR No. 2047, is former 'New C' Class 0-6-4T No. 5, built in 1915 and withdrawn in March 1934. In the right background is an unidentified former '159' Class. Note the NSR 6-plank wagons in the left background amongst various LM&SR wagons. *Manifold collection*

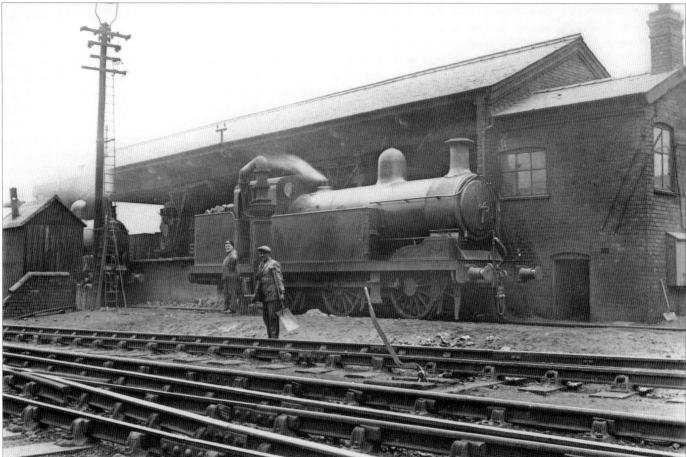

Former NSR 'New L' Class 0-6-2T No. 157, now as LM&SR No. 2249, alongside the coal stage in 1931. *Gordon Coltas*

Right: Former NSR 'M' Class 0-4-4T No. 12, now as LM&SR No. 1433, was photographed marshalling wagons at the coal stage on 23rd March 1932. This locomotive was built in 1908 and withdrawn from service in October 1935. The Round House appears in the left background, with the offices to its right. On the right of the picture is a former HSR eight-compartment bogie Third Class carriage, newly painted in LM&SR livery. *Manifold collection*

Above: The Round House, centre, and former locomotive works, far left, seen from a passing train in the mid 1930s. The tall chimney is part of the former works in front of which, left, is a store and, above it right, a shed. By this time, this part of the works, where the NSR had built and repaired locomotives, was leased to Robert Hyde & Son Ltd. Various locomotives can be seen stabled to the left of the breakdown shed, which was clearly a little on the short side for the breakdown crane within, the doors having had holes cut in them to accommodate the buffers.

Left: An unidentified former 'New M' Class 0-4-4T at the head of a short train of open wagons alongside the breakdown shed, again photographed from a passing train. Note the flared top to the locomotive's bunker. *Both The Transport Treasury*

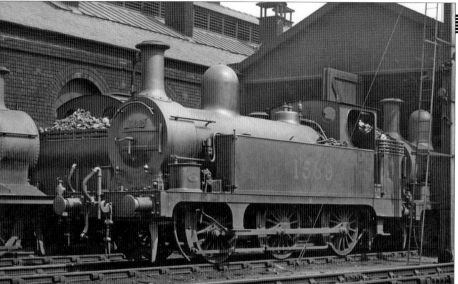

Left: A glimpse of the rebuilt rail motor shed in the late 1920s, with former NSR 'D' Class 0-6-0T No. 144, now as LM&SR No. 1589, well coaled and awaiting its turn. To the left and just peeping in to view is the smokebox of a Fowler Class '4F' 0-6-0, which at the time of this photograph had been recently allocated to Stoke shed. *Author's collection*

Below: A cast-iron Stoke (5D) shedplate, its later designation in the LM&SR period, which was retained throughout the British Railways years and up until closure. *Chris Knight collection*

Left: The new concrete coaler at Stoke in 1936, the year of its installation. It was of the No. 2 type, 150 tons capacity with twin feeds. On the right is Stanier 2-6-2T No. 130, which had been allocated to Stoke shed in November 1935. *W. Potter*

Right: Stanier 2-6-4T No. 2467 is seen here at Stoke shed circa 1937, with the new 1936 coaling tower looming large in the background. This locomotive was built at Derby and came new to Stoke in November 1936; it was one of twenty-three of the class that arrived here in that year, largely as replacements for twenty-one 'New L' Class locomotives that were withdrawn between 1934 and 1937, along with a further six that were sold out of service in 1936 and 1937. Six more of the Stanier 2-6-4Ts came between 1942 and 1945. At Nationalisation, there were twenty-seven of these attractive and versatile engines at work on the North Staffordshire Section. *Author's collection*

The Long Shed circa 1937, with former 'New L' Class 0-6-2T No. 2 all prepared for its next turn of duty, now as LM&SR No. 2271. This locomotive was built in 1923 and was sold in October 1937 to Lancashire Associated Collieries; it is now part of the collection of the National Railway Museum. In the background can be seen part of the overhead traverser of the ash disposal plant, with the girders serving two ashpits. On the left is an LM&SR 5-plank Loco Coal wagon and a Sneyd Collieries private owner, whilst on the far left can just be seen the end of Fenton Villa, the residence provided for NSR Locomotive Foremen/Superintendents. This view also allows us a glimpse of the interior of the six-lane shed. *National Railway Museum*

Right: Ex-NSR, Kerr, Stuart-built, 0-6-0T No. 74, now renumbered as LM&SR No. 1602 but not fitted with a shed plate, was photographed inside the rail motor shed on 22nd May 1932. It was one of two such locomotives acquired from the nearby Kerr, Stuart Company in 1919. They spent their lives working the various yards at Stoke and No. 74 was withdrawn from service in October 1932. *Leslie Good*

Below: This Engine Pass was issued by the NSR Loco. Dept. to Mr Gosling, Bridge Engineer of the NSR, on 22nd December 1922; it expired on 31st December 1923, after the start of the LM&SR era. *Manifold collection*

North Staffordshire Railway,

No. 873. LOCOMOTIVE DEPARTMENT,

Stoke-on-Trent, Dec. 30th. 1922.

ENGINE PASS

Allow the bearer Mr. Gosling (Permanent Way)
to ride upon the Engine

Between _____ all N.S. _____ Stations,

to Date December 31st. 1923.

N.B.—Not more than one person in addition to the Driver and Fireman must be allowed to ride on any Engine at one time.

This Pass is issued upon the understanding, and the use of it shall be taken as conclusive evidence of an agreement with the Company, that the latter are relieved from all liability in respect of any delay or injury to the person or property of the person using it.

The holder of this ticket must not in any way interfere with any part of the engine or with the duties of the Driver and Fireman.

John A. Hookham

Superintendent.

N. S. Ry.

ENGINE PASS.

Below: This September 1939 view of Stoke motive power depot was taken at the same time as the panorama of the Long Shed which appears on page 46. The photographer was here standing slightly further to the north and has also taken in the sidings for coal wagons on the right and the new concrete coaling tower in the background. *A.G. Ellis*

A September 1939 view from the new coaling tower; looking east to the Biddulph Valley Line in the left background. Re-roofing of the damaged part of the Long Shed is taking place but this work was shortly to be suspended due to the outbreak of the Second World War and was not finally completed until the early 1950s. On the left is the overhead traverser ash disposal equipment and, at the bottom of the photograph, a Stanier 2-6-2T just creeps in to view. Smoke on the right engulfs the site of the former wagon repairing shop. The building top left is the zinc oxide works of James M. Brown. *A.G. Ellis*

Two views taken at Newcastle Junction in September 1937 of the last locomotives in two NSR classes shortly before they were taken out of service.
Above: Former 'D' Class 0-6-0T No. 57 (now with LM&SR No. 1570) under the new LM&SR gantry; it was withdrawn from service in December 1937. A recently arrived Stanier 2-6-4T can be seen on the left.
Below: Former 'New L' Class 0-6-2T No. 1 (now with LM&SR No. 2270) on shunting duties with two Settle Speakman coal wagons in the right background. This locomotive was built in the spring of 1923, was withdrawn from service in October 1937 and was one of five locomotives then sold to Manchester Collieries. *Both Gordon Walwyn*

9

Locomotive Allocations and Use

The LM&SR standardisation policy for locomotive stock was toughly enforced. It was not just the small numbers in many classes of NSR locomotives that were affected but also, for example, the 'Precursors' (1904) and 'Atlantics' of the L&NWR, and the L&YR 'Atlantics' (1899). The NSR's four 'G' Class locomotives, built as late as 1910, started to disappear from 1928 onwards. With the grouping of seven constituent companies and a further twenty-seven subsidiary companies, the LM&SR had a stock of 10,396 locomotives and no fewer than 293 different locomotive types. The policy of phasing out older engines that were few in number and of building a relatively small number of new locomotive classes, impacted inevitably on the ex-NSR fleet. The LM&SR policy of building larger locomotives had also reduced the stock requirement. By December 1930, this figure had reduced to 9,319 locomotives, whilst a total of 2,972 engines that the LM&SR inherited had been withdrawn from service.

In 1923, the LM&SR introduced a renewal programme of 8.5 per cent of the locomotive stock annually. In 1930, they brought in the principle of storing locomotives that were in excess of current needs, rather than spreading them over available work, with the result that, across the network, 584 locomotives were stored in this way. At Stoke, the two-lane wagon repair shop (located alongside the Biddulph Valley Line and facing the Long Shed) was so used. For the LM&SR, in January 1938, 150 different types, or 38 per cent, had been eliminated. Between 1923 and 1938, 6,234 old locomotives had been displaced and 3,482 new ones had been built. The NSR handed over 192 locomotives (apart from three rail motors and the battery electric locomotive) and twenty-two different locomotive types. This stock remained relatively unchanged until 1927. There then followed a series of rapid withdrawals as follows:

Up to 1930 76
1931-35.... 104
1936-40.... 12

There were heavy withdrawals in 1928, with the loss of twenty-eight locomotives, in 1934 of twenty-one locomotives and in 1935 of twenty-four locomotives.

The NSR's 0-6-0 freight locomotives, many of them between fifty and sixty years old, were largely withdrawn between 1928 and 1930. The numerous 'D' Class engines saw their numbers reduced from fifty-one in 1927 to ten in 1933. There was a marked difference in the age of locomotives scrapped with, on the one hand, the twenty-three older locomotives with fifty to sixty years' service and, on the other hand, the many newer locomotives built after 1907 and scrapped within twenty-five

to thirty years. Seven locomotives were sold into industry in 1935 and 1936 (six 'New L' Class and one 'KS' Class). The last two 'New M' Class locomotives, No's 1434 and 1436, were scheduled to be cut up in the autumn of 1939 but, with the possibility of war breaking out, cutting at Crewe had been suspended in March 1939 and a number of condemned locomotives were reprieved. The decision was taken to repair them and to put them back into service and these included various L&NWR types and the two NSR locomotives. However, in the event it was not to be and the last NSR locomotives in LM&SR service were cut up in the spring of 1940.

Some NSR locomotives continued to work Summer Excursion services to holiday destinations such as Llandudno and Blackpool, whilst the introduction, from 1923, of the 'Eastern Counties Express' holiday trains to Great Yarmouth and elsewhere in East Anglia involved return workings from Nottingham. A small number of NSR locomotives were also transferred further afield. 'K' Class locomotives worked into Birmingham in 1924, whilst examples of the 'B' Class worked in London around Poplar in 1926-27. Members of 'D' Class were based at Birkenhead between 1926 and 1934, their narrow wheelbase being well suited for shunting work on the sharply curved lines in the docks; no fewer than six different locomotives worked there but never more than two at a time. Other 'D' Class locomotives and an 'E' Class were seen at Barrow Docks in 1926. Four of the 'New L' Class, part of a group of six allocated to Longsight (LM&SR No's 2261 to 2266), worked at Altrincham on the Manchester South Junction & Altrincham Railway for a period from August 1927 until 1930, a year before that line was

A view taken in Crewe Works, of No. 9 Erecting Shop, showing the West Street end and looking east in September 1935. Former NSR 'New L' Class 0-6-2T No. 10 (LM&SR No. 2272), seen in the process of being cut up, was the penultimate locomotive to be built at Stoke Works in the spring of 1923. The traverser can be seen in the foreground. This shop was built in 1903, when all new locomotive construction was transferred to the West End. *Manifold collection*

Stoke shed, a view looking east in 1931 with barely an NSR locomotive in sight. Far left is ex-L&YR Barton Wright Class '2F' 0-6-0ST No.11316. To its right is first the single lane shed known as 'The Parlour', then the six lanes of the Long Shed and, in the far right background, scarcely visible, the rail motor shed that had been restored after the 1924 fire. The locomotives that can be identified are LM&SR 'Mogul' 2-6-0 No. 13294, then a Fowler '3F' 0-6-0 and finally Fowler '4F' 0-6-0 No. 4306 with its Stoke 40 shedplate just discernible as a white dot on the smokebox door. *National Railway Museum*

electrified. Several 'K' Class locomotives were allocated to Derby in the early LM&SR years, working both north to Sheffield and south to Birmingham. They were later transferred to Manchester and Stockport where, in addition to pilot duties at the latter, they worked some of the south Manchester suburban services, until most were withdrawn in December 1933/January 1934.

From time to time, NSR engines were allocated to sheds away from the North Staffordshire Section. For example, in 1928 there was one 'New F' Class locomotive allocated to Crewe. In February 1933, five 'K' Class locomotives were allocated to Stockport Edgeley shed, whilst in 1934, there was one 'New M' Class allocated to Longsight shed. In 1935-36, Longsight shed was allocated one 'M' and one 'New L' Class, whilst Stafford shed had one 'New C' Class in 1925 and one 'K' Class in 1931.

So rapid was the rundown of the ex-NSR fleet that, in February 1931, of the total of 115 locomotives at Stoke shed, there were only sixty-three that had previously belonged to the NSR; the rest comprised of nine ex-LN&WR, seven ex-Midland, four ex-L&YR and thirty-two LM&SR builds. In February 1933, there were allocated to LM&SR Shed 40, encompassing all former NSR sheds in the LM&R Western Division, 132 locomotives, of which sixty-one were ex-NSR locomotives, twelve ex-L&NWR, five ex-Midland and forty-three LM&SR builds; at the same time there were four ex-NSR locomotives based at Burton Midland shed.

The first ex-L&NWR locomotives were allocated to the North Staffordshire Section from around 1928; the 0-8-0s of the 'G' Classes came and went, and one of these survived at Stoke into the British Railways era. Numerous members of these classes were allocated to the section over the years, mainly to Stoke but also to Macclesfield (several), Alsager (two) and Uttoxeter (one). These were followed by six 'George V' Class locomotives that had arrived by late 1928, replacing the 'H' and '100' Classes that were withdrawn around the same time. These 'George V' Class had been reduced to three by March 1931 and to one by April 1933. Seven 'Experiment' Class 4-6-0s had arrived by January 1929,

reducing to six in March 1931 and to four in April 1933; all had been withdrawn from service by the end of 1934. Three 'Prince of Wales' Class locomotives were allocated in October 1931 and four more came between September 1935 and January 1936, only a few months before their withdrawal from service; some of these may well have been sent to Stoke to go into store. Two 'Cauliflower' 0-6-0s were allocated in December 1939 and a further one in July 1942. These three survived in November 1945 but only two remained at 31st December 1947; one L&NWR Class 'G2a' also survived at Alsager at 31st December 1947.

Former L&YR locomotives also provided motive power to the North Staffordshire District, between February 1930 and the early 1940s, never more than four at any one time. They were Barton Wright and Aspinall 0-6-0Ts and 0-6-0STs. However, by November 1945, none were allocated to the North Staffordshire Section.

From the late 1920s until early 1931, there were at least seven older (1875) Johnson Midland 0-6-0s that were allocated to the North Staffordshire Section, with four remaining in 1933 and one or two of this class lasted until 1947. Other Johnson 0-6-0s came and went from July 1933 down to 1947 but did not last on the North Staffordshire Section into the British Railways era.

Trials also took place at Stoke and elsewhere in 1932, to test Michelin diesel railcars but these particular trials proved unsuccessful and the LM&SR abandoned this project in 1934.

In the 1926-1934 period, the new generation of LM&SR locomotives started to make their appearance on the NS Section in greater numbers. The Fowler '3F' 0-6-0s started arriving at Shed 40, at Stoke and Alsager, from 1927, carrying out shunting and light passenger duties. There were fourteen of this class in April 1931 and in April 1933, a number that barely increased, reaching fifteen in November 1945 and remaining at this figure in December 1947. Six Fowler 2-6-4Ts arrived new from Derby Works in the early summer of 1929 and this number remained unchanged until the spring of 1933; between then and the end of December 1937, a further twenty-one had arrived in the district. At the same time,

Johnson Midland Class '2F' 0-6-0 No. 2915 near the coaling stage at Stoke circa 1930; it is dwarfed by the Fowler Class '4F' 0-6-0 immediately behind. *Gordon Coltas*

Left: Six ex-NSR locomotives were sold out of service by the LM&SR between 1933 and 1937. Former 'KS' Class 0-6-0T No. 75 (LM&SR No. 1603) was sold in 1933 to Nunnery Colliery, Sheffield, where it remained in use until early BR days. Nunnery was located in the centre of Sheffield and in 1945 employed 1,381 miners. The colliery removed the vacuum brake gear along with the numbering and lettering, and painted the engine grey. The two locomotives in this class were built at the Stoke works of Kerr, Stuart & Co. in 1919 and were purchased by the NSR in that year, against the background of a considerable backlog of repairs and maintenance in the NSR workshops at that time. Their main duties were shunting the goods yard at Stoke. *Author's collection*

Left: LM&SR No. 2253, a former NSR 'New L' Class 0-6-2T, was sold in March 1936 to the Longmoor Military Railway, where it is seen at work at its new home and now named *Marlborough*. The LMR was a British military railway in Hampshire, built in 1903, whose objective was to train soldiers in railway construction and operations, and it had seventy-one miles of track. In 1942, *Marlborough* was described as being '*in constant use; is a firm favourite with the men, and looks very smart in its green uniform with red nameplates, and 2253 on its smokebox door.*' It was withdrawn from regular use in 1946 but remained at Longmoor, being brought in to use when required; it still retained its number plate. It was sold to J.N. Connell of Coatbridge in 1948 and was finally cut up in 1953. *Author's collection*

twenty-two new Stanier 2-6-4Ts had arrived and another two had been transferred from other sheds.

From 1927 and early 1928, a substantial fleet of twenty Fowler '4F' 0-6-0s had been allocated to Stoke; they replaced several NSR classes of 0-8-0 goods tender locomotives which had been built between 1871 and 1874, and that had been withdrawn from service between 1926 and 1929. The number of '4F's had increased by one to twenty-one by 1933, to thirty-two by November 1945 and to thirty-eight by December 1947. Three LM&SR Hughes/Fowler 'Mogul' 2-6-0s arrived in December 1930, working the newly introduced 8.45pm Stoke to Camden express goods, staying until that working ceased in the late 1930s, when they were then replaced by 4-6-0s. The larger LM&SR 4-6-0s also started to arrive, one 'Patriot' Class in February 1935, followed by new Class '5's in 1935 and 1937; other 4-6-0s were transferred in the years down to 1947, all based at Stoke. Stanier 2-6-2Ts started to arrive in April 1935 and, by 1937, there were thirty-five on the North Staffordshire Section; most arrived new at Stoke but some also arrived new at Macclesfield. They did not prove popular or successful and, by November 1945, the class locally had been reduced to fourteen, whilst at 31st December 1947, their numbers had dropped to only eight.

The first (eight) Stanier 2-6-4Ts to arrive at Stoke were in January 1936 and a further sixteen arrived there by February 1937, by which time nearly all the 192 locomotives inherited from the NSR by the LM&SR had been withdrawn from service. Thereafter, a further twenty-four had been transferred to Stoke

by January 1945 and transfers out were regular. Five Fairburn 2-6-4Ts, all Derby-built, arrived in 1945, one arriving new in May whilst the remainder were transferred to Stoke in November. At 31st December 1947, on the North Staffordshire Section, there were twenty-six Fowler 2-6-4Ts, nineteen Stanier, and five Fairburn. There were two Fowler 2-6-2T Class '3F's allocated to Macclesfield from 1944; between the time (1930-32) when they were built and 1947, only five of this class were allocated to the North Staffordshire Section, the first being seen in July 1930. In December 1940, three LM&SR 0-4-4Ts arrived at Stoke and stayed until February 1944.

The following table lists the arrival of new locomotives to the North Staffordshire Section between 1935 and 1947, all of which, except one Fairburn locomotive, were Stanier-designed:

Year	2-6-4Ts	2-6-2Ts	4-6-0s
1935		18 (Stoke)	3 (Stoke)
		6 (Macclesfield)	
1936	23 (Stoke)		
	5 (Macclesfield)		
1937	1 (Macclesfield)	3 (Macclesfield)	1 (Stoke)
1942	1 (Stoke)		
1943	4 (Stoke)		
1945	1 (Stoke)	—	—
	35	27	4

Of the sixty-six delivered new, fifty-one went to Stoke and fifteen to Macclesfield; no new locomotives went to Alsager and Uttoxeter and no new locomotives came to Macclesfield after 1937 during the LM&SR era.

Illustrations of the change in motive power include:

• Manchester-Macclesfield-Stoke	NSR 'B' Class replaced by 'M' Class, replaced by 2-6-2Ts and 2-6-4Ts
• Macclesfield-Uttoxeter	as above
• Stoke local services	'B' Class replaced by 2-6-2Ts
• Buxton-Ashbourne-Uttoxeter	'M' Class & 'L' Class replaced by 2-6-4Ts and 2-6-2Ts
• Alsager mineral trains	'H' Class replaced by '4F' 0-6-0s
• Stoke-Market Drayton	'L' Class replaced by 2-6-2Ts
• Caldon Low mineral trains	New 'L' Class replaced by '4F' 0-6-0s
• Llandudno excursions	'G' & 'KT' Classes replaced by '4F' 0-6-0s

The following table shows the locomotive allocation between the end of the NSR era and 1947:

Shed	1923	2/1929	11/1945	31/12/1947
Stoke	125	112	98	96
Alsager	15	20	15	16
Uttoxeter	8	11	8	8
Macclesfield	12	15	8	9
Leek Brook	2	7		
Market Drayton	2			
Crewe	2			
Burton	7			
Derby	9			
Ashbourne	2	(1)		
Caldon Low	3	(3)		
(Hulme End)	2	(2)		

Note: The information above is drawn from different sources and some are not strictly comparable.

By 1929, the NSR sheds at Crewe, Burton and Derby had closed and the remaining former NSR sheds were sub-sheds of Stoke.

An LM&SR shed numbering system was introduced in which Stoke (North Staffordshire Section) was given shed code 40 from 1926, though shed code plates did not start appearing on locomotives until the spring of 1929; this lasted until 1934. From March 1935 and throughout the remaining LM&SR era, under a new numbering scheme, Stoke became 5D, Alsager 5E and Uttoxeter 5F under Crewe North shed; Macclesfield became 9C under Longsight shed. Trip working at Grouping was based on thirty shunting engines (including two at Burton) at sixteen locations. In addition, there were two trip engines shared with the L&NWR at Burton, working mainly over the Dallow Lane Branch. Trip working expanded during the L&MSR era as follows:

Date	Stoke	Alsager	Macclesfield	Uttoxeter	Total
9/1927	35	9			44
9/1938	40	10	6	5	61
10/1947	49	11	7	8	75

Two Burton Midland Division locomotives were also engaged on some trip working throughout the period. The classes engaged on trip working in September 1938 were:

'4F's	2-6-4Ts	2-6-2Ts	0-6-0Ts	'G1's
23	16	16	8	1

Below: Crewe Works in May 1939 where, amongst the many engines being stored on the stabling lines, the last two former NSR locomotives that were used by the LM&SR could be found awaiting their fate. In front is former 'New M' Class 0-4-4T No. 15, here as LM&SR No. 1436, and behind is 'M' Class 0-4-4T No. 41, with LM&SR No. 1434. In the background are the chimneys of the steel works, mothballed at the time and awaiting re-commissioning. With the outbreak of war these two locomotives were reprieved from being cut up but, in the spring of 1940, they finally went under the torch. *W. Potter*

Right: The first of three photographs showing former NSR locomotives whilst engaged in working excursion trains shortly after Grouping. Here at Llandudno on 1st September 1923, former 'G' Class 4-4-0 No. 170 is being prepared for the return journey to Derby and Nottingham. The locomotive is still in full NSR livery and yet to receive its LM&SR number of 59. *Manifold collection*

Left: The Yarmouth to Liverpool return working of the 'Eastern Counties Express' at Nottingham (Midland) station in 1924. This service was introduced by the LM&SR in 1923 in direct competition with the L&NER excursions to the same area. On this occasion, former 'E' Class No. 67, built at Stoke Works in 1875, still in NSR livery and yet to carry its LM&SR No. 2340, is piloting ex-L&NWR 'Precedent' Class 2-4-0 No. 862 *Balmoral*. No. 67 was eventually withdrawn from service in 1928. *T.G. Hepburn*

Below: Former 'G' Class 4-4-0 No. 171 was photographed at Blackpool Central in the summer of 1924, with its new LM&SR number of 598 and the early LM&SR logo. The open wagons behind the locomotive appear to be still in L&YR livery. Beyond them, the roof peaks and ventilators of the shed can just be made out, with the water tank just in view on the right. *Author's collection*

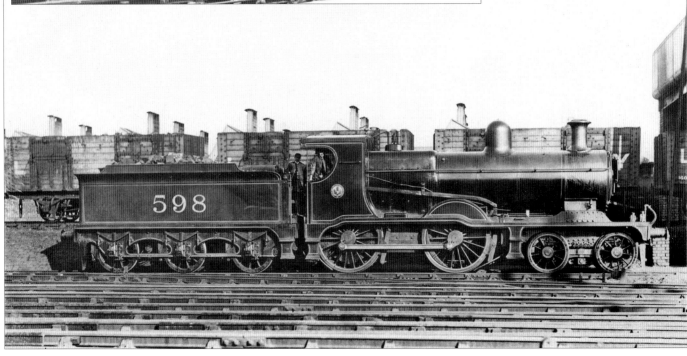

Left: Former NSR 'B' Class 2-4-2T No. 61 (now LM&SR No. 1459) is seen on shunting duties outside Birmingham New Street station circa 1930. This locomotive was built in 1887 and was the last of its class to be withdrawn from service, in August 1934. *National Railway Museum*

Below: Also at Birmingham New Street station, in June 1926 and engaged on station pilot duties, was former 'New C' Class No. 31, as renumbered in LM&SR days as No. 2041. This locomotive was built in July 1914 and was withdrawn from service in March 1935, after a relatively short life of twenty-one years. *J.T. Clewley*

Right: On the former North London Railway at Poplar station on 16th January 1927, former NSR 'B' Class 2-4-0T No. 7 (now renumbered as LM&SR No. 1451) is about to depart with a service for Broad Street. Around this date, several of these 2-4-0Ts, including LM&SR No's 1442, 1446, 1447 and 1451, were transferred to the North London District. This was the last 'B' Class locomotive to be built, in 1895, and was withdrawn in 1928. *H.C. Casserley*

Left: Former 'D' Class 0-6-0T No. 126 (now as LM&SR No. 1566) on shunting duties in 1931 at Duke Street, alongside Birkenhead Docks, with a GWR shunter's truck attached behind. The masts of several sailing ships can be seen in the background, whilst immediately behind No. 1566 are wagons belonging to the Ruabon Coal & Coke Co., right, and Lowell & Co., left. This particular locomotive was built in 1886 and withdrawn from service in December 1931. The 'D' Class, with their narrow wheelbase, were very suitable for dock shunting work on sharply curved lines and the first of them to come to Birkenhead arrived in January 1926. Several others came and departed after that, staying for different periods of time, although there were never more than three of the class at Birkenhead at any one time. The final one (LM&SR No. 1583) returned to Stoke in June 1934 and they were replaced on this work by Midland '1F' 0-6-0Ts. *Ian Bowland collection*

Right: The former Manchester South Junction & Altrincham Railway's platform and terminus at Manchester (London Road) is shown here in around 1930, with former 'New L' Class 0-6-2T No. 25 (LM&SR No. 2265) at the head of the morning Altrincham to Ardwick goods train. Six of this class had been allocated to Longsight shed in the summer of 1927 and four were transferred to Altrincham in July and August 1927. Above the train is the footbridge crossing over Fairfield Street into Mayfield station. *L.M. Hobdey*

Below: A view looking south at Longport on 30th August 1934, with the chimneys of the Shelton Iron, Steel & Coal Co. on the sky line in the left distance. The locomotive is a former L&NWR Bowen-Cooke 'G1' Class 0-8-0, now running as LM&SR No. 9273, and it is pictured at the head of a Down coal train. This particular engine appears to have been the first of the class allocated to Stoke shed, in February 1934, and others followed. Note the vegetable plots in the foreground, cultivated by local staff. *Gordon Walwyn*

Right: A busy view at Glebe Street, Stoke, as a North Wales to Derby express departs on 26th July 1930. It is powered by former L&NWR 'George V' Class 4-4-0 No. 5379 *Woodcock*, of Stoke shed. This locomotive was one of six of its class allocated to Stoke in 1929, though only two were still there in April 1931 and just one in April 1933. Far left is the emerging steelwork of the new goods warehouse and right is Stoke South signal box, later renamed Glebe Street. Hard at work to the left of the express train is a rare view of the former NSR Kerr, Stuart-built 0-6-0T locomotive, renumbered No. 1602 in 1923, which is seen actually actually at work, shunting Stoke South goods sidings. *Gordon Walwyn*

Below: Former L&YR Barton Wright 'F15' Class 0-6-0 No. 12015 at the head of a passenger working at Stoke station in 1930. Three of this class were allocated to Stoke in 1930 and 1931 but their stay was relatively short. *W. Leslie Good*

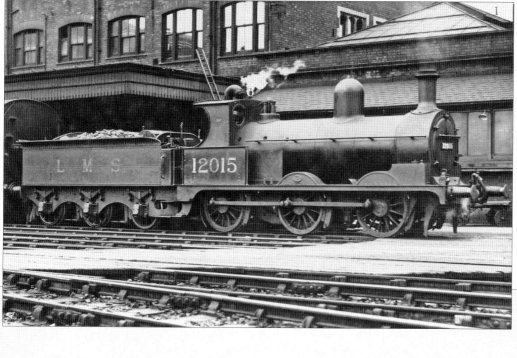

Below: Stoke carriage shed looking north on 27th February 1932, with former L&NWR 'Prince of Wales' Class 4-6-0 No. 5650 *Castor* backing on to its train; this locomotive was allocated to Stoke in October 1931. The shed was located on the Up side, two hundred yards or so north of Stoke station, and it was shortly after this photograph was taken that it was demolished as part of the remodelling of the goods yards. The smoke in the background, beyond the shed, is coming from Winton Pottery. On the right, behind the water column, is the newly built North Staffordshire Technical College. *Gordon Walwyn*

Right: This newspaper clipping carries a photograph of Stoke station Down platform taken on Sunday 10th April 1932. The view is looking south, with the roof over the Newcastle-under-Lyme bay platform visible in the background. Attracting the attention of the crowd is the arrival of *The Micheline*, a petrol-driven rail vehicle with pneumatic tyres, that had been invented by the Michelin Tyre Company. It had just completed a test run from Stafford to Stoke, having previously travelled up from Bletchley via Birmingham; this was the first public demonstration in England on the LM&SR network. Passengers were seated in 'easy armchairs' with Pullman style comfort. *The Micheline* stayed at the station for a while before stopping for several hours at the Campbell Road level crossing on the Michelin Works line. The choice of Stoke as a location for the trials was due to the presence of the substantial Michelin Works that had opened there in 1927. *The Sentinel Newspaper*

EVENING SENTINEL, MONDAY, APRIL 11, 1932

The arrival of The Micheline—a rail-car on pneumatic tyres—at Stoke Station yesterday afternoon.

Bravery

The "MICHELINE" on pneumatic Tyres (inflated like Motor Car Tyres) gives—faster, MORE FREQUENT, CHEAPER and more comfortable Travel. It very much reduces cost of Railway operation.

A "MICHELINE" will travel from STOKE-ON-TRENT to ASCOT on SUNDAY next, 24th April.

Arrival at LEAMINGTON STATION (G.W.R.), at 12-35 p.m.

It will remain on view for 15 minutes.

This is your FIRST OPPORTUNITY of witnessing the arrival and departure of this machine, which represents a REVOLUTIONARY ADVANCEMENT IN RAIL TRANSPORT, and we shall be pleased if you can come and see it.

MICHELIN TYRE CO., LTD.,
STOKE-ON-TRENT.

Right & Below: The front and reverse of a promotional postcard issued in April 1932 by the Michelin Tyre Co. Ltd, Stoke-on-Trent. It carries details of an intended run by the railcar from Stoke to Ascot via Leamington Spa. *Author's collection*

The "MICHELINE"—The first Train on Pneumatic Tyres.
In commercial use since 1931 : Born of the Michelin Tyre.

As run on L.M.S. Line (Bletchley-Oxford) 1932.

Left: Fowler Class '3F' 0-6-0Ts started to arrive in the North Staffordshire Section from 1927, becoming the mainstay of shunting duties and light passenger work in the area for more than thirty years. Seen here at Leek and about to depart with a passenger service for Stoke in 1927, the year it was built by the Hunslet Engine Co., is No. 16531. *Gordon Walwyn*

Below: Looking north through the arch of Porthill Bridge, at the south end of Longport station, on 30th August 1934, as Class '4F' No. 4505 clatters by with an Up goods train. This locomotive had been allocated to Alsager shed by August 1931, having come new to the LM&SR from the North British locomotive works in 1927. Top left can just be seen three of the bottle kilns of White Hall pottery. In the left foreground is the short headshunt for the long siding that ran several hundred yards to Midland Tileries. *Gordon Walwyn*

Right: Newly arrived Stanier 2-6-2T No. 76 is seen off the road between the turntable and the coaling stage at Macclesfield (Hibel Road) shed in April 1935. No. 76 was built at Derby and was allocated new to Stoke shed in March 1935, before being transferred to Macclesfield in the following month; the locomotive carries the shed code 9C, this being a sub-shed of Longsight. This engine was the first of its class to be sent to Stoke and, in 1935, no fewer than twenty-four of them were allocated to former NSR sheds. These, along with the Stanier 2-6-4Ts, replaced the fifty-two NSR locomotives that were withdrawn from service between 1934 and 1937. Performance over the years by the 2-6-2Ts was not considered to be satisfactory on the North Staffordshire Section and, by November 1945, the number had been reduced to fourteen and, by December 1947, it was down to eleven. *Author's collection*

Above: A lovely study of immaculate Fowler 2-6-4T No. 2348, almost straight out of Derby shops and standing in the middle lane at Stoke station on 10th August 1929. This locomotive was one of six sent from Derby in June and July 1929 and immediately set to work between Stoke and Manchester. The class started to be used for passenger and freight workings over a wider distance and replaced NSR locomotives that were being withdrawn at this time. Note that this locomotive has yet to have its shed code plate, No. 40, fixed on the smokebox door. The van in the background is a former L&NWR horse box, to its standard design and in L&MSR crimson lake livery. The L&NWR owned almost 700 such boxes and most lasted in service throughout the LM&SR period. In the centre of the vehicle is the horse compartment, with the groom's compartment to the right and the bedding/hay storage on the left. *Gordon Walwyn*

Right: Fowler 2-6-2T No. 55 is seen here circa 1945 at Ashton & Holmes' Sutton sidings, 800 yards south of Macclesfield Central station, on the wrong line, tow roping and manoeuvring a wagon into this small siding; the view is looking north. The white cloth on the buffers is likely to have been fixed for work in the wartime blackout. It is clear that a broad band on the edge of the buffer beam is also painted white and the use of white buffers was to alert shunters of the approaching locomotive in blackout conditions. This locomotive was built at Derby in 1932, allocated to Hibel Road shed in August 1944 and was still there in November 1945; however, by 31st December 1947, it had been transferred to Stockport Edgeley shed. Between the time (1930-32) when they were built and 1947, only five of the class were allocated to the North Staffordshire Section, the first being seen in July 1930. *Author's collection*

Endon station on 12th June 1948, looking north east towards Leek, with Fairburn 2-6-4T No. 2675, transferred to Stoke in November 1945 when only a few months old and still with its LMS lettering on the tank sides, at the head of a Leek to Stoke working. On the Leek Line, the original passenger service was Stoke to Leek but, in the 1890s, a combination of commuter and tourist requirements led the NSR to extend the service to Rudyard and Rushton; this pattern then continued into the British Railways era, some passenger services terminating at Leek and the remainder at Rushton. Workmen's tickets were available from all stations on the Leek line, whilst Cheap Daily Return tickets were available from Stoke to Rushton from 1935 every day by all trains on the day of issue only. The train here is passing over the level crossing, with the crossing keeper's house on the left and the roof of Endon signal box just visible above the locomotive. Note the NSR nameboard on the right. *W.A. Camwell*

Right: General view of the Control Office at Stoke in 1929, showing the telephone equipment in the centre of the table. In older control rooms the telephones were located around the walls of the room, on shelves at a convenient height, with small glass partitions between the instruments; in the more recently equipped offices, such as Stoke, the telephones ranged around the flat control table. Note the quality of the wood panelling around the walls, a reflection of the fact that it was located in the former NSR Board Room. *Allan Baker collection*

L.M.S. TELEPHONE CIRCUIT No. A 2125.

STOKE CONTROL—ALTON.

STATION.	SIGNAL.
Stoke CONTROL	Special Key.
Endon Box	—
Leek Brook South	■ ■ ▪ ■
„ „ Shed	■ ■ ■ ▪
Leek Yard	■ ■ ■ ▪
„ Telegraph Office	■ ■ ▪
Rudyard Office	■ ■ ▪ ■
Rushton Office	■ ■ ▪
Ipstones Box	■ ■ ▪
Cauldon Quarry Shunters ...	■ —
Waterhouses Box	■ ▪ ■ ■
Froghall Junction Box ...	■ ▪ ■
Oakamoor Box	■ ▪ ■
Alton Box	■ ▪

May, 1927.

Left & Right: Examples of the printed cards detailing Telephone Circuits for railway signalling, both of which include Caldon Quarry. On the left, issued in May 1927, is the circuit from Stoke Control to Alton, and, on the right, issued in October in 1938, is the circuit from Waterhouses to Leek. *Author's collection*

E.R.O. 20381/1134

L M S Telephone Circuit A2114

WATERHOUSES - LEEK.

STATION.	CALL.
Waterhouses Booking Off.	■ ■ ▪
„ Box... ...	■ ▪
Caldon New Face Weighbridge..	▬ ▬ ▪
„ Junction Box	
Winkhill Halt	■ ■ ▪ ■
Ipstones Booking Office.	■ ■ ▪ ■
„ Box	■ ■ ▪ ▬
Apesford Crossing ...	■ ■ ▪ ■
Bradnop Booking Office..	■ ■ ▪ ▪
Leek Brook East Box ...	■ ■ ▪
„ „ South Box ...	■ ■ ▪
„ „ North Box ...	■ ■ ▪
„ Booking Office ...	■ ■ ▪
Up Trains	■ ▪ ■ ▪
Down Trains	■ ▪ ■ ▪
CALDON QUARRY G FRAME	

October, 1938.

Left: A closer view of the control table. Note the two rows of lamps running down the centre. In order to avoid unnecessary noise and confusion, inward calls were announced by a single low-toned short ring; this was accompanied by the simultaneous illumination of the electric lamp near the telephone connected with the circuit that was calling. *Allan Baker collection*

10

Traffic Control

Prior to Grouping, most of the railway companies operated separate Control arrangements; these embraced the regulation of trains and traffic on the railway, so as to improve the effectiveness of passenger and freight movements, of engine power and of train loading. As part of a wider LM&SR reorganisation in 1927, the Chief General Superintendent's Department (based at Derby) assumed responsibility for 'Control', with Divisional Controls based at Derby, Crewe, Manchester and Glasgow, under which there were also District Controls. These divisions generally reflected the larger pre-Grouping companies, with Crewe being responsible for eighteen districts, including Stoke.

This structure remained intact until 1945, when new District Control arrangements for England and Wales were introduced, with District Operating managers in the Western, Midland and Central Divisions absorbing the forty-two District Control Areas. It was agreed in October 1944 that this national scheme would take three to five years to roll out; the Stoke Control area, almost identical with the former NSR boundaries, was selected as a pilot area where the new arrangements could be introduced within six to eight months. Stoke became operational in May 1945, with an implementation cost of £5,100.

During the LM&SR era, there were several improvements in telephonic links, including Stoke to Rushton, Waterhouses and Alton in 1928 at a cost of £1,900, and Stoke to Derby and to Crewe in 1930 at a cost of £8,140. In 1930, Creed Teleprinters were introduced between Crewe and Stoke in place of the existing single telegraphic apparatus, with four male staff being replaced by four female staff (at lower rates of pay, which was part of the economic justification).

At the time of Grouping, the NSR employed an Inspector-in-Charge of the Signal Section, working to the Civil Engineer (C.G. Rose) and the Telegraph & Electrical Superintendent (A.F. Rock). Post-Grouping, the NSR was made part of the new Western Division and Rose became District Engineer, losing responsibility for Signals & Telegraph, which went to Crewe; Western Division supplied the North Staffordshire Section with L&NWR equipment from the former L&NWR Signal Works at Crewe, such as signal boxes, lever frames and other equipment. Three English divisions and seventeen districts were established, with Stoke becoming part of the Western Division based at Crewe. There was a revised district organisation, with seventeen districts within a Signals & Telegraph Department, of which Stoke was one; the former NSR lines and the Crewe to Manchester lines were transferred to the Eastern Division. There was a further reorganisation in July 1938, with seventeen areas being reduced to twelve districts, with each district having its own Signals & Telegraph Area Technical Assistant; Stoke was retained as a district and still within the Eastern Division. This structure continued through the rest of the LM&SR era.

Frank Boden at the Head Controller's desk circa 1938. *Boden family collection*

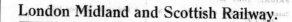

E.R.O. 53040.

London Midland and Scottish Railway.

Carriage Working Arrangements.

NORTH STAFFORDSHIRE SECTION
(WESTERN DIVISION).

STOKE-ON-TRENT WAKES,
Friday, July 29, to Friday, August 5, 1938.

The working shewn herein will be the diagrammed working of the local, regular and special trains during the above period, in conjunction with the arrangements laid down in R.S.D. Notices Nos. 10 and 11.

Station Masters and other concerned must carefully check the working shewn, and satisfy themselves that all trains starting from their Stations are provided for. All terminal points must telephone to Control, Stoke-on-Trent, each night before closing down, and state if requisite number of Sets are on hand for the following day's work.

Station Masters concerned are requested to see that the trains are strengthened as laid down.

EXPLANATION OF REFERENCES.	
†—Attached.	E—Empty stock.
*—Double train.	O—Ordinary train.
B—Bogie Stock.	R—Relief.
	X—Excursion.

Crewe,
July, 1938.

S. E. Parkhouse,
Divisional Supt. of Operation.

McCorquodale & Co., Ltd., Printers, London and Newton.

E.R.O. 3002/165.

LONDON MIDLAND AND SCOTTISH RAILWAY COMPANY.
WESTERN DIVISION.

STOKE-ON-TRENT CONTROL AREA.

SEPTEMBER 26th, 1938, and until further notice.

LOCAL TRIP AND SHUNTING ENGINE WORKING.

The timing and working of Trips and Shunting Engines in the Stoke-on-Trent Control Area will be as detailed in this Notice, and each Shunting and Trip Engine must carry a target corresponding to the number shewn.
The complete train times are shown in the Working Time Tables.

Stoke-on-Trent Trip Engines.
No. 1.
Class 4 Freight Engine (Standard 0-6-0).
4.5 a.m. (MO), 4.15 a.m. (MX) to 3.17 a.m. (MX), 3.28 a.m. (Sundays).

	arr. p.m.	dep. p.m.		arr. p.m.	dep. a.m.
Stoke Yard -	12 4	1 0 L.E.	Longton -	11 30	12 35 (MX)
Newcastle Junction -	1 15	1 30 (SX)			and (SuO)
Glebe Colliery -	1 45	...	Stoke Yard -	12 45	1 35L.E (MX)
Newcastle Jn. -	...	1 30 (SO)	Longton -	1 42	2 8 (MX)
Glebe Colliery -	1 52	3 3	Stoke Yard -	2 19	2 52 (MX)
Longton -	3 6	3 44	Pratt's Sidings -	2 58	3 15L.E (MX)
Glebe Colliery -	3 47	4 10	Stoke Shed -	3 17	...
Stoke Yard -	4 20	5 15	Newcastle Jn. -	...	2 0 (SuO)
Ketley's Siding -	5 29	5 45	Longton -	2 15	
Silverdale -	5 50	6 15	Longton -	...	3 10 LE (SuO)
Hartshill -	6 30	6 50	Stoke Shed -	3 28	...
Newcastle Junction -	6 54	...			
Cliff Vale -	...	7 45			
Grange Junction -	7 50	8 40			
Cliff Vale -	8 44	9 23			
Stoke Yard -	9 28	10 0 L.E.			
Newcastle Junction -	10 3	11 13			

After working 4.30 a.m. (MO), 4.40 a.m. (MX) freight, Stoke to Bushbury and 8.25 a.m. return.

No. 2.
Class 4 Freight Engine (Standard 0-6-0).
8.50 a.m. to 7.45 a.m. (MX), 6.50 a.m. (Sundays).

	arr. a.m.	dep. a.m.		arr. p.m.	dep. p.m.
Stoke Shed -	...	8 50 L.E.	Stoke Yard -	6 23	6 50
Pratt's Sidings -	8 57	9 5	Sideway -	7 0	8 55
Botteslow Jn. -	9 14	9 34	Trentham -	9 0	11 0 (SX)
Barlow's Sidings -	9 37	9 49	Sideway -	11 5	11 35 (SX)
Botteslow Jn. -	9 50	10 20	Stoke Yard -	11 45	1 15 (MX)
Mossfield Colliery -	10 30	10 40	Macclesfield -	3 58	5 0 (MX)
Adderley Green -	10 45	11 10	Stoke Yard -	7 13	7 40 (MX) L.E.
Mossfield Colliery -	11 15	11 40	Stoke Shed -	7 45	...
Botteslow Jn. -	11 45	1 20	Trentham -	...	10 1 (SO)
Mossfield Colliery -	1 30	1 40	Sideway -	10 6	10 30 (SO)
Adderley Green -	1 45	2 10	Stoke Yard -	10 38	12 10 (SuO).
Mossfield Colliery -	2 15	2 35	Cliff Vale -	12 15	1 30 (SuO).
Botteslow Jn. -	2 45 W	3 30	Longport -	1 40	2 10 (SuO)
Berry Hill -	3 34	3 55	Chatterley -	2 15	2 45 (SuO)E.&B.
Pratt's Sidings -	4 0	4 12 L.E.	Newcastle Jn. -	2 55	6 45 (SuO). L.E.
Stoke Yard -	4 15	4 30	Stoke Shed -	6 50	...
Sideway (Michelin's) -	4 39	6 15			

Above Left: The shift controller at work, with the board on which all the shifts were arranged on the wall to his right. Note the phone is held by an expandable metal trellis so it can be pushed back clear of the desk when not in use. *Allan Baker collection*

Working Instructions were issued for the operating of passenger and local goods traffic. These included:
Above: Carriage Working Arrangements for Stoke-on-Trent Wakes, 5th August 1938.

Left: Local Trip and Shunting Engine Workings, from 26th September 1938 until further notice.
Both Harold Bostock collection

11

The Smaller Canals and Rudyard Lake

The Caldon Canal

The justification for the building of the Caldon Canal in the 1770s, was to provide a connection between the limestone quarries of Caldon Low, via a succession of tramways, with the Trent & Mersey Canal and thence to the expanding markets of north and south Staffordshire and, later, south Cheshire. As the pottery industry diversified and expanded, in order to serve the increasing domestic market as well as the expanding markets of the Colonies and the United States, the Caldon Canal in the Hanley area – between Shelton and Ivy House – became an increasingly attractive location for pottery manufacturers and flint grinders. China clay brought coast-wise from Cornwall and flintstone similarly from Kent were conveyed from the Port of Runcorn and from Ellesmere Port to the various wharves at Tunstall, Burslem, Etruria, Shelton and Stoke, as well as to the wharves of individual firms. This reflected the situation at the time of Grouping. With the closure of the Caldon Tramroad in March 1920, limestone traffic by canal ceased, though small scale lime burning continued for some years at Froghall Wharf. Some limestone was carried by rail to the 1919 transshipment chute at Endon but this ceased in the late 1920s.

The principal carriers along the canal were the Anderton Company and its predecessor concern (from the 1820s) and the Mersey & Irwell Carrying Company (from the turn of the century). The Shropshire Union Railways & Canal Company established themselves at Etruria Wharf in 1866 but ceased carrying in 1921. The Mersey, Weaver & Ship Canal Carrying Company moved into the vacated premises and wharves very soon after, whilst the Manchester Ship Canal Company had established a base at Etruria Wharf by the early 1930s. As canal traffic contracted, from the late 1930s and during and after the Second World War, Anderton and Mersey & Weaver reduced their carrying activities, as did Potter & Sons, a Runcorn-based family firm of canal carriers and flint merchants.

The number of fleet carriers was small, as were the number of boats that they operated, and both began to be reduced from the 1930s onwards. The pottery firm of Meakin operated three boats in 1923 but this reduced to two when that firm ceased to carry its export traffic by canal in 1930. Thomas Bolton & Sons, copper and wire manufacturers at Froghall, had a fleet of five boats, all of which brought coal slack to its boiler house, adjacent to the canal,

A 1935 view, looking north, of the Anderton Wharf and related buildings at Etruria Wharf. In the background is the brick boundary wall, in front of which descended the 1802 tramway that commenced at the wharf and travelled on a rising gradient to Hanley. The wharfinger's house can be seen in the background framed by the crane. The bricks and stone in the foreground are part of the filling-in and rebuilding of Etruria Wharf that was taking place at this time. *The Waterways Trust*

Left: Bedford Street double locks in 1948, with Anderton boat *Millicent* about to enter and boatman Ernest Wood approaching the lock. *Millicent* was first registered at Runcorn in January 1892 and re-registered at Stoke in February 1923. Note how the bottom lock has had to be built up and reinforced, due to subsidence. *Author's collection*

Below Left: A delightful snowy scene between Cauldon Place and Lichfield Street, probably in the late 1950s but featuring an important canalside landmark, the Stoke-on-Trent Corporation Electricity Works. Opened in 1894 as the Hanley Electricity Works, following the creation of the new County Borough of Stoke-on-Trent, in 1910, it was agreed to reorganise the four electricity works, in Burslem, Hanley, Stoke and Longton, through the erection of this new central power house. Two wooden cooling towers appear in the foreground, with the chimneys of the original 1894 power station behind. In the right background is part of the flint works of Harrison & Son (Hanley), colour manufacturers, who located there circa 1912, one of whose other works, Victoria Mill, was located at Endon (see page 143). *The Potteries Museum &Art Gallery, Stoke-on-Trent*

continued at least until the late 1920s.

The commencement of the Caldon Canal, from its junction with the T&M at Etruria Wharf along the two-mile stretch to the east of Hanley at Ivy House Lane, was a heavily industrialised area, with a wide range of ceramic manufacturers located along the canal who received potters' materials by narrow boat. Household names included Meakin, Johnson, Wooliscroft, Buller and Taylor Tunnicliffe, and only one major firm, Cauldon Potteries, closed down during this period. Prominent flint millers included Goodwin and Harrison, along with John Ridgway & Co. and Jacob & Thomas Furnival, whose successor companies were located side by side at Etruria Wharf, merging in the mid-1930s to become George Mellor.

Etruria and Etruria Wharf was the hub of the NSR's canal activities, with the NSR owning seven houses, as well as operating facilities for boat repairs and for the maintenance of part of its canal system. There were several warehouses and two basins – Etruria basin and Anderton basin. The LM&SR era saw major changes to this area, with nearly all the houses, by this time being well over 100 years old, being taken out of occupation. All of the original warehouses alongside Etruria Basin were demolished between 1924 and 1938, and the basin itself reduced in size by half; only the Anderton warehouses survived, until the mid-1960s. However, Etruria continued to be an important depot for canal maintenance throughout the LM&SR era.

The canal from Etruria to Froghall is 17 miles 4 furlongs long. Cheddleton Wharf was strategic, historically, as it was located on the turnpike road to Sandon and therefore was an important 19th century canal/road interchange; it was the location for the maintenance yard on this canal but had been run down by the start of the LM&SR era. There is a junction with the Leek Canal at Hazlehurst and this canal will be dealt with separately.

but this traffic had ceased by the late 1940s. The Tomkinson family, of Stockton Brook, operated two boats until the mid-1930s, with George Tomkinson continuing until 1951 in carrying coal from Endon Wharf to Brittain's paper mill at Cheddleton. W. & A.J. Podmore had two works on the Caldon Canal, Caledonian Mills at Shelton and the flint mill at Consall; traffic between them, which started in 1918, ended around 1956. Many other firms, who had located along the canal east of Hanley, continued to receive coal and other minerals, and potters' materials, whilst sending out their finished products by water; this continued during the LM&SR era but on a much reduced scale. Such firms included Hardman Chemicals (at Milton), British Aluminium (at Milton), Stockton Brook waterworks, Stockton Brook brickworks, Wall Grange brickworks and Cheddleton paper mills. The small dry dock yard at Baddeley Green near Milton, established in the early 1850s,

The Eastwood Pottery of J. & G. Meakin Ltd, a view taken off the Lichfield Street bridge, Hanley, in 1948 and looking north east towards Milton. This factory was built in 1889, some thirty years later than the same firm's Eagle Pottery. Note the crated pots loaded into the narrow boat on the left, with both of the vessels seen here belonging to the Anderton Co. Ltd. The boat on the right is in the charge of a boatwoman, whilst that on the left is No. 229, behind which are two Meakin lorries bringing in clay. There were seven bottle kilns on this site, which were colloquially known as the 'Seven Sisters'. *Author's collection*

An aerial view looking north east towards Milton in the early 1930s, showing Hanley and its profusion of bottle kilns. The canal winds its way through the industrial landscape from left to right, between Lichfield Street, off picture to the bottom left, and Bucknall Street, at the top right of the picture, with bottle kilns, and earthenware and china factories on either side. Bottom left is the pottery works of Rigby & Stevenson, followed by Eastwood Mill and then the large Hanley Pottery of Johnson Brothers. At the top is the Nelson Pottery of Elijah Cotton and then Waterloo Pottery. On the right hand side of the canal, at the bottom of the picture, are the works of Bullers, next Taylor Tunnicliffe and then the large Imperial Pottery of Johnson Brothers, beyond which are Albion Flint Mill and Johnson Brothers' Trent Sanitary Works. Diagonally, facing Nelson Pottery, is one of the flint mills belonging to George Edwards. *Author's collection*

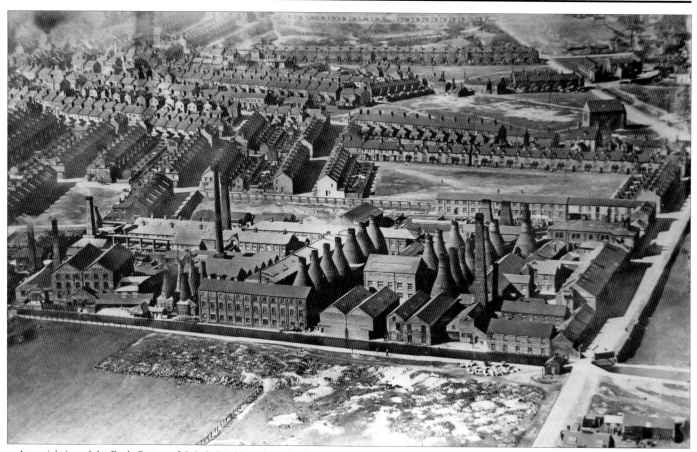

An aerial view of the Eagle Pottery of J. & G. Meakin, taken shortly after the end of the Second World War. In this factory, which was built in 1859 on a site previously occupied by a foundry, the company manufactured a wide range of ironstone china and earthenware products. Meakins was the only local pottery firm, in the LM&SR era, to operate its own fleet of narrow boats. The view is looking north, with the Caldon Canal running across the bottom of the picture, coming from Etruria, to the left, and going towards Milton. To the right of Meakin's factory is Ivy House Road, with its lift bridge over the canal and facing the works is the recently cleared foundry site belonging to Ralph Goodwin & Son. Partially in view bottom right is the works of George Heath, crate and packing case maker. To the left of Meakin's works is the 1827 Ivy House Paper Mills and, to the left of that and only partially in view is Dresden Colour Mills, cobalt manufacturers. The photograph was taken circa 1946. *Michael Dawson collection*

As noted above, Meakins ran their own small fleet of three narrow boats, bringing potters' materials from Weston Point docks at Runcorn, with return loads of crates and barrels of pottery for export via the Port of Runcorn. Most of the export traffic was carried by boat until 1930. Here we see pottery being loaded on to *Alice* at the Eagle Pottery circa 1950; the last of the boats were sold in 1953. In the background, across the canal, is Meakin's covered warehouse for china clay. *David Salt collection*

This second aerial view of Meakin's Eagle Pottery was taken facing south in 1950, four years after the picture opposite, and shows the substantial modernisation that had occurred in the factory during that short period of time. Following the end of the war, all seventeen bottle kilns have been demolished (all of which were shown on the 1879 OS), to be replaced by horizontal kilns; these can be seen in the centre of the pictures. The canal runs from left to right across the centre of the photograph, with Abbey Road visible at the top; Ivy House Road intersects with this to form the boundary of Eagle Pottery, with the lift bridge just visible to the left of the chimney. On the right on the south (far) side of the canal is the Encaustic Tile Works of George Wooliscroft & Son Ltd, diagonally facing the Ivy House Paper Mills, itself adjacent to the pottery. To the right of the paper mills, the works of Alfred Meigh, smalt manufacturer, which were established as the Dresden Colour Mills by Job Meigh in the early 1830s, can again be seen. Top left is the newly built engineering and foundry works of Ralph Goodwin and running across the very top is the Biddulph Valley Line. *David Salt collection*

Bullers Ltd was a firm that manufactured the ceramics for insulators and the company's first factory was established in Hanley alongside the Caldon Canal in 1860. A new factory was opened at Milton in 1920, located in the fork between the canal and the Leek Branch of the NSR, with access to both; it was the last new factory to be built with access to the Caldon Canal. Some traffic came by the canal but this had ceased by the late 1930s. This 1925 view is looking west across the canal with, from left to right, the slip house, the glaze ball mills, with barrels of clay beneath a partially-covered storage area and a pen to the right with three different stacks of china clay, then the turning department and finally the test room and chimney, in front of which is china stone. *Taylor Tunnicliff Ltd*

Left: A second view of Bullers Works, looking north along the canal towards Stockton Brook. A rather crude wharf can be seen, centre right, behind which china clay is stored on the side of the canal. Bricks and masonry in the foreground are evidence that some new construction was taking place. From left to right are the slip house, the blunger department and the glazed ball mills, in front of which are two canopies. Bullers used six horses, a couple of which can be seen here; they were supplied by a local farmer, Johnny Doxey. *Taylor Tunnicliff Ltd*

Right: A view of the Staffordshire Potteries waterworks at Stockton Brook in the late 1920s, looking towards Milton. Note the elegantly designed Victorian building and chimney; the buildings still stand, although currently have no use but the chimney has gone. The wharf and loading dock can be made out on the left, adjacent to Stockton Brook Lock No. 5; the wharf was principally used to receive coal to power the waterworks. The Leek Line runs to the left of the canal at this point, as indicated in the picture of the flood damaged track below. *Author's collection*

Left: The Stockton Brook floods which occurred on 11th July 1927 were the first of several, along with resultant storm damage, that occurred in north Staffordshire in July, August and September of that year, which cost £18,000 in total to repair. The nearby Stanley Reservoir rose six feet in two hours and overflowed, leading to the flooding of the cutting to a depth of three feet. The railway embankment was washed away for approximately 120 yards and in places to a depth of six feet. This view is looking towards Milton, with the waterworks visible in the background on the right. The canal side at Cheddleton was washed away and a train toppled over when part of the embankment was washed away by Hazlehurst Acqueduct. The floods also damaged Harrison's mill at Stanley and Brittain's paper mills at Cheddleton. *Author's collection*

Left: Looking along the Caldon Canal at Endon towards Cheddleton, around 1947. This is a rare photograph of the swing bridge here, which carried a standard gauge line of rails from the Leek Branch across the canal to connect with the line serving Harrison's Victoria Mill, a flint, glazing and colour business based at the village of Stanley. Solidly fixed to the canal bed, it was operated by rack and pinion and the circular rack is still visible today on the solid concrete boss in the centre of the canal. As the plan below shows, a short siding also ran back to a wharf on the right bank, between the swing bridge and the overbridge behind. This rail traffic ceased in 1961. *Author's collection*

Right: The tippler, seen here in 1919, transferred limestone delivered by rail from the new quarries at Caldon Low into waiting boats at Endon Basin to carry to the iron, steel and chemical works of north Staffordshire and south Cheshire. The tippler enabled the quarries to send large volumes of limestone to customers who wished to receive it by canal but without placing excessive demands for water on the canal system. Authorised by Act of Parliament in 1904, it was not until 1918-19 that it was built (in Stoke Works) and then commissioned. The tippler continued in operation until the late 1920s and this was one of four photographs taken at what was possibly a demonstration or trial; the NSR canal maintenance boat, in the foreground, seems badly loaded. Although taken at the end of the NSR era, it is shown here in order to compare it with the LM&SR Land & Rating Plan below. *Manifold collection*

Below: Part of the LM&SR Rating Plan of 1928, showing, left, the private siding from Endon station to Harrison's (Stanley Colour Works), with the swing bridge carrying the line over the canal and the wharf. Right is the limestone loading basin, showing the wooden staging, with a shed for boat horses and a cabin for boatmen. *Cheddleton Railway Museum*

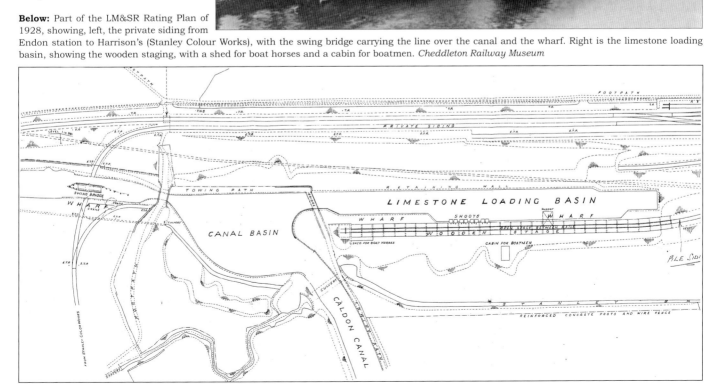

Hazelhurst, photographed here circa 1948, was the junction between the Caldon Canal, on the left, and the Leek Canal, on the right. The Caldon Canal at this point descends through three locks, whilst the Leek Canal maintains its level along the south side side of the valley. Leek, however, lies to the north of the Caldon and thus, just over half a mile further along, at Denford, the Leek Canal crosses over the Caldon on its way to the town. Note the cast iron bridge on the left, to the left of which is the lock-keeper's house. *Author's collection*

Hazelhurst Aqueduct at Denford in 1948, which carries the Leek Canal over the Caldon Canal. The bridge was built in 1841 when the Leek Canal was re-aligned at Hazlehurst Junction. The archway frames the canal cottages that can be seen in the background and this view has changed little down to the present day. *Author's collection*

Left: An aerial view of Cheddleton Paper Mills in 1922, looking north east towards Leek, with the Caldon Canal running from left to top right. The origins of this mill date back to the late 18th century and it entered into the ownership of the Brittain family in 1889. Brittain's were manufacturers of specialist tissues and other fine papers for the pottery industry. In 1932, they employed over 400 people. Top left is the entrance to Cheddleton Tunnel on the Churnet Valley Line. *Author's collection*

Below: Regular deliveries of slack were made along the canal from Endon Wharf to Brittain's by George Tomkinson of Stockton Brook, a third generation boatman. Seen here unloading at Cheddleton probably in the 1930s, this trade lasted until 1951. *Caldon & Uttoxeter Canal Trust*

Below: Looking up the Churnet Valley in 1918, showing Flint Mill Lock and the loading dock for the grinding mill of W. & A.J. Podmore, manufacturers and millers of materials for the pottery, glass, enamel, iron and brick industries. Podmores operated seven mills, at Rocester, Consall, Stone, Stretton and Stoke. With the closure of Froghall Wharf in 1930, they ceased to receive raw materials by rail to there and by canal to Consall; this was replaced in 1931 by a rail service to new sidings at the mill. The mill dated back to the 1680s, when its original function was iron slitting; Podmores had acquired it in 1918. The original buildings can be seen in the centre right background, to the right of which is a wooden crane surrounded by clay stone. *Author's collection*

FLINT MILLS, CONSALL.

C-13.

Right: An advertisement from *Cox's Annual Potter and Glass Trade Book*, 1926, for W. & A.J. Podmore, manufacturers and millers, in respect of their flint mills on the Caldon Canal at Shelton and at Consall. Around the end of the First World War, the Podmore family started acquiring existing flint grinding businesses, Consall Mill in 1918 as already noted and then at Shelton in 1920, also located alongside the canal. The bottom view is an artist's impression of the Caledonian Mills at Shelton, originally built as a brewery in 1888 for Hedge & Co. The top engraving shows the production and transport facilities at Consall. Note the siding arrangement, for a rail connection into the mill that was only installed five years' later! *City of Stoke-on-Trent Archive Service*

Far Right: *Beatrice,* one of a fleet of five boats owned by Thomas Bolton & Sons Ltd at Consall, decked out for a family pleasure trip circa 1930. Bolton's fleet brought slack to Froghall for the works boiler, located alongside the canal. This trade had commenced when the works opened in 1890 and lasted until 1951. *Wakefield family collection*

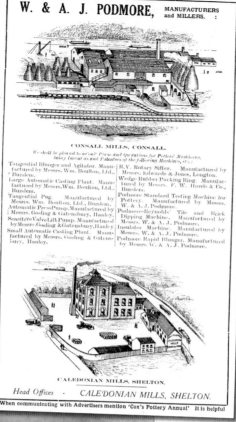

Above: Podmores' *Perpetual* at Froghall Wharf in the mid-1920s, loading china stone for the short journey to the mill at Consall. It was known as a 'buttermilk boat', since it was also used for carrying flint in a slop condition from Consall to Podmores' Shelton mill. *Author's collection*

Above: The Caldon Canal approaching its terminus at Froghall Basin, circa 1924, with the warehouse and cottages beyond the bridge, behind which can be seen the track bed of the former narrow gauge tramroad, which had closed in March 1920, passing above the limekilns. The limekilns remained in use and, during the late 1930s and the Second World War, limestone was brought down to the wharf by lorry and burnt to produce lime. Note the sawn timber, left, from the nearby Foxt Woods, awaiting movement by canal, probably to Cadman's saw mills at Bucknall. On the right is the entrance to the first lock on the former Uttoxeter Canal, with the Uttoxeter Basin just beyond; behind is the toll house and workers' mess room. Note the footbridge over the canal. *Thorne family collection*

Right: From the same viewpoint in 1938, most of the buildings seen above remain but nature has taken over. Prominent again behind is the route of the 1802 former tramroad, whilst centre right are the lime sheds at the foot of the kilns. *Harold Bostock*

The Uttoxeter Canal

The Uttoxeter Canal went from Froghall to Uttoxeter and was 13 miles 4 furlongs long. Opened in 1811, it was part of the Trent & Mersey Canal system but closed in January 1849, although was partially out of use by that date with a section of the canal having been used when the Churnet Valley line was constructed during the previous twelve months.

The bridge that carried the Ashbourne to Cheadle turnpike road over the former Uttoxeter Canal at Oakamoor. After the closure of the canal, a railway line was laid into what became known as Jimmy's Yard and this was used to provide coal and other provisions to the local community; this line remained in situ until the early 1940s and a short section of it, albeit long disused, is seen here, the siding now terminating at the other side of the bridge. Note the oval Uttoxeter Canal bridgeplate, No. 1, still fixed to the side of the bridge. *Wilson family collection*

The house and stables built at Oakamoor for the Uttoxeter Canal in 1811 and seen here in 1935 when decorated with bunting celebrating the Silver Jubilee of King George V. The stables, on the right, continued to be used after the Uttoxeter Canal officially closed in January 1849, for horses engaged in shunting the internal railways of the copper and brass works of Thomas Bolton & Sons, a practice that continued until 1941. These horses were the last to work on the North Staffordshire Section of the LM&SR. *Heath family collection*

The Leek Canal

The Leek Canal was 3 miles 2 furlongs long and passed through very pleasant countryside, along with a short 130 yards long narrow tunnel; in the LM&SR era very little traffic passed along the waterway. Leek Wharf had for many years been a centre of activity, with several coal merchants being located there, serving the domestic and industrial markets, as well as the municipally-owned gas works, established in 1826, before the coming of the railway in 1849. By the 1920s, these merchants (usually six) and the gas works received nearly all of their coal via the adjacent railway sidings at Leek station. Although the Anderton Company advertised a carrying service from Leek Wharf during the LM&SR era, traffic had all but ceased at this time. The carrying of coal to Leek from Norton Colliery via Foxley Wharf, amounting to 5,000 tons per annum, ceased in 1934. The last commercial traffic on the canal was a trade in tar from Milton to Leek and this finished in 1939.

Right: Departing from the Caldon Canal at Hazelhurst Junction, as we saw a little earlier, this 1930s postcard shows a section of the Leek Canal at Longsdon, a view typical of the scenery through which the canal passes, with Sutherland Road bridge in the middle distance. *Author's collection*

Below: The north portal of the Leek Canal tunnel, seen here in 1948. The canal had deteriorated since its legal abandonment in 1944 but, following restoration work begun in the 1970s, the canal and this tunnel are navigable again today. *Author's collection*

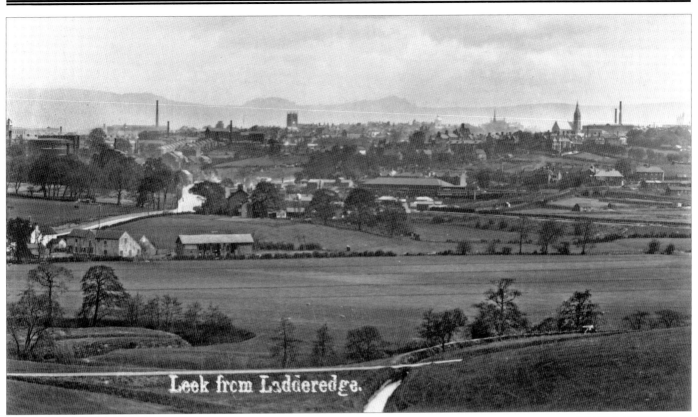

Leek from Ladderedge.

Above: A postcard view of Leek from the late 1920s, taken from Ladderedge. In the centre is the railway goods warehouse and coming in from the right is the line of the canal. The gas works can be seen to the left of the Newcastle to Leek road. *Author's collection*

Right: Leek Wharf circa 1947, a view looking east showing the canal terminus. On the right is the canal warehouse and on the left dominating the skyline is the imposing Leek Gas Works. To right of the gas works in the centre background is the Churnet Valley Hotel, formerly owned by the NSR and thought to have been sold by the LM&SR in the late 1920s; in front of it was the site utilised by the six coal merchants who operated here. The wharf offices can be seen on the left. By this date, the canal had been legally abandoned under the 1944 LM&SR Canal Act. *W.S .Heaton*

Left: The redundant canal warehouse at Leek Wharf in 1958, when it was becoming increasingly derelict and with the surrounding area used as a scrap yard; the view is looking west to Ladderedge. The canal terminus was between the dilapidated warehouse buildings and the wooden sheds to the right. *Peter Norton*

Rudyard Lake

Rudyard reservoir, or lake, was built between 1797 and 1800 to serve the Caldon Canal, via the Leek Canal. It holds water that flows down from the Peak District via the Dane Feeder and then flows past the Leek Arm, the entrance to Leek Basin, and into the Leek Canal; its capacity in 1942 was 121,795,000 cu. feet. With the rest of the T&M Estate, it was sold to the NSR in January 1847. The NSR sought to commercialise its operations at the lake through a 1904 Act of Parliament, in order to exploit the Edwardians' desire for railway travel and leisure opportunities. To this end it owned and leased several cafés and a boat landing stage, and the Company widely promoted lakeside fishing, as well as a newly-established golf course on the Cliffe Park Estate, which it had purchased in 1905 for that purpose. The NSR also enlarged the Hotel Rudyard, which it had run since 1851.

Changes occurred soon after Grouping. The golf course closed in 1926, unsupported by the LM&SR, whilst the Hotel Rudyard and surplus adjacent land was sold in 1927. The golf club house was leased out from 1933 to 1969 to the Youth Hostels Association. Some of the café leases continued through the LM&SR era, as did the boating license and the angling facilities. Whilst Rudyard Lake continued to be an attractive tourist location, its popularity did wane in the 1920s and the 1930s, especially as the nearby Alton Towers became established as one of the premier tourist attractions in England. The LM&SR retained the boat hiring concessions until 1940. During the Second World War, the lake was used by the American Army for training in amphibious landings prior to D-Day, whilst Rudyard Woods were used for training in guerrilla warfare for the war in the Far East.

Right: Handbill advertising the auction of the LM&SR Estate at Rudyard on 27th August 1927, which included the Hotel Rudyard and eight building sites. This was part of a general policy being pursued to dispose of properties and assets that were peripheral to its business. The price realised was £6,350. *Author's collection*

RUDYARD LAKE, Near Leek

In the Parish of Horton

NORTH STAFFORDSHIRE

Amidst Beautiful Woodland and Lake Scenery.
Within a few minutes of Rudyard Lake Railway Station,
2 miles from Leek.
Congleton, 6 miles ; Macclesfield and Stoke-on-Trent, 10 each ;
Buxton, 14 ; Crewe, 19 ; Stafford, 25 ; Manchester, 27 ;
Derby, 30 miles.

Plan, Particulars, and Conditions of Sale

OF

The Hotel Rudyard

Villa Residence and

Building Land

To be Sold by Auction by

J. OAKES ASH & SON

At the Hotel Rudyard (Lot 1)

On Thursday, 25th August, 1927

At 6·30 o'clock prompt.

THE PROPERTIES COMPRISE A MODERN COMMODIOUS
FULLY-LICENSED HOTEL, known as

THE HOTEL RUDYARD

AND

EIGHT ATTRACTIVE BUILDING·SITES

With Vacant Possession on Completion; also

A PICTURESQUE VILLA IN RUDYARD VALE

As more particularly described within.

Further information may be obtained from the following —
Solicitors : **BEALE & Co.,** 12, Newhall Street, BIRMINGHAM.
Estate Agent : **F. J. STANNARD,** Euston Station, LONDON, N.W. 1.
Auctioneers : **J. OAKES ASH & SON,** 43, St. Edward Street, LEEK.

Hotel Rudyard.

Left: Hotel Rudyard on a commercial postcard published in 1924. The property began life in the early 19th century as the water bailiff's cottage but became a hotel in 1851. Successive enlargements of the building took place subsequently, leading to a top floor being added in 1907, which is the section seen here beneath the Hotel Rudyard name. Still open today, the front of the building has remained unchanged. *Author's collection*

Right: From the same set of postcards comes this view of T.A. Stone's Kingswood store, which faced the hotel. The popularity of Rudyard Lake as a tourist destination led to the growth, from 1900 onwards, in the number of cafés and stores on the road leading to it, as well as bric-a-brac stalls on the dam. Kingswood store was built by Tommy Stone, who was allegedly a former spy and a Private Secretary to Queen Mary. Prominently advertised is Rudyard Rock, which was widely available in the village. Also advertised are Kodak Film and Three Castles cigarettes, neither of which are available to buy today. *Author's collection*

Cliffe Park Golf House. Rudyard.

Above: This is the second photograph to illustrate the changing use of Cliffe Park during the LM&SR era (the first appears in Vol. 2, p.58); this early 1920s postcard shows it as Cliffe Park Golf House. It was originally Cliffe Park Hall and was part of the Cliffe Park Estate at Rudyard, which was acquired by the NSR in 1905 as a springboard for leisure developments that they intended to introduce to the area. The hall, built in 1810, became the club house for the Rudyard Lake Golf Club in 1908 and this view of the entrance was taken from the 18th green. The club fell upon hard times after the end of the First World War and closed in 1926; it was sponsored originally by the NSR but neglected in later years by both the NSR and the LM&SR. The hall was briefly considered by the LM&SR Board in 1936 as the location for its proposed School of Transport but was rejected on the grounds that its location was inaccessible. *Author's collection*

Above: The sale of land adjacent to the Hotel Rudyard by the LM&SR in 1927 provided the opportunity for small scale development here. A garage was built (still there) and, in the early 1930s, a new timber tearoom, affectionately known as Brasso's, it having been opened by the family of the Reservoir Attendant, Arthur Brassington. This building was the last of the many Rudyard tearooms to survive as such, finally closing in 1982. *Author's collection*

Right: A view of Rushton in the early 1930s, looking towards Macclesfield, at a point where the feeder from the River Dane, near Wincle, passes under the Macclesfield to Leek road, before flowing into the north end of the Lake. *Author's collection*

RUSHTON .

Right: Two late 1920s postcard views of the lake and the landing stage. *Author's collection*

KEY
1. Ravensclough Brook
2. Bungalows
3. Dingle Brook
4. Feeder
5. Sgt Brooth (?) landed
6. Drowned man found
7. Fishing cabin
8. Cliffe Park station
9. Wolf Dale
10. Sgt Wise landed
11. Old Hill
12. Barnswood
13. Lake View garage
14. RAF men landed
15. Hunt House
16. Over flow
17. Hotel Rudyard
18. Shir Khan's lair
19. Miners' Home
20. Fair View
21. Rea Cliff
22. Logs
23. Horton Lodge
24. Rocks
25. Sandypoint
26. Fortside
27. Fort
28. Rocks
29. Waterfall
30. Bracken
31. Dragons den
32. Chalet
33. Birch Trees
34. Plane crash
35. Cliffe Park
36. Pilot found
37. Weeds
38. American camp
39. Barnsite

This map was hand drawn in 1944 and depicts Rudyard Lake during the Second World War. It shows the location of the wires installed across the lake to prevent enemy invasion. Also visible (38) is the camp used by American servicemen during the war, for training in amphibious landing prior to D-Day; they were based at Blackshaw Moor in the Staffordshire Moorlands. Around 100 yards south of Cliffe Park Hall (35) is the site of a crash in Rudyard Woods of an RAF bomber (34) that was on a training flight. These woods were used for training in the art of guerrilla warfare for fighting in the jungles of the Far East. The Dane Feeder (4) from the Dane Valley can be seen coming in at the north end of the lake and the LM&SR Churnet Valley Line runs down the east side, after passing Cliffe Park station (8). *Christine Chester*

12

The Leek Line

The Leek Line, as it was generally known, was six miles 1,408 yards in length and ran from the junction with the Biddulph Valley Line, at Milton Junction, through to Leek Brook, where it joined the Churnet Valley railway. It was an important component for the NSR strategy of linking Stoke with a satellite of towns up to twenty miles away and it opened in 1867, with intermediate stations initially at Milton and Endon; further stations were opened subsequently at Wall Grange (1873) and Stockton Brook (1896), with Leek Brook Platform (serving St. Edward's Hospital at Cheddleton) opening in 1904. The line passes through open countryside and small villages, and these increasingly became commuter suburbs of the Potteries. Industry was concentrated around Milton, with aluminium, chemical and porcelain insulator manufacture at locations that had rail access to the line as well as to the Caldon Canal.

The line was single between Milton Junction and Endon, and the gradients were gentle apart from the 1 in 123 climb from Milton to Stockton Brook. The opening of St. Edward's Hospital in 1899 in turn led to the opening of Leek Brook Platform, which comprised an island platform situated jointly on the Leek Line and on the Down Churnet Valley Line; a small number of trains stopped at the island platform each day and this enabled passengers to get off and walk to the hospital or the nearby Wardles Dye Works. The doubling of the line between Endon and Leek Brook provided extra line capacity for excursion traffic to Waterhouses (for the Manifold line) and to Rudyard Lake and to Leek, as well as being able to handle the increasing traffic from the new quarry faces at Caldon. The NSR had started a programme in 1920 of demolishing and rebuilding timber trestle bridges but two bridges of this type on the line were not replaced until 1930.

Passenger services from the 1890s were timetabled to go to Rudyard and Rushton, and that arrangement continued throughout the LM&SR era. They were a mixture of Stoke to Leek and Leek to Rushton workings. In October 1922, there were twelve daily and three on Sundays, with four calling at the 'Platform'; the NSR rail motor service still worked one train a day and this carried over but only into spring 1923. With the closure of the Biddulph

Valley Line in July 1927 for passenger traffic, Fenton Manor and Bucknall & Northwood stations remained open and were incorporated into Leek Line timetables. In the summer of 1930, there were six daily passenger workings from Stoke to Leek and these were supplemented by market trains to Leek on Wednesdays and Saturdays, and to Rudyard on Saturdays; in the summer of 1947, there were six Stoke to Leek and six Leek to Rushton trains, with an extra train on Saturdays. The motive power seen on the branch was very varied and was often used to break in new locomotives coming into Stoke shed. There was also a 1,330 yards long electric tramway between the 'Platform' and the hospital. The passenger service on it had ceased by 1920 but its use for coal and other supplies continued until the tramway's closure in 1954; the hospital had sidings at Leek Brook.

At Grouping, there was only a modest availability of Third Class Workmen's Weekly tickets – between Endon and Bucknall & Northwood, and from both Milton and Stockton to Bucknall, Fenton Manor and Stoke. By September 1924, this had been expanded to include Leek to Wall Grange and Endon; Stockton Brook and Milton issued these tickets to other stations on the Leek line and to Bucknall, Fenton Manor and to Stoke. There were also Weekly Workmen's tickets available from Stoke to Milton, Stockton Brook and Wall Grange. This pattern continued through until 1929 at least. From summer 1935, there was a package of Cheap Daily Return tickets between Stoke and all the eleven stations to Rushton, and to each other, every day and by all trains on the day of issue only; this promotion continued until the outbreak of war.

Freight working on the Leek Line was never very heavy, the daily pick up freight from the NSR era being replaced by a daily trip working between Pratt's Sidings and Leek Brook Sidings and Leek. The other workings over the line were mineral trains from Caldon Quarry to Pratt's Sidings and other destinations beyond. Wagon accomodation on the line comprised, at Milton, 98 wagons in the yard on the Up side and, at Endon, 63 wagons in the yard, also on the Up, and at Leek Brook, 63 on the Leek line and 67 on the Churnet line.

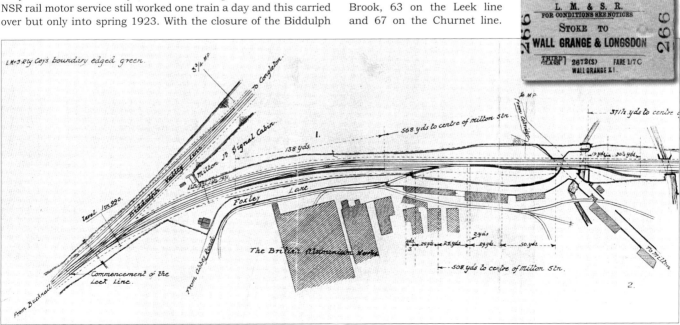

Above: A Private Siding Agreement dated 31st July 1922, between the NSR and British Aluminium, which details the arrangements for maintaining the sidings of Hardman Chemicals and of British Aluminium. Note the length of the sidings in the extensive chemical works. *Author's collection*

Inset Above Right: An LM&SR Stoke to Wall Grange & Longsdon Third Class ticket. *Author's collection*

A fine circa 1930 aerial view of the industrial complex to the north of Milton Junction, located between the single track Leek Line, running from bottom right to top left, and the Caldon Canal, also coming in bottom right but turning ninety degrees right, facing the Foxley Arms, at the top of the picture; the Foxley Branch canal to Ford Green, heading off to the top left, was built to serve the collieries and iron works of Robert Heath & Son. At bottom left is the continuation of the Biddulph Valley Line, with Milton Junction signal box in the fork between the two railways. In the centre of the picture is the British Aluminium Works; rail access was via a backshunt, across Redhill Road, with Milton Road coming in top left. The original works was built in 1888 by the American-owned Cowles Electric Smelting Company. It was the first plant in Europe to use the electrolytic methods to extract aluminium metal from bauxite ore but was closed in 1894, then taken over by the British Aluminium Co., who used the plant as a rolling mill and foundry. Above this factory is the works of Midland Tar Distillers, formally Josiah Hardman Ltd, coal tar distillers and manufacturers of tar and ammonia products. John Hardman was a local landowner who established his own chemical works at Milton in 1864; the first private siding agreement dates back to February 1883. The Hardman plant closed in 1933 and at least part of the site was later taken over by British Aluminium; it was closed in the late 1950s. At the very top of the picture can be seen the oil works of Cooper & Adams, beyond which is the aluminium foundry of Jackson Bros (Milton) Ltd. The three lines, for both works, are, from top to bottom: (i) traffic awaiting removal; (ii) marshalling; (iii) the Leek Line (single). Whilst Hardman's had its own locomotive, British Aluminium did not and at some period it would appear that the former did the shunting of the latter. This is a photograph full of interest; notice there are plenty of railway wagons in the sidings, suggesting a healthy traffic and at least one canal boat either loading or unloading at the aluminium works, probably bringing coal from a local colliery. *Steve Grudgings collection*

There was no booked mineral traffic at Milton, where the British Aluminium Co. Ltd, Hardman Chemical works (closed in 1933 with its plant being taken over by British Aluminium) and Bullers all took materials by rail, nor at Endon where Harrison & Sons, potters' millers, had a quarter mile spur line off the Leek Line and over the Caldon Canal. Only Endon had coal merchants at the station yard, namely Lloyd & Co. and William Rogers. Motive power used in the LM&SR era for freight work was Class '4F's and 2-6-4Ts. Limestone transshipment at Endon Wharf from railway wagons into narrow boats commenced in 1919 but did not last many years into the LM&SR era.

Finally, the LM&SR Country Lorry scheme covered such villages as Baddeley Edge, Bagnall, Longsdon and Stanley, as well as the villages that had stations.

Above: *Josiah Hardman Ltd*, an outside cylindered 0-4-0ST built by Yorkshire Engine in 1908, is seen at the Milton chemical works of Josiah Hardman Ltd circa 1930. The open smoke box door allows an interesting view of this part of the boiler. In the background and off the rails is a chemical tank wagon belonging to Tar Residuals Limited. John Hardman was a well established local landowner who founded the chemical business in the early 1860s; it became a subsidiary of Midland Tar Distillers in 1929 but the works closed soon afterwards in 1933. This locomotive was then transferred to the Chesterton Chemical Works of Midland Tar Distillers which, in turn, closed some time before the start of the Second World War. The siding officially closed in March 1940. *H.W. Robinson*

Right: An early 1920s rearward view of the Milton Works of Bullers Limited, manufacturers of electrical porcelain at Hanley and Milton. Looking towards Cheddleton, the newly built (1920) factory was served by both rail and canal. The test room is to the right of the chimney and to the right of that is the office block. Beyond these works, the Leek Line can be seen to the right and the Biddulph Valley Line to the left of the chimney. The Newcastle to Leek road runs across in the middle background. Two further views of the works, taken from the Caldon Canal can be found on pages 127-8. *Author's collection*

Right: An early photograph of Bullers' new factory showing the railway sidings on the left and the Leek Line running across the foreground. The long building on the left is the office block, whilst the buildings to the right are the blunger department. Several 5-plank open wagons can be seen on the left, at the side of which is a small lorry; beyond these is the test room, above the covered area where coal was received and put into bays; some private owner wagons are also just visible and there is an NSR home signal on the right. *The Potteries Museum & Art Gallery, Stoke-on-Trent*

North Staffordshire Railway.
THIRD CLASS WORKMAN'S TICKET
STOCKTON BROOK
TO
LEEK
AND BACK   Revised Fare 4

LEEK RD.   STOCKTON BROOK.

Above: The exterior of Stockton Brook station, looking along Leek Road towards Endon in the mid 1920s. The bus on the left was probably owned by the Potteries Electric Traction Co. Ltd, which had a frequent daily service between Hanley and Leek via Stockton Brook. In the centre are the station buildings, to a design found also at Cliffe Park and on the line to Waterhouses. Note that the nameboard is, unusually, on the awning above the buildings, which still survive, now in use as showrooms. The station was renamed Stockton Brook & Brown Edge during the LM&SR era. *Author's collection*

Insets – Above: An NSR Workman's ticket, Stockton Brook to Leek; **Below –** An LM&SR Bicycle/Cloak Room ticket for Stockton Brook *Author's collection*

Below: A delightful view of Stockton Brook station in the 1930s, taken from the Leek to Newcastle road bridge and looking towards Endon. Opened in 1896, it was one of several new openings by the NSR around the turn of the century on existing lines, to service the expanding population in the Potteries suburbs; other stations included Meir (1893), Rolleston-on-Dove (1894) and Aston-by-Stone (1901). This later design of waiting shelter, all in timber, could be seen at many of the stations on the NSR network. The nameboard reads 'STOCKTON BROOK FOR BROWN EDGE'. *WA Camwell/SLS collection*

685
L. M. & S. R.
BICYCLE CLOAK ROOM
WEEKLY TICKET
Not transferable.
Mr Copped
having signed the usual
Agreement is entitled
to deposit day by day
his/her Bicycle at
STOCKTON BROOK
From 5/6/56
To
FEE 1/8 P
TO BE GIVEN UP ON EXPIRY
685

Above: A circa 1930 aerial view of Victoria Mill, Stanley, near Endon, owned by Harrison & Son Ltd. This was a firm of potters' millers located near the Caldon Canal, which William Harrison purchased in 1867 for his son, Thomas William Harrison, to run. William Harrison took over Stanley Forge Mill, a water mill for grinding flint stone and established a works manufacturing ceramic colours and glazes; production in later years was '*for outside and foreign markets*'. The firm originally relied on the canal for the delivery of potters' materials and the despatch of its products but, in 1885, they laid down a short railway line of approximately ¹/₄ mile, which crossed the canal via the swing bridge seen on page 129 and overleaf, and connected with the Leek Line at Endon station. The line was operated down to 1925 on the overhead electric wire system, including the section over the swing bridge. In the late 1920s and early 1930s, the business prospered and an additional siding was put in to provide extra storage and loading facilities, and to serve new modern steel and brick buildings (centre right). The branch heads off top right towards Endon. *Mark Mills collection*

Right: Harrisons owned their own shunting engine; *Nina* was a standard gauge battery electric locomotive, of a similar design to the NSR's shunting locomotive at Bolton's Works at Oakamoor. It came new to Harrison & Son from its builders, Electromobile Ltd of Otley, Yorkshire, in 1925 and was sold to the Brookfield Foundry & Engineering Co. in 1961. On the left is a 3-plank wagon loaded high with china stone. *Allan Baker collection*

Below: A surviving nameplate from *Nina*. *Mark Mills collection*

Right: A view looking west towards Stockton Brook, showing the canal swing bridge at Endon carrying the branch to Harrison's Victoria Mill. There was a gate across the branch on the right, with the Leek Line visible beyond the hedge.

Below: The LM&SR Private Siding Agreement with Harrison & Son that was prepared in July 1929. It refers to an earlier agreement with Harrisons dated 10th January 1885, when the mill was first rail connected. The agreement is interesting because it shows the length of track (111 yards) from the end of the siding off the Leek Line until it crossed the canal via the swing bridge on which LM&SR locomotives were not permitted to work. Note the canal basin and the ¼ mile line from Endon station to the transshipment wharf for limestone traffic; this became operational in 1919 but, by the date of this agreement, had been taken out of use. *Author's collection*

Bottom: Looking east towards Endon circa 1950, with the station building just visible in the background. Fowler 2-6-4T No. 42418 is working a Leek-Stoke freight train and is passing the line to Harrisons' mill at the point where it curves away south to cross over the swing bridge. Note the NSR cast iron trespass notice on the right. *Gordon Walwyn*

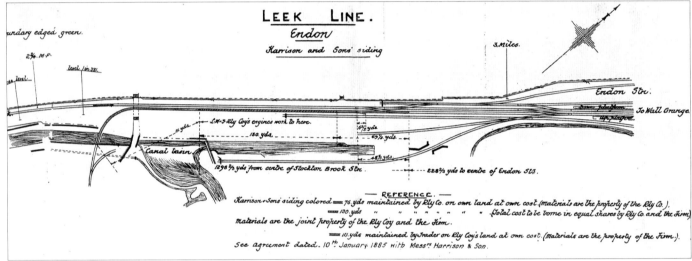

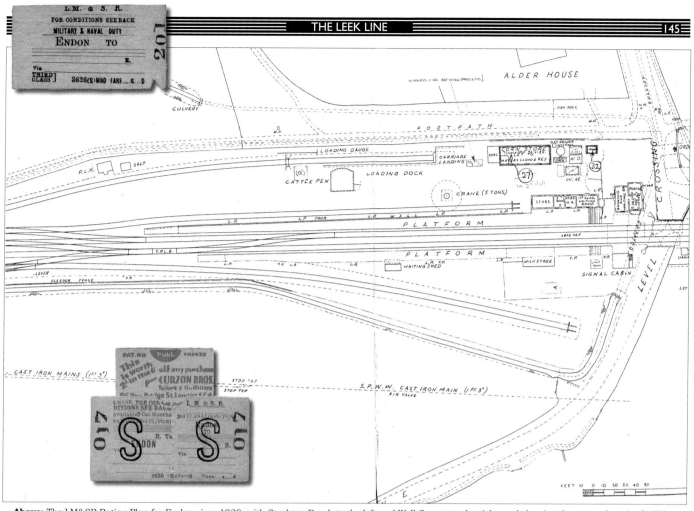

Above: The LM&SR Rating Plan for Endon circa 1928, with Stockton Brook to the left and Wall Grange to the right, and showing the comprehensive facilities available for passengers and for goods traffic. On the Down side (to Wall Grange) there was a cattle pen, loading gauge, a carriage landing, corn store, store, ladies' waiting room, First Class waiting room, a booking and waiting room, an office for the station master and clerks, and a room for porters. On the Up side was a waiting shed, landing stage, the lamp room and the signal cabin. A photograph of Endon can be found on page 119. *Cheddleton Railway Museum*
Insets Above: An LM&SR Military & Naval Duty ticket for Endon; an LM&SR Third Class & Foreign Saloon ticket with advertising insert. *Author's collection*

Wall Grange & Longsdon station looking west towards Endon circa 1948; note the nameboard reflects the name change from Wall Grange but the LM&SR had maintained the NSR design. Note the length of the platforms, extended to accommodate long excursion trains. The platform on the right is built of timber, a later addition when the line was doubled in 1910, unlike the facing platform. The station did not have its own signal box, just a ground frame positioned in front of the main buildings and the station house. *Author's collection*
Inset: An LM&SR Privilege ticket for Wall Grange. *Author's collection*

Wall Grange & Longsdon station looking towards Leek from the bridge carrrying Sutherland Road over the line, seen in the previous picture. Taken circa 1947, a three coach Stoke to Leek train is about to depart from the timber Down platform. Note the station master's vegetable garden in the right foreground and the tower of St. Edward's Mental Hospital in the distance. *Author's collection*
Inset Right: An NSR Wall Grange to Leek Workman's ticket. *Author's collection*

North Staffordshire Railway.
THIRD CLASS WORKMAN'S TICKET
WALL GRANGE
TO
LEEK
AND BACK

Choddleton Mental Hospital (Nr. Leek) from the Air.

St. Edward's Mental Hospital circa 1930, with the Leek Line coming in bottom left and curving round the spacious cricket ground and nurses home. It then makes a left to Leek Brook Halt, top centre, and the junction, where it connects with the Churnet Valley Line which runs from left to right. Top left is the triangle of lines, in the middle of which, barely visible, is Leek Brook engine shed. There was an island platform on the Down side of the Churnet line, where passenger rains to Leek were never booked to stop; the other side of this platform was for passengers going by tram to the hospital. The route of the electric tramway leaves the Churnet Valley line near the Leek to Stone road bridge and climbed on a rising gradient of 1 in 120 to the hospital. The passenger service, via the tramway, lasted until around 1920, whilst the goods service ceased in 1954. *Author's collection*

Right: Looking across to the timber-built Leek Brook platform on 13th August 1932, with former L&NWR 'G1' Class 0-8-0 No. 9384 working a Pratt's Siding to Leek freight. Just behind the locomotive is the platform where workers for Wardle's works could alight and join. This arrangement only featured in the Working time tables and never in the Public time tables; only two trains a day each way would call there. *Gordon Walwyn*

Left: The passenger service on the Leek Line was an easy turn and a wide variety of motive power was used, often some of the older and larger L&NWR locomotives just prior to their withdrawal. The following sequence of pictures looks at a selection of the classes to be found on these services in the 1920s and 1930s. Here, former L&NWR Webb '18ins Coal Tank' 0-6-2T No. 599 is seen approaching Leek station from the south on a Stoke to Rudyard working in 1925. *Gordon Walwyn*

Right: With its better days some years behind it, former L&NWR 'George V' Class 4-4-0 No. 25409 *Dovedale* was photographed at the head of a Leek to Stoke passenger working on 21st August 1937. In the right background part of Leek gas works can be seen, whilst on the left are two of the wagons owned by Henry Machin, coal merchant of Leek. *Gordon Walwyn*

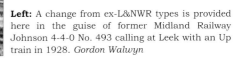

Left: A change from ex-L&NWR types is provided here in the guise of former Midland Railway Johnson 4-4-0 No. 493 calling at Leek with an Up train in 1928. *Gordon Walwyn*

Left: Former L&NWR 'Experiment' Class 4-6-0 No. 5456 *City of Chester* at Leek on a Stoke passenger working in May 1931. It was one of seven of this class that came to Stoke early in 1929; one remained there in April 1933 and another was in store at Stoke in June 1935.

Below Left: Former L&NWR 'Experiment' Class No. 5539 *Lancashire* with a passenger working for Stoke on 1st May 1930.

Below Right: Former NSR 'A' Class 2-4-2T No. 35, now LM&SR No. 1455, on a Stoke passenger train at Leek in 1927. This locomotive was built as a 2-4-0 in 1882, rebuilt as a 2-4-2T in 1898 and withdrawn from service in October 1932.

Bottom: Former L&NWR 'George V' Class 4-4-0 No. 5328 *P.H. Chambres* departing with a Stoke passenger train on 5th June 1930. It was one of seven of the class that came to Stoke in late 1928; only one remained there by April 1933 but a later arrival survived until July 1936. There is the usual busy scene in the goods yard here on the right. *All Gordon Walwyn*

13

The Leek, Caldon & Waterhouses Railway and Caldon Quarries

The Leek, Caldon & Waterhouses Branch was nearly 9³/₄ miles long, single track throughout and consisted of two lines, one from Leek Brook to Waterhouses which measured 8 miles 1,496 yards, and the other from Caldon Junction to Caldon Quarries which was 1,342 yards. It was the last major branch line to be built by the NSR, opening in July 1905, standard gauge and, along with the Leek & Manifold Valley Light Railway, built under the 1896 Light Railway Order Regulations, being authorised by an Order of the Light Railway Commissioners on 6th March 1899. It was a difficult line to engineer, climbing steeply out of Leek Brook at 1 in 45 and 1 in 59 to Ipstones, followed by the descent to Waterhouses at 1 in 40 and a further climb, on the Caldon section from Caldon Junction, to the newly opened Bottom and West End quarries at 1 in 79. The branch opened in June 1905, a year after the Manifold line.

There were three passenger stations on the branch, at Bradnop,

Ipstones and Waterhouses, and two halts, at Winkhill and Caldon Low. There were coal or corn merchants serving each station, whilst the branch passed through bleak and exposed countryside, and sparsely populated villages. Local passenger traffic was small but the branch did provide a feeder service to the Manifold line at Waterhouses. The economic rationale for the branch was the large volume of limestone traffic from the quarries that passed over it, bound for industrial customers and for use as permanent way ballast. Milk was collected through the early part of the LM&SR era from all the stations except Caldon Low but this declined, following national trends, during the mid-1930s; there was a special milk collection point at Apesford Crossing, between Bradnop and Ipstones but this closed in 1939. Milk traffic from the Manifold Valley passed over the branch to Leek Brook, whence some went to Manchester, via Leek, and some to London via Uttoxeter.

The LM&SR did not attempt to promote the line as a tourist

Left: Former NSR 'D' Class No. 144, now as LM&SR No. 1589, on a Waterhouses milk train at Leek station during the period of the 1926 General Strike. It is backing on to an ex-L&NWR milk van. *Gordon Walwyn*

Right: Advertisement for 'Cheap Trips from Leek to the Autumn Illuminations at Blackpool', on Sunday 14th October 1934. The train started at Waterhouses and picked up from all stations to Bosley. It was a long day for excursionists, because the train did not return from Blackpool until 11.50pm; despite this, it was advertised as a 'Half-day Excursion'! *Leek Post & Times*

Below: The last passenger train for the Waterhouses Branch at Leek station on 28th September 1935. Former NSR 'New L' Class 0-6-2T No. 157, now as LM&SR No. 2249, is seen here backing on to the passenger stock that will form its train. *Manifold collection*

CHEAP TRIPS FROM LEEK.

AUTUMN ILLUMINATIONS at BLACKPOOL
SEPT. 15th, to OCT. 22nd.

HALF-DAY EXCURSION TO

BLACKPOOL

SUNDAY, October 14th, 1934.

From	Times of Departure.
WATERHOUSES	11-30 a.m.
WINKHILL HALT	11-40 a.m.
IPSTONES	11-43 a.m.
BRADNOP	11-58 a.m.

Return Fare (Third Class), 5/6.

LEEK	12-14 p.m.
RUDYARD LAKE	12-22 p.m.

Return Fare (Third Class), 5/-.

RUSHTON	12-27 p.m.
BOSLEY	12-35 p.m.

Return Fare (Third Class) 4/6.

BLACKPOOL
(North) arr. 3-20 p.m.

Children under three years of age, free; three years and under fourteen, half-fares.

RETURN ARRANGEMENTS.
Passengers return same day from BLACKPOOL (North) at 11-50 p.m.

Third Class
Return Fare.

MONDAY, OCTOBER 15th.
12-18 p.m. UTTOXETER ... 2/-
(STEEPLECHASES).

Above: A rather cruel enlargement from another photograph which provides a rare view of Leek Brook engine shed, in the centre background, in around 1932. It was situated alongside the south to east curve at Leek Brook. The scarred landscape behind is a casualty of the construction of the Waterhouses Branch in the early years of the 20th century. *Gordon Walwyn*

Right: Another rare glimpse is also provided here, of Leek Brook East signal box, on the left in this late 1920s photograph, behind which can be seen part of the engine shed again. The passenger train on its way from Waterhouses to Leek is checked at a signal on the east to north curve, which runs behind the engine shed in the view above. The photograph was taken from the window of one of the six railway cottages built at Leek Brook in 1914; the cottage garden is in the foreground and the mile post can be seen on the left. *Fleming family collection*

An aerial view of Leek Brook, looking towards Leek, in the late 1930s, with the line to Caldon and to Waterhouses going from left to right across the top of the picture, on a climbing gradient as it crosses the Leek to Stone Road (top right). On the left, the railway passes behind some wooden huts that were originally built to serve the navvies engaged on the construction of the line from 1902 to 1905 and continued to be occupied as dwellings for many years afterwards. To their right are the 1914 NSR cottages. Dominating the picture are the two dye works of Joshua Wardle Ltd, the furthest one to the right having been built in the 1870s and the nearest one in the mid-1930s. The engine shed is just off picture to the left. *Author's collection*

Right: Former NSR '100' Class 0-6-0 No. 102, renumbered in LM&SR days as 2349 and then 8671, at the head of a short Waterhouses goods train passing Leek Brook in 1927. This locomotive was built in 1897 and withdrawn from service in March 1929. Once the Class '4F' 0-6-0s were introduced into the North Staffordshire Section from 1927 onwards, the heavier NSR locomotives were taken out of service, ten of the '100' Class going between 1928 and 1931. *Gordon Walwyn*

Centre Right: Longbottom former 'DX' Class 0-6-2T No. 77, now with LM&SR No. 2237, approaches the short railway viaduct at Leek Brook on 25th October 1928, with a morning goods train for Waterhouses. This locomotive was built in 1902 and withdrawn in June 1929. At this time, Waterhouses was served with morning and afternoon goods services. *Gordon Walwyn*

Bottom Right: Bradnop station on 28th April 1926, the morning after the fire that completely destroyed the original buildings, offices and waiting room. The station was used at this time largely for milk transport. On the right is a young Robert Keys, later a well-known historian of the NSR, and his father, an Inspector at Leek station. *Robert Keys collection*

destination for the obvious reason that there were no tourist attractions; it did benefit from the national tourist travel promotions of 1933 but to little effect. The NSR never provided Workmen's tickets on the branch but, by September 1924, they were issued from Leek to Waterhouses and, by March 1929, from Ipstones, Winkhill Halt and Waterhouses, all to Leek. Passenger services to Waterhouses in the main coincided with connections with the Manifold service. Even the modest NSR service, three on weekdays, a market train on Wednesdays and Saturdays, and one on Sundays, was whittled away with no Sunday service from 1931, and two daily passenger trains and one Saturdays only from 1932, until the line was closed for passenger traffic on 30th September 1935.

The LM&SR era saw the steady decline of the branch, partly through the national economic circumstances of the depression from 1929 onwards and partly from the growing competition from other forms of transport – for carrying goods, milk and other merchandise, and for carrying passengers be it to work or for pleasure. To some extent, the decline in all forms of traffic on the branch had already occurred before Grouping and this trend continued after 1923. On the Manifold line, the closure of the creamery at Ecton in 1932 undermined the viability of that route, as well as the viability of the Leek, Caldon & Waterhouses Branch, the Manifold line closing on 10th March 1934.

The closure of the passenger service between Leek and Waterhouses in September 1935 followed a decision of the LM&SR Traffic Committee on 24th July 1935. The reasons were not hard to see, with passenger receipts amounting to £86 per annum against operating costs of £763 per annum. The freight service limped on for a few years and, early in 1943, the LM&SR reviewed the viability of the section from Caldon Junction to Waterhouses. To avoid the costs of relaying that section and also having regard to the wartime shortage of materials, the decision was taken to close it in March 1943, with goods and mineral traffic being transferred to the Caldon freight activities. Signal boxes were shut between then and 1947 at Waterhouses, Caldon Junction, Leek Brook East and Leek Brook North. The goods depots at Bradnop, Ipstones and Winkhill were closed on 4th May 1964.

Apesford Crossing was a collecting point for milk and milk empties, this being a Waterhouses goods turn, and it was used for milk collection until 1939, though the level crossing continued to be operational, when limestone traffic passed through, until February 1989. These two photographs were taken near Apesford Crossing, which was situated between Bradnop and Ipstones, on 13th September 1935.

Left: At the head of a train of fifteen empties for Caldon Quarries was former 'New C' Class 0-6-4T No. 70, now as LM&SR No. 2043. This turn was for the heavier NSR locomotives but Class '4F' locomotives were introduced on the branch from October 1935, lasting until the end of steam, more than thirty years later. This turn was shared in the early 1930s by members of the 'New L' and 'New C' classes.

Right: The lightly loaded Waterhouses goods train is seen here hauled by a new arrival, Stanier 2-6-2T No. 82, off Macclesfield shed. This class did not work the Waterhouses goods service for long, giving way to the '4F's. *Both Gordon Walwyn*

Right: A Down Caldon freight being worked by Fowler '4F' 0-6-0 No. 4508, off Stoke shed, passing Ashenhurst level crossing on 25th August 1947. The '4F's started to be allocated to Stoke during 1927 and, by January 1928, there were twenty shedded there. Their numbers increased to twenty-one in 1933, thirty-two in 1945 and thirty-eight in 1948. At the time of their first arrival, they replaced the 1870s built 0-6-0s. *Gordon Walwyn*

Below Left: In the first of a short sequence of three views of stations on the branch, all taken shortly after the cessation of passenger services in September 1935, Bradnop is seen from the 117ft long milk dock that faced the station building. From left to right, the accommodation comprised the booking office, waiting room, ladies' waiting room and the water closet, with the platform being 100 yards long. There were two goods sheds, situated on a slope leading up from the milk dock which, in the late 1920s, was let to Stubbs & Co. and to Cattle Foods Ltd. *Brian Morris collection*

Below Right: Ipstones from the goods yard, with coal wagons in the siding. It was a small country station, with the same arrangements as for Bradnop. There were two LM&SR warehouses and a 20cwt Avery portable weighing machine; the majority of available warehouse space was let, in the late 1920s, to Derbyshire Farmers Ltd for the storage of grain. There were also three coal stacking grounds that were leased to Biddulph & District Agricultural Society. Until the early 1930s, all these stations were also served by a daily milk train. *Brian Morris collection*

Left: The LM&SR Rating Plan for Winkhill Halt, which was carried out in the late 1920s. Note the later additions recording the withdrawal of the passenger service and the Station Corn Stores Agreement of 14th November 1939, which was presumably a renewal of J.E. Bull's previous letting. *Cheddleton Railway Archive*

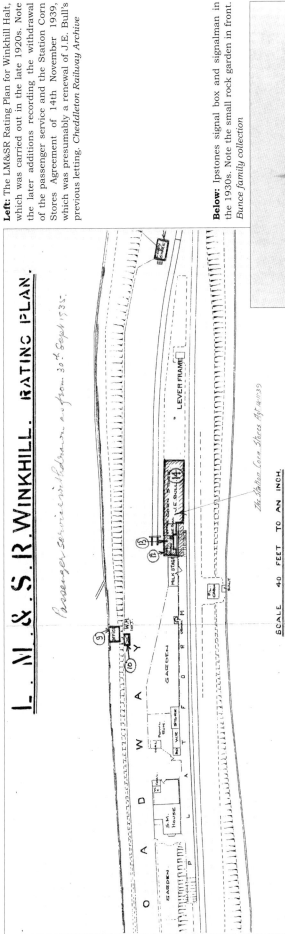

Below: Ipstones signal box and signalman in the 1930s. Note the small rock garden in front. *Bunce family collection*

Above: Completing the sequence of three 1935 views is this picture of Winkhill Halt, looking towards Caldon Quarries. There is a garden in the foreground, behind which is the station master's house. Facing on to the platform, the edge of which had been demolished by this date, and only just glimpsed was the booking office, waiting room and store, behind which is what was described as the 'Fowl Run' - presumably where chickens were kept. Then comes the garden urinal and at the end of the platform is the milk stage and the corn store, let in the late 1920s to J.E. Bull; a lever frame worked the siding to the corn store. On the far left was the location for a Pooley 10-ton weighing machine. In the background another smaller corn store can also be seen. This station opened in 1910, some five years after the others. The originals of these three views are hand coloured lantern slides, which explains the very grainy nature of the images; the picture above is also reproduced in colour on the rear cover. *Brian Morris collection*

Caldon Junction in the early 1930s, with the line descending to Caldon Low Halt and to Waterhouses on the left on a 1 in 40 gradient. Adjacent to the junction is an LM&SR notice advising drivers to pin down brakes before the descent. Heading straight on is the single line (1,067 yards) to the quarries and on the right, tucked into the bank, is Caldon Junction signal box, which had a very limited view of trains leaving the quarries. The box was taken out of use shortly after the goods service to Waterhouses ceased in March 1943. In the background is the jagged ridge of the hill at Caldon, indicating the extent of the extraction that had taken place since these quarries opened in 1905-06. *Jim Plant*

Caldon Low Halt, looking down the gradient towards Waterhouses in the 1930s, opened in June 1905 and featured in the opening time table. It was built to serve quarry workers and villagers in Caldon, and passengers could join or alight on request. The halt's only building was a Third Class passenger carriage body, installed at the rear of the wooden platform. The tall elegant NSR distant signal dominates the halt. *Jim Plant*

Waterhouses station on 9th September 1933, looking east towards Ashbourne. The rear of the narrow gauge Leek & Manifold Railway's wooden waiting shelter is in the left foreground, with the standard gauge track of the Leek & Waterhouses Branch running across the foreground to the right. Beside the shelter, and to the rear of the station's starting signal is the sloping ramp connecting the two platforms, which were at different levels. On the Waterhouses platform next to the station building is an old carriage body that served as a lamp room and cycle store, with the gentlemen's toilets at the far end. Adjacent to the occupation crossing, the gradient board marking the end of the 1 in 40 descent from Caldon Junction and the short section of 1 in 260 through the station can be made out. In the right background is the distinctive long face of Brown End Quarry. *S.H.P. Higgins, courtesy of the National Railway Museum*

Right: An unidentified Stanier 2-6-2T, with a strengthened train, approaches the rear of the waiting shelter on the narrow gauge side of Waterhouses station as it nears the bottom of the steep $^3/_4$ mile of 1 in 40 gradient from Caldon Junction in the summer of 1935. This is a rare photograph of this class of locomotive working on the branch, as they had only arrived at the former NSR sheds in the spring of 1935 and the line to Waterhouses was closed in September of that year. An LM&SR bridge plate is just visible on the left. *Jim Plant*

Above: The following sequence of photographs, all taken at Waterhouses, illustrate the different motive power used on the branch. As the older and smaller ex-NSR locomotives were withdrawn from service, they were replaced by heavier former NSR types, often still relatively young. The usual passenger loading was one 8-wheeled coach, to which was often added goods traffic to form a mixed train. Former 'D' Class 0-6-0T No. 153, now as LM&SR No. 1598, with the 2.50pm Wednesdays and Saturdays only working to Leek on 11th July 1928. The train has been strengthened to four coaches and note the reporting number on the buffer beam. The forty-nine members of the 'D' Class, built between 1883 and 1899, comprised the largest NSR class. No. 1598 was the last to be built and was withdrawn from service in November 1929. *W Potter*

Left: Another 'D' Class, No. 150 as LM&SR No. 1595, on a mixed train for Leek on 24th September 1930. Behind the L&NER van are two NSR 6-wheeled coaches. No. 1595 was built in 1897 and withdrawn in March 1932. *Dr Jack Hollick*

Left: Former 'New C' Class 0-6-4T No. 173, now LM&SR No. 2044, with a goods train including an LM&SR van. Built in 1913, the engine was withdrawn from service in March 1936. *Author's collection*

Below: On 29th April 1933, former 'New L' Class No. 69, now as LM&SR No. 2257, waits to depart with a three coach train. The station nameboard dated from the opening in 1905 and read 'WATERHOUSES CHANGE FOR FROGHALL QUARRY'. Strictly, this was incorrect on two counts, firstly, it was Caldon Quarry and secondly, Caldon Low Halt was the closest passenger stop for the quarry. No. 2257 was built in 1913 and was sold to Lancashire Associated Collieries in May 1937, along with four others of the class, where it was named *King George VI*. They were stationed at Mosley Common Colliery (Boothstown), Walkden Yard or Sandholes Colliery (Walkden); on working days, they were employed at Mosley Common or Sandholes, returning to Walkden Yard each night. No. 2257 finally ceased service in 1966. *H.C. Casserley*

Right: LM&SR No. 2053 was former NSR 'F' Class 0-6-4T No. 119. It is seen here, at the head of a more usual one-coach train, also on 29th April 1933 and appearing to need banking assistance up the 1 in 40 climb to Caldon Junction. The reason for this unusual combination is unknown but it was a far cry from this particular locomotive's work in the pre-Grouping era, when it was often rostered to haul the 12.05pm L&NWR London express from Manchester (London Road) as far as Stoke. Built in 1918 and one of a batch of eight locomotives whose building was delayed because of the war-time shortage of materials, it was withdrawn from service in April 1935. It is carrying shed plate No. 40 beneath its rather bent smokebox door handrail. *H.C. Casserley*

Should tentative plans by the Moorland & City Railways and Churnet Valley Railway project ever come to fruition, the largely vacant old station site at Waterhouses could once again become the terminus of the line running up on to the moors from Leekbrook Junction and scenes such as this could once more be a reality. In September 1933, former NSR 'C' Class 0-6-4T No. 53, now renumbered as LM&SR No. 2042, stands at the platform at the head of a train for Leek. The three immaculate looking coaches are not, as they appear at first glance, a set. Leading is an L&NWR 57ft five-compartment non-corridor Brake Third to Diagram 333, seating 60 passengers and the last design of L&NWR non corridor stock built before the Grouping. Although a neat match with the other two carriages, the underframes and other features reveal these to be early LM&SR standard non-corridor designs, built in large quantities in the late 1920s at Wolverton, Derby and Newton Heath. In the middle is a 57ft nine-compartment Composite to Diagram 1701, seating 24 First Class and a total of 72 Third Class in the three at each end. Last comes a 57ft six-compartment Brake Third to Diagram 1703 seating 72. One of the original buildings survives in use here by a cycle hire shop, at the start of the Manifold Trail. *S.H.P. Higgins*

Above: Waterhouses station on 28th July 1940, nearly five years after the withdrawal of passenger services but before its final closure for goods traffic in March 1943. The main station building stands on the single platform that was provided here in the centre, with the run round loop on the right. The buffer stops can be seen in the background and the NSR Down starter signal is partially in view behind the waiting shelter in the left foreground, which served the Manifold line and is still in excellent condition over six years after the complete closure of that route. *Neville Fields*

Below: Waterhouses station in June 1941, starting to look rather neglected and much the worse for wear. The Manifold waiting shelter has now gone and the narrow gauge trackbed, in the foreground, is overgrown with weeds. *John Marshall*

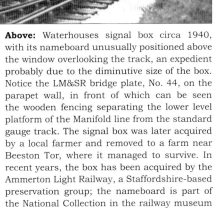

Above: Waterhouses signal box circa 1940, with its nameboard unusually positioned above the window overlooking the track, an expedient probably due to the diminutive size of the box. Notice the LM&SR bridge plate, No. 44, on the parapet wall, in front of which can be seen the wooden fencing separating the lower level platform of the Manifold line from the standard gauge track. The signal box was later acquired by a local farmer and removed to a farm near Beeston Tor, where it managed to survive. In recent years, the box has been acquired by the Ammerton Light Railway, a Staffordshire-based preservation group; the nameboard is part of the National Collection in the railway museum at York. *Author's collection*

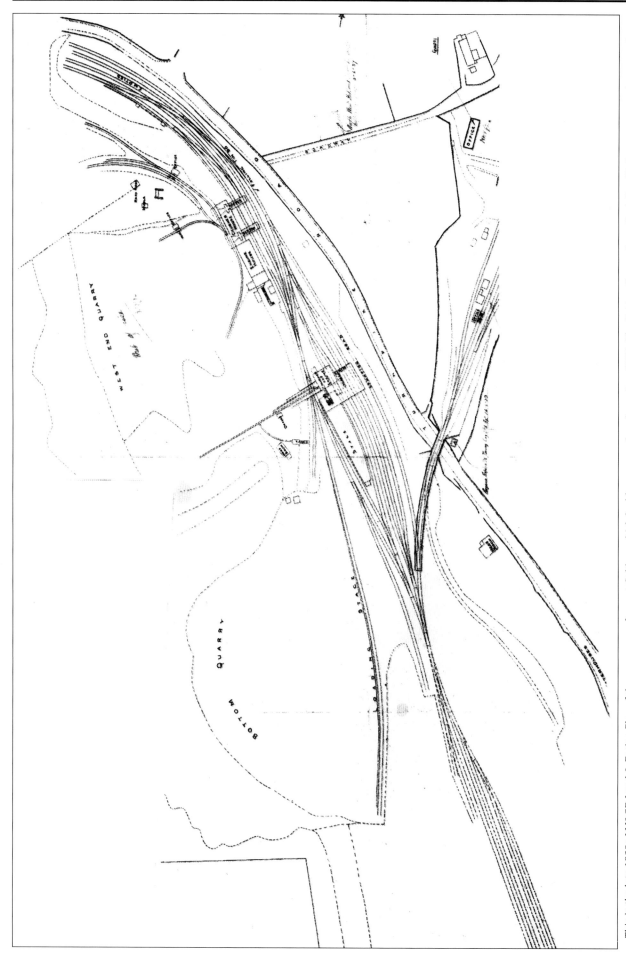

This is the late 1920s LM&SR Land & Rating Plan of the new quarry faces at Caldon, which had been opened up from circa 1906. The Bottom Quarry is on the left, with its mess room, chute, crusher and engine, and two screens. The West End Quarry is on the right and the plan shows an engine house, crusher house, weighing machine, and two screens. The plan here has a note appended to it, indicating that this quarry was taken out of use on 31st March 1932. This will only have been a temporary cessation, however, because of the economic depression. The tender documents issued in the following year offered a lease for working both quarries. Note the 1 in 80 falling gradient. The Bottom Quarry was served by a narrow gauge railway line from a higher level, whilst the West End Quarry was served by a winch-operated cable railway. Sadly the other two notes that can be seen, right and bottom, containing the dates in 3rd June 1937 and 16th June 1939 respectively, cannot be otherwise deciphered on this copy of the plan. *Cheddleton Railway Archive*

The Limestone Quarries of Caldon Low

The limestone quarries of Caldon Low are located in the bleak landscape of the Staffordshire Moorlands, 1,100 feet above sea level. Following an agreement with four local landowners and four lessees of land, the Trent & Mersey Canal were granted a 999-year lease to work the quarries on payment of a royalty. There was a distance of approximately $3^1/_4$ miles between the quarries and the terminus of the 1778 Caldon Canal, which was 670 feet lower.

In order to connect the quarries with the Caldon Canal, the T&M built a succession of plateways or tramways. The first was a wooden wagonway in 1778; next, in 1785, this route was realigned and rebuilt using cast iron rails on wooden baulks; then, in 1804, a double track plateway, laid on stone blocks, with four self-acting inclines was built; finally, in 1847, a 3ft 6ins gauge single track railway was laid, divided into four self-acting inclines and gravity worked. The development of the tramway systems reflected not only the wish to introduce the changing technology but also the need to have a transportation system capable of moving the substantial increases in tonnage quarried. All four of these systems entered the quarries (known as the Old Quarries, Nick and Dunkirk) at the same point, adjacent to the Stoke to Ashbourne Road. Improved quarrying practice was introduced following the employment of a small number of Welshmen from Anglesey from the mid-1850s onwards, and they held down all the senior managerial and administrative posts, and the skilled mining posts, until the 1930s.

Quarry output reflected some of these changes: 1794 – 48,220 tons; 1817 – 59,112 tons; 1849 – 104,028 tons; 1864 – 186,334 tons; 1883 – 231,382 tons (possibly the year of peak use of the tramways); 1891 – 192,262 tons. The Old Quarries progressively became worked out and the NSR, to whom the leased passed on

An aerial view of the new quarries looking towards Waterhouses, taken in June 1938. The line from Caldon Junction comes in on the left (centre) to provide a headshunt into the works. The square building is the original 'Knotty' crusher, installed in 1915 and taken out of use circa 1937; to the left is the tar plant, installed in 1936-37 to replace an earlier plant. Next come the engine room and screening plant, installed by the NSR in 1914. The first sidings put in were nearest to the line from Caldon Junction; additional sidings were added circa 1915 and these can be seen bottom right, just above which is the Swynnnerton chute. Also visible, centre right, are various incline railways that were internal to the quarry site, the most visible of which had become derelict by the early 1930s. On the right of the picture, leading up to the quarry faces, are 2ft 6ins gauge tramroads on which ran tipping wagons or 'jummers', each with a capacity of two tons. This system fed materials to the standard gauge sidings at two levels, the upper tracks from the main quarry face (to the right of the photograph) terminating alongside the crusher. An incline with a power operated winch enabled the jummers to be transferred between the two levels when required. The face of Nick Quarry can be seen (top right) as its contours come round in an arc from the old quarry; beneath it was what was known as 'The Ledge' and beneath that was Bottom Quarry. Far right is the section of the quarry known as the West End and below that can just be seen the incline from Nick and Dunkirk quarries, redundant after 1931. Wagons were let down this incline by a windlass, thereby providing an outlet for the limestone after the 1847 incline railway closed in March 1920. *Manifold collection*

its acquisition of the T&M in 1847, opened a new quarry face about half a mile to the east, from 1905, called the West End and Bottom Quarries, which were connected to the Caldon section of the Leek, Caldon & Waterhouses Railway. Output, subsequently, was from both quarries until December 1931, though traffic down the incline tramway to Froghall ceased in March 1920.

As regards the long lease on the quarries that the NSR had inherited from the T&M in 1847, this in turn was passed on to the LM&SR. However, the older Dunkirk and Nick quarries adjacent to the A52 trunk road from Stoke to Ashbourne were becoming run down and a report in October 1922 indicated that '*the P. Way is in a very bad condition, the engine rolls and jumps in a frightful manner.*'.

The top of the standard gauge incline railway that led from the new (1909) quarry faces to the NSR stone crushers, on 28th June 1933. *H.C. Casserley*

Caldon West End and Bottom Quarries

The 1905 mineral line into the (new) West End and Bottom quarries started to yield limestone in 1909, with the first dedicated train for limestone running in December of that year, shortly after the installation of a new crusher and sidings. Over the next few years there was further investment in the new quarry face, this coinciding with the progressive run down of the Dunkirk and Nick quarries about half a mile away alongside the Stoke to Ashbourne Road.

The LM&SR, in its early assessment of the future of the quarries, was projecting a probable output of 250,000 tons per annum, of which 150,000 tons would be needed for the chemical, iron and steel industries, with 100,000 tons for railway ballast; the quarries were the only ones operated by the LM&SR. Although the NSR had considered the possibility of limestone burning and crushing at Caldon Low, this had always been rejected in favour of the facilities at the foot of the incline railway at Froghall. Very early on in the LM&SR era, in 1925, a proposal had been received from the Carbo-Lime Company at a time when the LM&SR was considering an increase in the output and the policy of the general development of the quarries. The proposal was for the company to obtain limestone for crushing into carbo-lime; the limestone used would be the small chippings initially being crushed in the 1915 'Knotty crusher' in the new quarries. This project would have been beneficial to the LM&SR but unfortunately it was not proceeded with.

In the late 1920s, the mining operations here were hit with both the economic depression and the exhaustion of reserves at the

Top quarries, and these factors led to a rundown of activities. The Dunkirk and Nick quarries were closed at the end of December 1931 and the Caldon locomotive shed officially closed on 1st January 1932; the locomotives were cut up on site in 1936. Personnel records from 1st January 1931 to December 1934, show the rundown of employees, something which had actually commenced before 1931. Against a normal complement of 243, the numbers at January 1931 were 214; January 1932 – 205; May 1932 – 41; October 1933 – 40; finally, the remainder of the employees were discharged on 1st December 1934.

The following table details output and profitability in the LM&SR era:

Year	Output Tons	Revenue £	Expenditure £	Net Revenue £
1923		45,728	42,125	3,603
1925		37,215	34,960	2,255
1926	165,201			
1927	168,500			3,304
1928	150,761			1,366
1929	165,000			
1934	37,571			
1938	188,206			

In the early 1930s, the LM&SR decided to reassess the merits of their '*engaging in the extraneous business of operating a quarry*';

under the 1841 Agreement by the T&M Canal with local landowners, a royalty payment per ton of 2d (5s 6p) was to be paid. The NSR had, since 1866, operated the quarries itself, with all the key posts being occupied by Welsh miners from Anglesey and their descendants; this practice continued until the LM&SR ceased to operate the quarries in 1934. Therefore, the LM&SR sought, against the background of a substantial falling off in contracts for the supply of limestone to outside customers, to transfer the lease and the responsibility for working the quarries to another party. It was agreed in December 1933 to advertise in the press for tenders for the lease and for the right to work the faces, known as the Bottom and West End quarries that had been producing stone since

MONDAY NOVEMBER 13 1933

CONTRACTS AND TENDERS

4 lines 20s. (minimum)

THE LONDON MIDLAND and SCOTTISH RAILWAY COMPANY INVITE TENDERS for a LEASE of the QUARRYING RIGHTS in the BOTTOM and WEST END LIMESTONE QUARRIES at CALDON LOW in the COUNTY of STAFFORD. Tender forms, plan and conditions of Lease can be obtained on application to Mr. W. H. C. Clay, Chief Estate Manager, Euston Station, London, and all tenders must be delivered to the Secretary of the Company not later than 12 noon on the 30th November, 1933. The Company do not bind themselves to accept the highest or any tender.

1909, the Top quarries having already closed. The lease was for a fourteen year period to December 1947, with a guaranteed output of 85,000 tons per annum, with the output to be consigned by LM&SR routes where possible; the lessees were also to supply the railway company with any quantity of ballast, limestone chippings and lump stone to the maximum requirements of 80,000, 1,000 and 1,000 tons respectively, to be paid by the LM&SR at certain specified prices, with them further guaranteeing to take a minimum quantity of 40,000 tons per annum.

The tender from John Hadfield & Sons Ltd was accepted. The payment was to be 1s $0^1/_4$d (5p) for the first 85,000 tons per annum, 6d (2.5p) per ton on private sales and 1s $0^1/_4$d for sales to the LM&SR. This was estimated to yield an annual rent of £4,338, with the LM&SR continuing to remain responsible for the 2d per ton royalty on all stone sold or taken away under the 1841 Act.

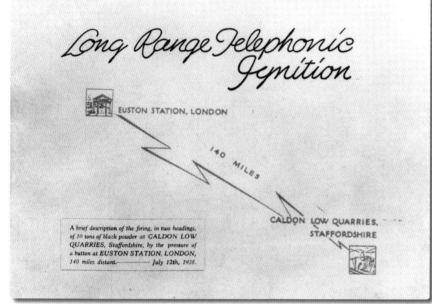

Above: The advertisement that appeared in *The Times* of 13th November 1933, inviting tenders for the lease of the quarrying rights in the Bottom and West End limestone quarries at Caldon Low. *National Archives*

Left: A major blast at the new quarries took place on 12th July 1938 when Lord Stamp, Chairman of the LM&SR, pressed an ignition button at Euston and activated the detonation of part of the limestone hill at Caldon 140 miles away. Some 100,000 tons of limestone were blown up in this way. Such was the novelty in the way the blast was ignited that a commemorative booklet was published recording the event, of which this is the front cover.

Below Left: Taken from the booklet, this is a view of the quarry face following the explosion.

Below Right: Sir Francis Joseph (in helmet), an LM&SR Director, and W.H. Hamlyn, the LM&SR Architect, select a 25-ton block intended to be used as the foundation stone for the new Euston station. *Manifold collection*

Right: The explosion was national news, as this extract from the *Daily Express* of 13th July 1938 shows. *Manifold collection*

In February 1936, Hadfield (Hope & Caldon Low Quarries) Ltd sought an extension to the existing lease (which was granted), so as to convert it into a twenty-five year lease expiring on 25th December 1959. In support of the request, Hadfields stated that £9,500 had been spent in installing new plant and machinery, and the company expected by December 1936 to have spent £20,000, with output anticipated to be 200,000 tons per annum; it was clear that the LM&SR would benefit from increased royalties and freight charges. Around this time, Hadfield established Derbyshire Stone Ltd, an amalgamation of its Derbyshire and Staffordshire quarrying interests.

Hadfields seemed happy with the terms of the lease and during the Second World War supplied stone to the munitions industry; at the west of the quarry a chute was installed, known as the 'Swynnerton chute' (named after the munitions factory near Stone), for ease of loading.

In 1947, Hadfields indicated that they wished to increase output from these quarries and to modernise and extend its plant. Inevitably, the company was seeking security of tenure, given that its existing lease was due to expire on 25th December 1959; as the LM&SR had a surface lease expiring in 1990, it was agreed to grant a new lease to expire on 29th September 1990.

The LM&SR also inherited from the NSR two other assets at Caldon Low. First was the provision of water supply that served its quarries and the sixty-eight cottages it acquired from the NSR. These assets (reservoir, pumping station and pipe lines) became no longer an economic proposition after the Top quarries were closed and so were sold to the Cheadle Rural District Council in 1936 for £140. Hadfields undertook to maintain existing obligations. Secondly, July 1947 saw the sale for £3,000 of the Yew Tree Inn, an ancient pub directly facing the Bottom Quarry, to Ind Coope & Allsopp. The NSR, in almost its last act, had acquired the pub in December 1922 but it never featured in the list of hotels owned and promoted by the LM&SR. Its acquisition seemed to fit in to the strategy at the time of acquiring land and property around the quarries as and when they became available, a policy not continued by the LM&SR, who sold off local property which it considered surplus to its requirements.

The number of daily mineral trains fluctuated over the years, according to the level of demand for limestone. In December 1922, there were three, by 1927 there were four and, at the time of Nationalisation in 1948, there were two, one morning and one afternoon. At this time, wagons left the sidings marshalled in order of destination and the trains were split up at Leek Brook Junction; the afternoon train ran through on the Leek Line to Grange Sidings, Etruria, with wagons for the Shelton Iron, Steel & Coal Company's works.

This view was taken from 'The Ledge' some time after the major explosion in 1938, showing the 'jummers' being loaded right up against the quarry face. Visible are thirty roads of 2 foot gauge track, the normal arrangement being two roads off one turnout, from the main feeder line, on which a train of up to fifty jummers would be assembled by one of two Ruston & Hornsby diesel locomotives (arrived autumn 1936) and worked forward to be tippled into the crushers and hoppers. In the background is Derbyshire Stone's new tarmac plant, the old 'Knotty' crusher, and the rail line to Caldon Junction. *Tarmac archives*

Above: West End Quarry at Caldon in 1941, following Hadfield's modernisation and expansion of operations here. From left to right the principal buildings are the tar plant, engine house, the crushing plant and hoppers. *Tarmac archives*

Right: A photograph taken in West End Quarry in the late 1930s, with former NSR and LM&SR quarrymen, now employed by Hadfield's, posed in front of the quarry face. Following the rundown and closure of the Top quarries between 1932 and 1934, 85 per cent of the workforce were made redundant; some returned to North Wales, some travelled to the quarries in the Buxton area and others went to work in the mills in Leek. From left to right are Billy Lees, Ned Harrison, George Ratcliffe, Bill Davies, ?, Percy Allcock, Roland Jones, ?. *Phillips family collection*

Below: LM&SR stamp, Caldon Low Goods Department. There was trade in agricultural products and coal at Caldon. *Author's collection*

Above: A view of Froghall above the basin in 1935, with the track of the incline coming up from the wharf in the right foreground to run between the stones which formed the bed plates of the winding drum. The wharf manager's house is on the left, in front of which is the weighbridge hut. On the right are the wharf houses; behind them was the smithy and beyond that, and climbing sharply, ran the 1804 incline tramway. *Author's collection*

Left: The route of the 1847 railway, worked by cable, is seen here in 1935, passing under the main Stoke to Ashbourne road. The water tank on the right can still be seen today. *Author's collection*

Below Left: The brakesman's cottage, situated at the top of the Cotton Plane, at the summit of the 1804 plateway, is seen here circa 1970, with its trackbed still visible in the foreground, before it merges a few hundred yards further along with the 1785 wagonway and then enters the quarries. The cottage dates back to 1804. *Goldstraw family collection*

Below Right: An aerial view of the Top Quarries taken in the 1970s, looking east. The photograph is a time warp of the condition of these quarries after the LM&SR abandoned them at the end of 1931, as they became worked out. Note the routes of the numerous tramways running right to the face of the quarries; at the face, the dynamited stone would be broken up (the larger rocks by being dynamited again) into somewhat smaller pieces of limestone that were more easily handled. It was then transported in horse-hauled narrow gauge wagons, to be assembled at the top of the incline by the quarry locomotives. *Tarmac Archives*

Right: An illustration of the bleak Moorlands landscape at Caldon Low in September 1954, with the worked quarries and the former reservoir in the background. On the left of the picture is the cutting in which both the 1785 wagonway and the 1804 plateway ran, before passing to the left of the 1832 cottages built by the T&M Canal. This row was known as Newhouses, to the left of which are the 1873 row of cottages known as Bangor Houses or Bangor Terrace, named after the part of North Wales where many of the quarrymen came from. *Manifold collection*

Left: The Calvinist Methodist chapel at Caldon Low was built in 1878-79 with the financial support of the Flintshire Presbyterian Church and the NSR. It was sold in 1938 to the Cheadle Methodist Circuit, with the LM&SR donating the land on which the chapel was built. In the right background part of Bangor Terrace can just be seen. *Author's collection*

Left: Toad was one of three 0-4-0 saddle tanks used at the quarries. Built by Henry Hughes of Loughborough in 1877, it was photographed outside the engine shed at Caldon Low on 30th September 1923, soon after coming in to LM&SR ownership. Hughes' worksplate is visible on the cab side and the company supplied a second very similar locomotive to the quarries, named *Frog*. After the quarries closed, both locomotives were offered for sale but were apparently only of interest to the scrapmen; they were scrapped on site in May 1936. *W.H. Whitworth*

Left: The 0-4-0ST *Bobs* awaiting its turn to shunt wagons at Caldon Low in 1924, between the quarry face and the marshalling yard near the winding drum at the top of the incline. This was the last of the three locomotives acquired by the NSR for the quarries, in this case from W.G. Bagnall Ltd of Stafford, in 1901. It was reboilered in 1923 and, having been unsuccessfully offered for sale in December 1935, it was also scrapped on site in May 1936. Note the spoil from the quarry workings in the background. *W.H. Whitworth*

Above: Arthur Richardson was one of nine horse drivers working in the quarries. He joined the workforce at Dunkirk Quarry in 1923 and was one of 162 quarrymen dismissed early in 1932, after the Top Quarries had been exhausted. He later rejoined Hadfields, again as a horse driver. He is seen here at Dunkirk in the late 1920s in front of a workmen's croft, with a 6-ton load in a 3ft 6ins gauge side-tipping wagon. *Thacker family collection*

Right: A view of the 1847 railway as it crossed the Stoke to Ashbourne Road (just visible in the centre) at Caldon Low on 1st October 1936; there was an ungated level crossing at this point that was worked by flags, the limestone trains running over it to the top of the incline. The 1877 engine shed can be seen on the left, with the extension to accommodate *Bobs* jutting out. Behind the shed are the stables, part of a workshops complex that dated back to the time when the 1804 plateway was built. By 1936, the railway connection to the engine shed had been lifted, with only the rutted track bed left. *Manifold collection*

Right: The gunpowder magazine at the Old Quarries in 1938. It was located in an isolated spot and connected to the quarry railway system but in order to avoid any sparks from friction on the iron rails, wooden rails led up to the magazine. *Manifold collection*

Above: In the first of two further views which again illustrate the bleak Moorlands landscape at Caldon Low, both taken on 21st May 1936, the workshops and gated yard are seen on the left, with the former engine shed in the centre. The line from the old quarries appears centre bottom, while a row of now redundant tippler wagons awaits destruction.

Below: A close up view of the former engine shed, in front and to the right of which are derelict tippler wagons. Part of the workshops can be seen on the left. *Both W.A. Camwell*

Waterhouses on 9th September 1933, looking towards Leek, with the standard gauge line climbing steeply away on the left. In the foreground is the station home signal and the wooden platelayers' cabin, with five bull head rails stored on skids alongside. Siding No. 1, alongside the main line, served both the wooden goods shed (transferred from Fenton station in the autumn of 1905) and the gravelled access road from the rear of the Crown Inn in the village; behind the goods shed is a Manifold low-sided wagon in the headshunt and the NSR station master's house. Sidings to the right of the goods shed are, respectively, 'Empties No. 2': 'Loads No. 3' and 'Loads No. 4'; the covered goods van and a transporter car are on the narrow gauge line butting up to it. Adjacent is the narrow gauge running line ('No. 5) and, beside it, the loop ('No. 6), which joined to form a long headshunt. Between 'Empties No. 2' and Loads No. 3' was a capstan, provided in the 1920s, that enabled a Manifold locomotive to rope-pull a loaded 6-wheeled milk van from a transporter on to the standard gauge siding. *S.H.P. Higgins, courtesy National Railway Museum*

14

The Leek & Manifold Valley Light Railway

The Leek & Manifold Valley Light Railway was promoted by local worthies under the 1896 Light Railway Act and was engineered to lower operating standards by that Act. It attracted a large number of local shareholders and received financial backing from the Treasury and Staffordshire County Council. The narrow, 2 foot 6 inch gauge, line connected scattered villages in north east Staffordshire along the narrow, twisting valleys of the rivers Hamps and Manifold, and met with the standard gauge line, promoted by the NSR at the same time from Leek Brook to Waterhouses and, more importantly, to the limestone quarries of Caldon Low. The NSR operated the rolling stock, ran the services, and employed drivers and firemen, and the permanent way gang, passing over 55 per cent of the gross receipts to the Manifold Company.

The line, whilst popular in its early years, never attracted sufficient passenger and freight traffic to trade at a profit, yet alone pay any dividends to shareholders. Whilst substantial volumes of milk were carried a few miles to Waterhouses for transfer initially to the NSR network, for onward movement to London and Manchester, very little other merchandise was carried.

The Manifold line was swept along with the proposals for Grouping. The issue in 1922 for the L&NWR (by then the predecessors of the LM&SR) was whether to acquire the Manifold line direct, or whether to let the NSR make the acquisition. The bleak financial situation was reflected in the Manifold Company's Balance Sheet as at 31st December

1922, with accumulated liabilities of £50,157 and an accumulated revenue deficit of £15,294. The NSR did offer, on 8th March 1922, to purchase the line free from all liabilities for £15,000. Discussions continued for some months but proved to be unsuccessful, the Manifold Directors having a much exaggerated assessment of the worth of their undertaking. When the NSR met the LM&SR on 22nd January 1923, the LM&SR were of the mind that the line should be closed there and then, and could see no justification for paying any more than the £15,000 offered earlier by the NSR.

The Manifold Directors submitted a claim for £80,000-£100,000 to the Railways Amalgamation Tribunal on 27th March 1923, in respect of a line that Barnwell (the NSR General Manager) described as *'a millstone round the neck of the North Staffordshire Company and would never be a paying proposition'*. The LM&SR rejected the claim, and discussions and negotiations continued, mainly about the amounts to be repaid in respect of the loans to the County Council and to the Treasury, for a further twelve months – a full year after the LM&SR had agreed compensation with the eight constituent companies and twenty-seven subsidiary companies. The final compensation agreed by the Tribunal on 29th June 1924 for all claimants was £29,969 and all sums were included in the London Midland & Scottish Railway (Leek & Manifold Valley Light Railway) Absorption Scheme, 1924. This was the fragile background to the Manifold line's life in the LM&SR era, a life that ended in 1934.

The line had been given a boost with the opening in Ecton in 1908 of a creamery, owned by F.W. Gilbert Ltd. This attracted local milk to the creamery, which was then sent from there to Uttoxeter and further afield. The creamery was owned by the United Dairies group who had acquired it from Gilbert in 1915 and, from 1929, there was the introduction of 2,000 gallon capacity glass-lined tanks for the conveyance of milk by rail. After the creamery closed in September 1932, a victim

Above: A set of fourteen specimen tickets were printed by the LM&SR for use on the Manifold line but were in fact never issued. These are examples of five of them. *Author's collection*

Right: Waterhouses goods yard in the summer of 1936, after closure of the line, looking towards Caldon Junction. In the centre, a transporter car and one of the two low sided wagons stand on the narrow gauge line that abuts the end of the standard gauge 'Loads No. 3' siding, in the distance behind which are three carriages. To the right of the transporters is the covered van and on the far right the sheeted up narrow gauge locomotive, *E.R. Calthrop*. In the foreground is the rodding for the home signal. *Author's collection*

Left: *E.R. Calthrop* at the head of a single coach train, a Brake Composite, at Waterhouses in the early 1930s; the view is looking towards Caldon Junction. By this time, traffic was very light and only justified a single coach – passenger revenue in 1931 was only £554. The eight mile journey to Hulme End had eight stops; in 1924, the journey time took 40 minutes, in 1930, 50 minutes and, in 1934, 53-60 minutes. The gate to the signal box can be seen on the left and the Leek to Ashbourne Road is on the right. *Author's collection*

Below: *J.B. Earle* in the 1930 LM&SR black livery at Waterhouses in 1933. Clearly visible is the line of snap head rivets securing the new smoke box fitted in 1930. This is a good close-up of the highly ornate gates and balcony of the Third Class open carriage, also in black livery, and the small steps up from the platform. In the background is the NSR signal giving the right of way to Ashbourne Road level crossing and to Sparrowlee, the first station up the line. *Author's collection*

of the concentration of manufacturing facilities in larger units, the LM&SR decided that there was no justification to retain the Manifold line for the remaining traffic – the few passengers carried and the ability to transfer the small amount of freight traffic to Ashbourne and Hartington. The losses in preceding years were: 1929 – £3,449; 1930 – £3,805; 1931 – £3,493. The LM&SR put the case for closure to the Ministry of Transport and, once this was accepted, the formal abandonment of the railway was included in the London, Midland & Scottish Railway Bill, 1933. The line continued in operation through the winter of 1933, closing on 10th

March 1934. In the meantime, the fight was joined as to the after-use of the route. The North Staffordshire Ramblers Association sought, in 1933, to have the line retained as a footpath within a new national park embracing the Dovedale and Manifold valleys. The controversy over footpath versus roadway continued until the autumn of 1936, when the LM&SR gifted the track bed to the County Council and paid for the construction of a footpath; the formal opening occurred on 20th July 1937. Subsequently, in 1939, Staffordshire County Council obtained an Order preventing the use of the track bed as a roadway.

Two views of Waterhouses station, after the line's closure in March 1934, both looking towards Caldon Junction. In the first picture, **Left**, vegetation and the crumbling platform edge can be seen in the left distance but the running line and the run round loop, originally put in for the temporary 1904-05 station, are still in place. High on the left is the toilet on the standard gauge platform, the back of a carriage body (that served as a lamp room and cycle store) and then the rear of the standard gauge station building. The second picture, **Right**, is later, possibly in the summer of 1937, after the rails had been taken up. Prominent is the narrow gauge line waiting shelter, still in situ, which survived for a while but was demolished by the summer of 1941. By this time, the NSR signal on the Manifold line had been removed but that on the standard gauge line was still in use. *Both Author's collection*

Above: A 1920s postcard view of Waterhouses village, with the station master's house featuring prominently on the right. It was distinctive in being a brick building, surrounded by a large number of stone cottages. The view was taken from the top of the embankment of the standard gauge line and the station master served both stations. The house still survives and the Crown Hotel on the left is still open for business. *Author's collection*

Right: The level crossing gates protecting the Ashbourne Road, circa 1934, with Waterhouses station off picture to the right. The crossing was located a little more than a quarter of a mile from Waterhouses signal box. To this point, the line had descended on gradients of 1 in 60 and 1 in 41, before crossing the road on to a more favourable gradient of 1 in 144. The gates were worked by Waterhouses station staff, this crossing being the only one on the Manifold line that had gates. The original of this picture is again a tinted lantern slide and is reproduced in colour on the rear cover. *Author's collection*

The L&MVLR had distinctive rolling stock and these two pictures, taken in the LM&SR era on 28th June 1933, attempt to capture the flavour of this. The carriages were built by the Electric Railway & Tramway Carriage Works Ltd of Preston. This is Brake Composite No. 14989 in LM&SR livery. Access to the First Class compartment was by the end balcony on the left, with the guard's compartment at the other end. The carriage had eight First Class and twenty Third Class seats. *H.C. Casserley*

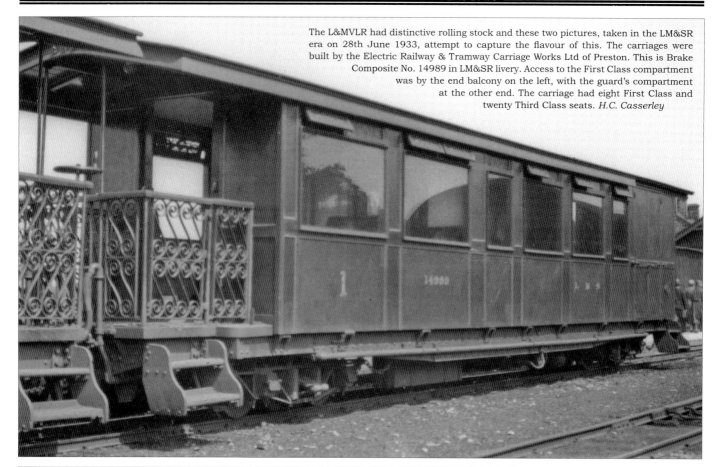

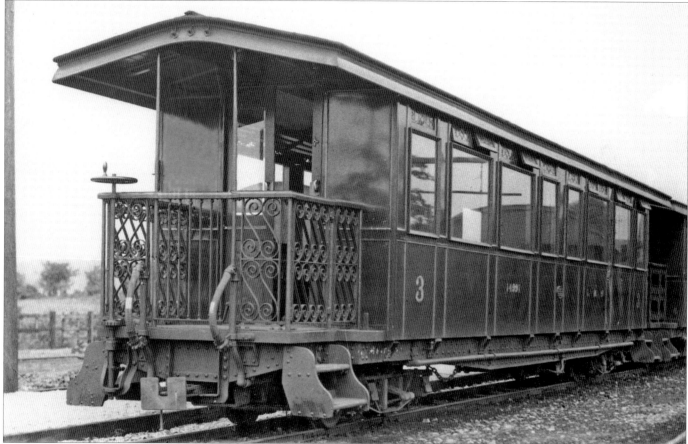

Third Class Open Brake carriage, with 40 seats and carrying LM&SR No. 14991. This view shows off the balcony to good effect, with the brake clearly visible on the left; note that the balcony was narrower than the main carriage body, to allow for the passenger steps on both sides, which also indicate the very low nature of the Manifold line platforms. Both of these pictures were taken at Hulme End. *H.C. Casserley*

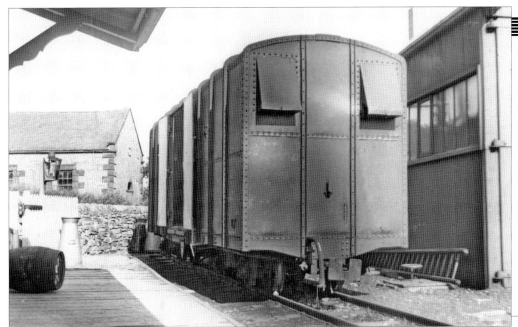

Left: The covered van in the head shunt at Hulme End. A one-off on the railway and numbered 3 in the L&MVLR stock list, it was virtually identical to a vehicle supplied by the Leeds Forge Co. to the Barsi Light Railway in India. On the platform are three milk churns, dropped off by one of the local farmers through the small wicket gate from the adjoining road, for onward delivery by railway via the L&MVLR and the Waterhouses Branch. At ground level, between the van and engine shed, is the control wheel for the headshunt water column. *Author's collection*

Right: The transporter cars were bogie vehicles designed to convey standard gauge wagons over the narrow gauge railway. Two, No's 4 and 5, were ordered from Craven's of Sheffield in 1903 and a further two, No's 6 and 7 in 1907. This is one of the later vehicles at Waterhouses in 1927. The view is looking towards Caldon Junction and shows a coal wagon owned by Nathaniel Attrill Ltd, colliery agents of Chesterfield, clamped on to the transporter car. A fifth, longer transporter car was also later added to the railway's meagre fleet of goods vehicles. *Dr. Jack Hollick*

Left: An LM&SR 12-ton mineral wagon loaded on to a transporter car at Hulme End on 24th June 1933. The wagon is still laden with coal so is presumably waiting to be unloaded here. The wheel securing clamp can be seen under the nearer axle and note, too, the hinged angles fitted after milk tanks were introduced at Ecton Creamery in 1929. *H.C. Casserley*

Right: Beeston Tor station in 1937, with the line curving to the left in the background as it heads towards Grindon. This is a view taken immediately before track lifting in March of that year and shows piles of limestone and barrels of tar that had been brought to site in order to construct the footpath after the track was lifted. Note the low platform, the original station name board and the carriage body supplied in 1907 to serve as a waiting room. Just visible on the far right is part of a small toilet at the edge of the field, which was provided when the line opened. *Author's collection*

Above: A postcard produced circa 1925 by the Alpha Publishing Co. Ltd, showing a train for Waterhouses approaching Thor's Cave. The first carriage is a Brake Third and the other two are composites. This card was colour printed but was based on an original photograph taken by Edwin Harrison of Newcastle, who was commissioned by the NSR to take photographs for use on its 'Official' postcards and in its 1908 guide *Picturesque Staffordshire*. The NSR devoted eight of its twenty-three sets of 'Officials' to the Manifold line but none after 1914 and this particular photograph appears in both sets 8 and 11. *Author's collection*

Above: Grindon station, probably in the late 1920s, looking towards Thor's Cave; this section of the line was very wooded, as the photograph shows. The line has descended from Waterhouses nearly 3³/₄ miles to Grindon and the remainder is a 4¹/₄ mile climb to Hulme End. The narrow gauge line in the background had a 25 yard standard gauge section for storing two wagons prior to loading on to a transporter. After closure, Grindon continued to be served by the LM&SR Country Services for goods, traffic being consigned to Waterhouses. *Author's collection*

Right: Redhurst Crossing on 24th June 1933, looking towards Waterhouses, with the milk churn loading stage in the background. This halt opened in 1915 and still has the original L&MVLR station nameboard, albeit the name had been changed from plain Redhurst on 2nd April 1923; trains stopped here by request. Again a carriage body served as a waiting shelter here. In the left background is an NSR Trespass notice. *H.C. Casserley*

Wetton station on 24th June 1933, looking towards Redhurst Crossing. The running line is on the right, in the centre is the passing loop and the line on the left was a siding with capacity at the end for a standard gauge wagon unloaded off a transporter. The platform was the longest on the line at 372 feet and 12 feet wide. The building, a chalet type waiting shelter, was the standard one for most stations on the line and was provided by the Portable Building Co. Ltd of Fleetwood at a cost of £40. The station nameboard, a replacement in the NSR era for the original, was to a standard NSR design. After closure, cartage under the LM&SR Country Services continued to be provided for Wetton, goods being consigned via Alsop-en-le-Dale. *H.C. Casserley*

J.B. Earle at the head of a Third Class and a Composite, all in LM&SR black, leaving Butterton on a Waterhouses train in the early 1930s. This station was second only to Hulme End for originating traffic. Note the substantially constructed bridge, typical of many on the line. *E.R. Morten*

Right: F. W. Gilbert Ltd became part of United Dairies in 1915 when it was based in Waterhouses and the transfer to Ecton, using some buildings that had been used by the copper works, enabled the operation to expand. However, later on, when it became clear that substantial costs would be involved in modernising and expanding the site, United Dairies closed the plant, in September 1932, although rail traffic from the creamery had ceased a short while earlier. From 1919 to 1926, the milk van from Ecton formed part of a milk train that ran via Waterhouses and Leek Brook to Finsbury Park in north London. Shunting at the creamery was by the train locomotive and up to 10 minutes was allowed for this purpose. This view shows more of the extensive scarring caused by a century of copper mining and smelting. *Author's collection*

Below: A panoramic view of Ecton Creamery, in the foreground, with the station in the centre distance, taken after 1918 and again showing the effects of the former copper mining operations. The creamery made use of the former Clockhouse smelter (centre) and the former South smelter (foreground). The private siding is clearly visible in the centre of the picture as it leaves the Manifold line and goes as far as the loading dock beside the former Clockhouse smelter. *Author's collection*

Below: A letter sent on 30th October 1923 from Uttoxeter Dairies (Wholesale) Ltd to its Ecton Dairies branch, advising of the need to send sixty churns of milk from Hulme End to Finsbury Park or Hornsey in London. *Author's collection*

UNITED DAIRIES (Wholesale) LTD.

BRANCH:

UTTOXETER, Staffs.

TELEGRAMS "CREAMERY, UTTOXETER."
TELEPHONE 43 UTTOXETER

October 30th 1923. 192

Mr. T. Dainton,
United Dairies (Who.) Ltd.,
Ecton.

Dear Tom,

Will you please see the Station master at Hulme End first thing on Wednesday morning and tell him that there will be 60 churns of milk to go from Hulme End to Welfords & Premier Dairies, Finsbury Park, or Hornsey, I do not quite know which station yet, but it will be one of the two, commencing November 1st. One load will arrive about 10 o'clock, or 10.30 a.m. and he will want help to unload it and put it somewhere in the shade. The driver will than go back again to Glutton Bridge and bring their milk in, which will get to Hulme End about one or two o'clock.

You had better arrange to stop there another day or two, after Miss Thomas comes back, so as to get these two factories into working order. It will be as well to go over and see them, and see the milk is all right when it comes in at each place, and all properly made up and labelled and everything in order, and see as to what time it may be worked.

You will also want to find some lodgings for the driver Stevenson, as I propose transferring the lorry from Waterhouses to Ecton altogether, as it will be as much as one lorry will do in the daylight in the winter, in that country.

I think we could manage to put it somewhere at Ecton, and the petrol and oil could be stored in the same way as it is at Waterhouses.

Please make all these arrangements and let me know that you have got it all in order when I arrive about 2 o'clock on Wednesday.

Yours faithfully,

John Dann

---

m r s rly Coy's boundary edged green.

L. & M.V. LINE. (2'6" Gauge.)

Ecton.

F.W. Gilbert Ltd Siding.

To Hulme End

River Manifold

Leek-Manifold Valley line

Ecton Station

Platform

110 yds to centre of Stn

7¼ miles.

From Butterton

Yds 23¾

— REFERENCE. —

F.W.Gilbert's siding colored. 237 yds maintained by Rly Co on own land at Traders cost. See agreement dated Aug 20th 1918 with F.W.Gilbert.

Above: The LM&SR Private Siding diagram of July 1929 covering the provision of F.W. Gilbert's siding and replacing an earlier agreement of 20th August 1918. The line to the creamery goes off to the left, beyond the LM&SR boundary. *Author's collection*

Left: Ecton Creamery sidings and milk loading dock, looking towards Butterton on 14th September 1930. In the left foreground is an NSR 6-wheeled milk van carried on the long transporter car, whilst beyond are two 4-wheeled United Dairies milk containers, carried on two of the short transporter cars. Behind are the slopes of the copper mines spoil tips and gleaming white in the right background are the buildings of Ecton Creamery, with the new siding entering the works. There was no standard gauge siding at the creamery and any wagons worked in had to remain on the transporter awaiting loading and subsequent collection. *Dr. Jack Hollick*

Right: Hulme End station on a busy day, with passengers queuing to have their tickets checked and the main building behind. Although the line was heavily promoted by the NSR, none of the LM&SR summer timetables advertised it at all. The two locomotives, *E.R. Calthrop* and *J.B. Earle*, are seen here back to back in the headshunt, the consequence of the former having been returned from Crewe Works in 1929 facing the wrong way, there being no turntable at either end of the Manifold line. Note the water pipe on the side of the timber engine shed on the right. *Author's collection*

Inset Below: An LM&SR Hulme End to Butterton ticket.
Inset Bottom: An LM&SR Hulme End to Waterhouses ticket. *Both author's collection*

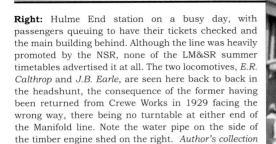

Above: A panoramic view of Hulme End station, representing its final layout. On the left is the five-lever ground frame that controlled the combined home and starting signal. Beyond the ground frame and the trespass notice is the wooden boarded urinal and enclosed earth closet. On the headshunt at the end is a wagon on a transporter, with on the right, the engine shed, store, coal stage and carriage shed. On the far right is a former L&NWR carriage body used as a platelayers' mess room and store. *Author's collection*

Left: A busy scene in the goods yard in the early 1930s. A 1907 transporter car sits in the narrow gauge portion of the platform siding with two lorries loading up on the hard standing between the standard gauge sections. At closure in 1934, there were two coal merchants trading from the station, Kirkland & Perkin and J.W. Bassett & Son, each of whom had small offices. After closure the LM&SR Country Services cartage arrangements continued to deliver to Hulme End and to Ecton, with goods consigned via Hartington.

Right: A snowy scene at Hulme End in February 1934, the month before closure. In front of the station building is a carriage body which was used as a bicycle store. *Author's collection*

Below: Another busy view of the yard in the early 1930s, with a Chatterley-Whitfield coal wagon and an LM&SR van on transporters, with another van on the standard gauge section. Two carriages sit at the platform, whilst the locomotive takes on coal and water prior to its next trip along the line. *Author's collection*

Insets Below: LM&SR tickets for trips from Hulme End to Redhurst Halt and Grindon. *Both author's collection.*

N.S.R.—THIRD CLASS.
HULME END to
REDHURST HALT
AVAILABLE FOR ONE JOURNEY ON DAY OF ISSUE
Turn over   Redhurst Halt 98   Fare 3d.
MY10 33   485

L. M. & S. R.
Issued subject to the conditions & regulations
in the Time Tables Books Bills Notices & in the
Railway Company's regulations relating to traffic
by Passenger Train or other similar service.
HULME END   TO
GRINDON
THIRD
CLASS]   2698 (S)   FARE -/7
GRINDON
784

Driver Harry Robinson on the footplate of *J.B. Earle* with a two coach train at Hulme End on 29th April 1933. On the right is the 1904 two-lane engine shed. Above it towers the water tank on its brick base, in front of which is the locomotive crane and the coal stage. Veering round to the right is the siding to the carriage shed, with the loading gauge provided to remind drivers that it had limited clearance for wagons on transporters. The nameboard indicates that the station also served the neighbouring villages of Sheen and Hartington. *H.C. Casserley*

Leek & Manifold Light Railway. 2'-6" Gauge.
(2 Engines.) 2'-6"Dia. Wheels Two 11½" x 16" Cyl⁵

B.P. 150 lbs

Total Water 600 Galls.
9'-6" Barrel
Coal 1 Ton.

Weight Light. With Water in Boiler
Weight in Working Order. 2-16 4-18 4-18 4-19 9-5 26-16
TOTAL 23-3

Left: The General Arrangement drawing, prepared by the LM&SR, for the Manifold locomotives, *E.R. Calthorp* and *J.B. Earle* – named after the railway's Engineer and Resident Engineer respectively. Such arrangement drawings or GAs were prepared by the LM&SR for all the NSR locomotives transferred over, the Manifold engines being treated as an NSR locomotive for this purpose. Incidentally, when they were built, they were the first locomotives of the 2-6-4 wheel arrangement to operate in Great Britain. *Author's collection*

Right: *E.R. Calthrop* wearing LM&SR livery at Hulme End on 15th September 1930. Behind, is part of the carriage shed (with the corrugated iron sides and roof), the water tower and, on the right, the store. In the foreground is a single lever ground frame. *D.S. Barrie*

Left: Following the closure of the NSR's Stoke Works by the LM&SR in 1927, Manifold locomotives were sent to Crewe Works for repair. *E.R. Calthrop* is seen here on a low loader, outside Crewe Works in the summer of 1929, before returning to the Manifold line. It is in the LM&SR crimson lake that both locomotives carried between 1923 and 1930. It is also still carrying its works plate, which was later replaced by an LM&SR transfer. In the left background is former L&YR 'N1' Class 4-6-0 No. 10468. *Whitworth collection, courtesy Neville Fields*

Right: *E.R. Calthrop* undergoing repairs inside the No. 9 Erecting Shop at Crewe Works in 1929. Everard Calthrop had previously engineered the Barsi Light Railway in India, hence the somewhat Colonial design of the two locomotives, including the two large front headlamps, which in reality were never used. *Author's collection*

PUBLIC NOTICE

Notice is hereby given that the
Manifold Valley Light Railway Section
of the Company's Line
WATERHOUSES to HULME END
will be CLOSED for the conveyance
of ALL classes of traffic on and from
MONDAY, MARCH 12th, 1934

BY ORDER.

District Goods and
    Passenger Manager's Office,
        Stoke-on-Trent.
March 1st, 1934.

The Company have excellent facilities for dealing
with PASSENGERS, GOODS and MINERALS
Traffic at the following Stations, covering the
WATERHOUSES to HULME END area:—

ALSOP-EN-LE-DALE   TISSINGTON
HARTINGTON   WATERHOUSES
IPSTONES   WINKHILL
THORPE CLOUD

(E.R.O. 55392.)

P.N. 117.   2,000 H.   Bemrose & Sons Ltd., Derby and London.

Above: The LM&SR Closure Notice for the line, dated 1st March 1934, to take place on 12th March. *Author's collection*

Top Right: On the first day of track lifting and construction of the footpath, the first demolition train prepares to leave Hulme End in February 1937. The picture shows rolls of netting being loaded in the background and the conveyor can be seen beyond. The netting was inserted between the limestone and the tarmac top surface. By this date, the watering facilities along the line were out of use, and a portable pump and motor was mounted on the front buffer beam of *E.R. Calthrop*, along with sandbags acting as counterweights. *Author's collection*

Above Right: These two snaps were taken by one of the workmen engaged on track lifting duties in the spring of 1937. Mechanical equipment was not used to dismantle the track, all the rails and sleepers being laboriously recovered by hand. Fork ended crowbars are here being used to lift the track and release sleepers for loading on to the demolition train, in the background. The rutted trackbed in the foreground will soon become a footpath, using the limestone chippings piled on the left. This photograph was taken in the Hamps Valley between Beeston Tor and Sparrowlee.

Right: The train carrying the lifted sleepers is seen working its way towards Waterhouses. *Both author's collection*

Left: The demolition train, headed by *E.R. Calthrop*, climbs the 1 in 60 section past the platform at Waterhouses on its way to the goods yard in May 1937, having left behind the 1 in 40 section at Ashbourne Road. This locomotive was cut up on site after dismantling of the line was completed. Note that the locomotive no longer carries the water pumping equipment on the buffer beam, which was removed as track lifting neared Waterhouses, as water supplies were available from the water column in the goods yard here. The train comprises two of the transporter cars, sandwiching one of the railway's two low-sided wagons, No's 1 and 2, which on the opening day had been converted for passenger use by the simple expedient of bolting wooden benches to them. *Author's collection*

Lifting and Disposal

After the line closed, it quickly became rusty and overgrown. The locomotive *J.B. Earle* was taken to Crewe Works in 1934, where it stayed until moved to Stanningley in 1937 for cutting up. In the spring of 1936, the LM&SR put out to tender the track, bridges, locomotives and rolling stock. There was disagreement locally as to whether the line should be converted into a roadway from Waterhouses to Redhurst Crossing or a footpath. The LM&SR gifted the abandoned formation to Staffordshire County Council in the autumn of 1936 but were only prepared to sanction a footpath and advertised a revised tender for the track, locomotives and rolling stock. This was awarded in January 1937 to William Twigg, a Matlock scrap merchant, who almost immediately sold it on to George Cohen & Sons & Co. Ltd, of Stanningley near Leeds. Dismantling of the line, starting at Hulme End, commenced in the spring of 1937. Limestone from Caldon Quarries and tar was brought in advance of the track being lifted and stockpiled beside the line; it was used to construct a seven foot wide path behind the demolition train. The footpath, known at that time as the National Pedestrian & Cycle Track, was opened on Friday 20th July 1937.

Above: A rally at Thor's Cave station on Sunday 18th June 1933. It had been organised by the North Staffordshire Ramblers Association and attracted ramblers from all over the country. It took place against the background of the forthcoming line closure, the growing pressure to create a National Park in land between the Manifold and Dove valleys, and a resolution urging the Government to adopt the Dovedale area as a National Park. Note the large loudspeakers on the left. *Author's collection*

EVENING SENTINEL, SATURDAY, JULY 21, 1937.

L HISTORY MAY BE MADE NEXT WEEK

A general view of the ceremony at the opening of the National Pedestrian Path which has been provided on the site of the former Leek and Manifold Valley Light Railway; and (right) Sir Josiah Stamp declaring the path open. Also on the platform are the Earl and Countess of Harrowby; and Alderman R. G. Patterson (Chairman of the Staffordshire County Council).

LEEK & MANIFOLD VALLEY LIGHT RAILWAY.

A view of Thor's Cave taken from above the old Railway Track.

STATEMENT

the Chairman and Members of the AREA
MMITTEE representing the Parishes served by
LIGHT RAILWAY.

23rd July, 1937.

Above: A newspaper clipping of the opening of the National Pedestrian Path on 20th July 1937, which had been created on the trackbed of the L&MVLR. The Chairman of the LM&SR, Sir Josiah Stamp (right) declares the path open, whilst also on the platform were the Earl and Countess of Harrowby, and the Chairman of Staffordshire County Council. The footpath was 7 foot wide and cost £7,269. It was claimed at the time that the national scenery was not affected and that the surface was ideal for rambling. *Evening Sentinel*

Above Right: Statement by the area committee representing the parishes served by the light railway, a pamphlet published on the same day as the trackbed was opened as a footpath. The area committee was founded at the instigation of Cheadle Rural District Council and the objective of the statement was to declare the surfaced footpath as a road. This was opposed by Staffordshire County Council and, after a Ministry of Transport Public Enquiry, they successfully applied to the Ministry of Transport, resulting in the Manifold Valley Road (Restriction Order) being approved by the Minister on 2nd March 1939. *Author's collection*

Far Right: Swainsley Hall was the weekend home of Thomas Wardle, a Director of the L&MLVR, owner of dye works in the Churnet Valley and of Joshua Wardle Ltd at Leek Brook. However, not wanting his view of the valley spoiled by the railway, he had Swainsley Tunnel built, which took the railway beneath his home. This view, of the south portal looking from Butterton, was taken after conversion of the line to a footpath. The tunnel was 164 yards long and was brick-lined; the bore was 12ft wide and 15ft 3ins high. *Author's collection*

Right: Hulme End station building and engine shed on 29th July 1940. Incidentally, a short ciné film of the line was made in 1930. Now in the British Film Institute collection, it can be viewed on line. *Neville Fields*